Faith and Freedom

Faith and Freedom

The Life and Times
of Bill Ryan SJ

Bob Chodos and Jamie Swift

NOVALIS

NOVALIS

Cover design: Caroline Gagnon and Suzanne Latourelle
Cover illustration: Eyewire
Layout: Caroline Gagnon and Christiane Lemire
Credits for photographic section: Center of Concern (p. 6 – T); Jesuit Archives, Rome
(p. 7 – B, p. 8); Archives of the Jesuits, Upper Canada Province (p. 9 – T); Tony Clarke
(p. 14); Dennis Murphy (p. 15 – B); Art Babych (p. 16). All other photographs are
courtesy of Bill Ryan.

Business Office:
Novalis
49 Front Street East, 2nd Floor
Toronto, Ontario, Canada
M5E 1B3

Phone: 1-800-387-7164 or (416) 363-3303
Fax: 1-800-204-4140 or (416) 363-9409
E-mail: cservice@novalis.ca

National Library of Canada Cataloguing in Publication Data

Chodos, Robert, 1947–
    Faith and freedom : the life and times of Bill Ryan SJ / Bob Chodos and Jamie Swift.

Includes bibliographical references.
ISBN 2-89507-246-9

    1. Ryan, Bill, 1925- 2. Jesuits–Canada–Biography. I. Swift, Jamie, 1951– II. Title.

BX4705.R93C48 2002   271'.5302   C2002-902276-2

Printed in Canada.

We acknowledge the financial support of the Government of Canada through the
Book Publishing Industry Development Program (BPIDP) for our publishing activities.

10 9 8 7 6 5 4 3 2 1   10 09 08 07 06 05 04 03 02

Contents

For Mary Hamilton SP
Martin Royackers SJ
Joan Whittingham SP

Acknowledgments

Many people contributed to this project – most notably Bill Ryan himself, who was unfailingly co-operative. We interviewed some sixty people and would like to thank all of them, including present and former officers and staff members of the Canadian Conference of Catholic Bishops, staff members of the Center of Concern and members of the Upper Canada province of the Society of Jesus. Bill Ryan's family was especially forthcoming with information and insights, and numerous others contributed observations about Bill, about the Jesuits and about the Catholic Church. Any writer needs libraries, and this project owes much to the CCCB library, the archives of the University of Notre Dame (where the Center of Concern papers are housed), the Regis College library and the archives of the Upper Canada Jesuit province. This was our first experience working with Novalis, and we are grateful for the encouragement and guidance of Michael O'Hearn and Kevin Burns.

Jamie Swift would like to thank Janet Pearse, who was new to the experience of living with someone who rises every morning dark and early and doesn't always seem quite there. While Andrea Leis has been living with a variant of this experience for twenty-five years, Bob Chodos is no less appreciative of the grace with which she endures it.

Foreword

This engaging book chronicles the life of one of the most remarkable men I have ever known. Growing up in a devout Roman Catholic family, Bill Ryan experienced the rigours of life under the frontier
conditions of the Ottawa Valley. His early exposure to the hardships of
working families, to racial and religious prejudices and to social injustice clearly shaped his decision to become a Jesuit priest and to manifest
his spirituality in social action. The story of how he did this is an utterly
compelling one that provides intriguing insights into how the profound
changes occurring in Canadian life and in the larger world were affecting politics and people in Canada, in the Jesuit order and in the Roman
Catholic Church. Father Bill was on the leading edge of these changes,
probing the limits and expanding the social horizons of his faith, reaching out to people of other faiths and cultures and then to people of
other countries as he expanded his activities and concerns to the poor
and underprivileged of the developing world.

Father Bill brought to his vocation a rare combination of personal and professional qualities. His brilliant mind was disciplined and
reinforced by a rigorous program of education that included a doctorate
in economics from Harvard. His natural affinity for people evolved into
superb diplomatic skills that enabled him to build bridges between people of diverse views and interests. And his respect for the beliefs of others made him an effective champion of ecumenism while deepening his
commitment to his own faith and extending its horizons.

I first got to know Bill Ryan through our shared interest in international development co-operation and ecumenism, where we had a
number of mutual friends – Barbara Ward, Joe Gremillion, Marvin

Bordelon, Irving Friedman and others who figure prominently in his life and in this book.

The interests we have shared over the years have brought us together in the several different roles through which we have each pursued these interests. As a member of the Society for Development and Peace (SODEPAX – jointly convened by the Vatican and the World Council of Churches), I learned of his ecumenical work and the high esteem in which he was held by both his Roman Catholic colleagues and leading Protestants. I became aware of and impressed with his enlightened and effective championing of issues of poverty and justice both in Canada and in the developing world when he held a major post at the Canadian Catholic Conference (now the Canadian Conference of Catholic Bishops) and I was with the Canadian International Development Agency in Ottawa. Through mutual friends who had established the Center of Concern in Washington, D.C., as an instrument of spiritually inspired social action, we were again brought together. I stayed in touch with him and continued to share interest and platforms with him – when he returned to Canada as leader of the Upper Canada Jesuit Province, and since then in our various respective roles.

I am sure that Father Bill does not realize how very much I have learned from him and have benefited from his work, his wisdom and his example over the years. This book has filled in for me many of the gaps in the events of his life that occurred before I met him and during the periods in which we had little opportunity to see each other. It has helped me to understand better and to deepen my appreciation for the ways in which he has transcended the many barriers to change that he encountered in his own Church and in society and the multiplicity of achievements through which he has become a leading agent of change in our time.

I have learned much, too, about how he has managed his own doubts, setbacks and frustrations. He has demonstrated in his own life a deep faith and abiding commitment to his vocation as a Jesuit priest that is not only fully compatible with his passion for social justice, but is its primary source and driver.

Father Bill's is a story of true leadership – how it began, emerged and has been so effectively exercised to make a real and positive difference to the prospects for a better world. It is a story from which we can all derive many lessons and much inspiration. This is certainly true for me. There is no one whose influence and example have meant more to me in my own career or whose friendship and counsel continue to be among the most precious benefits I have had from my public service career. We can all rejoice in the knowledge that Bill Ryan's commitment and his energies are undiminished as his influence continues to be multiplied by his unique qualities of wisdom, experience and an abiding, pro-active faith.

Maurice F. Strong
April 2002

Introduction

When Bill Ryan reviewed a preliminary version of this story of his life, one of his comments didn't quite fit. He wanted there to be something in the book about Jim McSheffrey.

From the time we undertook this project, Bill made it clear that he did not want veto power over the final manuscript. He did, however, want to review it for factual accuracy, and most of his suggestions were of a factual nature. It was, for example, gin that Cardinal Carter was drinking when Bill phoned him after learning in 1981 that the pope had appointed his own trustee to run the Jesuit order, and not scotch as we had originally written. But there were also a few points of interpretation, which we were free to ignore, and that one odd suggestion that didn't really fall into any category.

Jim McSheffrey was a Jesuit brother who lived among the poor in St. John's, Newfoundland, and died there in 1999 when he fell from a cliff while picking berries. At first glance, the worlds of Bill Ryan and Jim McSheffrey are about as far apart as they could be. Bill Ryan spent a good part of his working life in positions of authority – director of the Center of Concern, superior of the Upper Canada province of the Jesuits, general secretary of the Canadian Conference of Catholic Bishops. He played a prominent role in two Jesuit general congregations and a landmark Roman synod, as well as a variety of international conferences under United Nations and other auspices. He enjoys the company of cabinet ministers and World Bank economists. Jim McSheffrey would have been very uncomfortable in all those settings. He worked in very small worlds – in the Ignatius Farm Community in Guelph, Ontario, in the early 1980s, where he was one of several Jesuits living with people who had been in prisons or psychiatric institutions, and later in Brophy Place, a public housing neighbourhood in St. John's, where he was described as the "angel," the "conscience" and the "spirit." Loved by the residents of Brophy Place, he was often shunned by his fellow Jesuits, who found his singlemindedness and lack of concern for social graces difficult to live with. It would have been inconceivable for Jim to live Bill's life, or Bill Jim's.

And yet, Bill was suggesting, there was a connection between his world and McSheffrey's, one that was sufficiently close that his life story would not be complete if McSheffrey was not part of it. Institutional operator, international traveller, mover among the Top People – Bill Ryan is all of that, but not only that. A tireless advocate throughout his career for what has become known in the Catholic Church as the "preferential option for the poor," he has spent very little time (as his good friend Janet Somerville has pointed out) actually working with the poor. But those who do work with the poor have a secure place in his heart, and have often come under his wing. He sees this as an important part of his legacy, and he wanted to make sure that readers of this book were aware of it.

⟶➣◦⟨⟵

This book had its origin in a conversation between Bill Ryan and some Jesuit friends in the fall of 1999. Bill was approaching his seventy-fifth birthday and was recovering from prostate cancer; it occurred to the Jesuits that Bill's life was the stuff of a book and that now might be a good time to have it written. Our names came up as possible candidates to undertake this project: it is characteristic of Bill that he would think of a practising Jew and a lapsed Anglican as appropriate authors of his life story. Neither of us was in a position to take on the task on his own, and so we proposed a collaboration. Long-time friends and colleagues, we had worked together in a variety of capacities over the years, although never on a project of this magnitude.

Initially the project was conceived as a short "interview book," but it soon became clear that there was enough material for a full-fledged biography. Even with this expanded conception, our primary source was, of course, Bill himself. The very first time we met, he said, "As I look back over my life, what strikes me is that in all the positions I've held, I've always been able to maintain my freedom," an observation that puzzled us at first but eventually worked its way into the title of the book. In addition to a number of extensive interviews, Bill took us on a guided tour of his childhood haunts in the Ottawa Valley, both on the Ontario side where his family lived and on the Quebec side where his father worked in sawmills and logging camps. We walked down a logging road that his father had staked out six decades earlier to a lake where we came across an abandoned piece of machinery. Throughout the tour his reminiscences were interspersed with expositions of the thought of Pierre Teilhard de Chardin and comments on the current state of the World Bank. We also peppered Bill with e-mail questions during the writing stage, and without fail he responded promptly and fully.

At the same time, we sought to augment and balance Bill's narrative with the accounts of others who had participated in the same events. We interviewed several of his surviving siblings, close friends, and people who had worked with him in settings ranging from the Jesuit novitiate in the 1940s to the International Development Research Centre in the 1990s. We also spoke to people who could help us place Bill's career in the context of a changing Roman Catholic Church in the late twentieth century. For while Bill Ryan's life story is well worth telling in itself, it also provides a window onto some of the major events and developments that have taken place in the Church and especially in the Jesuit order over the last four decades: the Second Vatican Council and liberation theology in the 1960s, the synod on Justice in the World and the Jesuits' 32nd General Congregation in the 1970s, the "Dezza affair," in which the pope appointed his own delegate to head the Jesuits in the 1980s, and the leaner times and difficult struggles of the last years of the century.

Although both of us had worked with the Jesuits (and on projects initiated by Bill Ryan) before we began work on this book, our research was truly an education for us. For readers who are deeply familiar with the Catholic Church from the inside, we hope that we can provide a fresh perspective on at least some of the events described here. For those of you who are outsiders like ourselves, we hope that we can be your guides to one extraordinary traveller's journey through interesting times.

Bob Chodos and Jamie Swift

Chapter 1

Great Expectations

The boy with the spectacles and the thickening forearms had risen just before first light. Something about the woods at this time of day attracted him. Back home in town, where the CPR main line ran not far from the house, you grew used to the dull roar of the heavy freights trundling by, but it was different up here in the hills. Instead of his mother's busy puttering in the downstairs kitchen as she prepared breakfast, you woke to the song of the hermit thrush and the gurgle of a woodland stream. If you got up before the rest you could grab a few minutes to watch a ghosting mist rising from the calm surface of the swamp. The wiry kid hoped a stiff breeze might spring up to drive away the black-flies.

The blackflies. They say that the flies were the one thing that had tested the faith of the Jesuits when they had first arrived in these parts three centuries earlier, compared even to the persecution by the "Idolators" whom they were attempting to convince of God's glory and the king's "incomparable greatness." The energetic priests described the flies as "troublesome in the extreme...disagreeable beyond description." The only way to get rid of the little beasts, the Jesuits felt, was to clear and inhabit the countryside. After all, wrote Father Paul Le Jeune to his provincial back home, "already there are but few of them at the fort of Kebec, on account of the cutting down of the neighbouring woods."[1]

Thirteen-year-old Bill Ryan, Jr., knew little of the Jesuits beyond the usual lurid tales of the martyrdom of Lalement and Brébeuf, stories he had heard from the nuns at St. Francis Xavier School in Renfrew. He did, however, know about the cutting down of the woods. His father had spent his entire working life logging in the winter, driving timber downstream in the spring, and milling logs in the summer. From where Bill was standing in the Gatineau Hills that morning in 1938, he could now see the forest of pine, spruce, maple, birch and basswood emerge around him as the mist burned off. The majestic white pine that had enriched the Ottawa Valley's famous lumber barons – the term reflected the feudal grip they had on the early settler communities – were long gone, rafted away by armies of Frenchmen and Irishmen, some just as famous as their storied bosses. The Americans could talk about their Paul Bunyan, but kids growing up on both sides of the Ottawa River had heard the yarns about Jos Montferrand, or "Big Joe Mufferaw" as he was known among the English, the fabled lumberjack whose woodcutting ability was rivalled only by his boxing skills. The story had it that Montferrand had once taken on twenty English-speaking troublemakers all by himself.

Bill had just graduated from St. Francis Xavier, and since there was no Catholic high school in his hometown in those days, he would begin classes at Renfrew Collegiate Institute in the fall. But in the meantime, he was expected to spend the summer working in the small sawmill where his father was the foreman. Reflecting the divisions of earlier days, some sixty years later Bill Ryan would still describe the millowner, Jack Argue, as "a Protestant from Shawville." Not long before Bill Jr. began working at the mill, Argue made a special trip down to Hull to get his foreman's nearsighted son his first pair of eyeglasses.

"Even though he never left Dad anything for pension and even though Dad had made his whole enterprise possible and profitable," Ryan would recall, "it was one of the times I realized how deeply he cared for Dad and us boys."

⚬

There are a number of places in Canada – such as Cape Breton, Newfoundland, francophone Quebec, or New Brunswick's Miramichi (portrayed in the novels of David Adams Richards) – that have a culture and character that can truly be termed "distinct." The Ottawa Valley is one of those special places. And although that distinctiveness has sometimes been romanticized or distorted through modernity's commercializing lens, its roots and staying power can be traced to a time when the people were very much part of the land. As Richards says, "They've seen how physical work can lead to death on the job and to them life is pretty special."[2]

The Valley's local lore includes the legendary Renfrew Millionaires hockey team, led by Cyclone Taylor, reputedly the only player ever to score a goal while skating backwards. It includes tales of old-timers who can tell by the way an Ottawa Valley Irishman does the step dance whether he comes from Eganville or Shawville, by the way he talks whether he grew up in Carp or Mount St. Patrick. It includes the "hard but happy days" of a man whom one of the countless local histories describes as the last of the lumber-camp cooks. The rich accounts of fiddlers and farmers, raftsmen and loggers compete with rumours of what the massive stone houses built for this "great lumber family" or that "lumber king" really looked like inside. And how is it that Catholics who became Protestants were once called "soup-eaters"? The answer: when the starving Irish arrived in Quebec City in the 1840s, they were confronted by "converters" calling, "A bowl of soup if ye'll turn!" And what about all those long winter nights in the camboose shanties where your hair froze to the walls while you slept? According to the testimony of Renfrew's Syd Pottinger, who made it good in the timber business, "Those men were in there all through the winter, and they were happy. They had lots of fun amongst themselves."[3]

There are, however, accounts that paint a different picture of life in the Valley in the old days. A nineteenth-century engineer named Thomas Keefer told Montreal's Mechanics' Institute that he had hardly come across a single portage or bit of land jutting into a river where there wasn't a rude wooden cross carved with the initials of some unfortunate logger who had been drowned or crushed as he tried to free a log jam in the springtime river drive. As many as eighty men were killed this way each spring.[4] Hector Vaillancourt of Deep River recalled that he didn't remove his underwear for seven months on account of the lice, that the smell of the camps at least helped to keep the flies away. Vaillancourt was able to secure a job as a camp foreman at age seventeen because his father knew the boss. Jake Stewart of Point Alexander, who had sixty years in the trade, described the lumber industry as "the crookedest business in the world."[5] Allan Huckabone described a world in which you could get rich simply by owning the rights to crown timber. Although labour was cheap, a small operator could lose his shirt. "It was great to be rich but pretty bad to be poor," recalled Huckabone. "They glorify the lumber camps and shanty towns now but they were pretty rough: hard work, little food, less rest. It was pretty bad for a twelve-year-old boy up in those camps."[6]

Bill Ryan, Jr., came to spend his summers in a lumber camp just after he turned twelve because his father, William Patrick (Bill Sr.), was a woodsman born and bred. Like so many men who grew up on scratch farms near the forest frontiers of Ontario and Quebec, Bill Sr. was still a boy when he learned skills that were useful in the fields and in the woods. He could wield an axe, mend harness, drive a team and size up a stand of timber. His own parents, Michael Ryan and Catherine Bulger, were themselves farmers and the children of farmers, Michael having been born in rural Tipperary in 1853.

Many of the Irish who settled the townships around the upper reaches of the Ottawa and its tributaries in the latter part of the nineteenth century found themselves on land that could be described generously as not well-suited for agriculture. Even from the earliest days of Upper Canada, immigrants from Ireland got the short end of the stick, farms where the fields were as likely to produce a harvest of stones as they were to yield decent crops of potatoes or wheat. Harold Neil, a Renfrew high school chum of Bill Ryan, Jr., who later became a geologist, remarked that "just outside Renfrew you get right into the shield – Mount St. Patrick and Dacre and Eganville and all that rough country where people should never have settled."

Upper Canada's comfortable class liked to entertain an image of loyal Irish farmers (they were reported to have "behaved well" during the Rebellion of 1837) hard at work on barren land, but this conceit did little to feed families living in the hinterland. To do that, you needed cash money. Patrick Kennelly of Mount St. Patrick, who like Bill Ryan, Jr., was born in the 1920s, recalled the story of his great-grandfather who came out from Ireland in 1838: "They say he had nothing to work with. All he had was a little packsack and a couple of handspikes, and he chopped the big maples down and burned them for potash.... They didn't intend to farm."[7] Settlers reluctant to live on marginal land were a recurring problem for the lumber interests and the authorities. Time after time, new arrivals quickly sized up the situation and, realizing the grim prospects of farming the edge of the northern boreal forest, cut the standing timber, sold it off and moved on to do the same thing again or perhaps sought regular wage labour in the bush.

William Patrick Ryan was born in Mount St. Patrick, about twenty-five kilometres west of Renfrew, in 1893. It was the same year that the Ontario government established Algonquin Park, thereby protecting the watersheds of several important tributaries of the Ottawa as well as those of the Muskoka River. While there was some deft publicity about the need for nature sanctuaries and recreation areas, the authorities were in fact heeding the calls of Ottawa Valley timber interests anxious to prevent settlement on the crown lands that they had obtained through patronage or straight corruption. The creation of Algonquin Park assured the orderly liquidation of its timber by the companies that had already leased the rich stands of white pine that clung to the Precambrian granite. It was here that Bill Ryan, Sr., a son of immigrants who had attended school for only a year, began his working life. Since farming was simply not an option, the natural thing was to work in the woods. Bill Sr. would become a logger, timber cruiser, sawyer, millwright and general organizer of anything else remotely connected to the business of "hurlin' down the pine." It was a hard life. The work was rugged and dangerous. You lived in isolation, far away from town, church and school. All right for a bachelor, perhaps, but a different thing for a married man.

Bill Ryan, Sr., met Lena Donig during one of his visits back home. The Mount St. Patrick parish had been established in 1830 and in the mid-nineteenth century the area was, in the words of one priest who ministered at the church there, "100 per cent Irish." Though Lena had been born in a place called Shamrock, she was of German descent. Her parents, Theodore and Pauline Donig, had arrived in Canada in the 1880s, apparently from Alsace-Lorraine. They already had a family of five children, and Pauline died giving birth to Lena in 1893. Theodore remarried and young Lena remained with the family only long enough to complete two years of school before leaving home to help her older sister Mary, who kept a hotel in nearby Dacre. It is possible that it was at this "stopping place," as such establishments were known in the Valley, that Lena met Bill Sr. as he returned from another long stint in the bush.

Whatever the case, they married in 1916. The old church at Mount St. Patrick had been completed in 1869 by masons using stones from surrounding fields for the walls. The parishioners had local girls pose as models for the angels in the hand-painted frescoes that decorate the sanctuary and, despite their limited means, brought in a pipe organ all the way from Montreal. The day before her marriage, Lena Donig, who had been brought up Lutheran, went to the church and converted to Catholicism, though she would not let her own children know what she must have regarded as some sort of secret until they reached adulthood.

The Ryan-Donig union produced nine children, five girls and four boys.[8] The first three, Bernadette, Eileen and Katherine, were born some eighty miles west of Mount St. Patrick at Madawaska, one of the settlements closest to Algonquin Park, where their father was working near the main railway line at Mink Lake. After Katherine was born in 1921, the Ryans decided that it was time to move to a larger centre where "Bernie," now five, and the rest of the children could receive a proper education and attend church regularly. By the time their second son, William Francis, arrived in 1925, the Ryans had moved to Renfrew, a town on the Bonnechere River that had first been settled by timber squatters in the heyday of the white-pine boom nearly a hundred years before.

⇒⋙•0•⋘⇐

"Everything was O'Brien," shrugged Bill Ryan when he returned at age seventy-five to the town that hosts an annual Lumber Baron Festival. "It's as if they did everything. It just doesn't work like that."

It happened that the famous Ambrose J. O'Brien, the mining magnate who backed the Millionaires hockey team and so much else that moved in town, lived right around the corner from the house where the Ryan brood grew up. Their new neighbourhood was also home to local grandees like Guy French, Bill's employer at Mink Lake. After the Ryans moved to Renfrew, French kept Bill on the job as foreman at his lumber mill at Masham "on the Quebec side." The family occupied a detached clapboard house at the corner of Quarry and Lynn, a block away from the CPR main line and a short stroll from St. Francis Xavier Church and the downtown shops on Raglan Street, the main drag. Though it was a small place for what would be such a large family, it was quite respectable for a young working-class couple in the 1920s.

Their new house had a parlour and kitchen downstairs and four small bedrooms on the second floor. The children found it scary when the stovepipes that threaded through the upstairs rooms began to glow red on cold winter nights. The boys slept over the kitchen in a room with a doorway no more than five feet high. They had to navigate a narrow back staircase where Lena stored bulging sacks of flour, sugar and oatmeal. After the bags were empty, she would use the cloth to fashion sheets and aprons, their origins disguised by careful bleaching and the addition of elaborate embroidery. At the threshold of the store-bought era, she stuck to a homespun life.

Lena Ryan was a devout woman with large eyes that often displayed concern about her children. Slightly heavy-set and endowed with boundless energy, she would be up by four in the morning in warm weather to sweep a side yard that she kept as smooth as glass. In the winter her predawn efforts were devoted to getting the wood fire up and baking. According to her son Bill, "She was like a nun in the sense that she did everything around the house." Her world was wrapped up with her family and its needs, and she relied on her own family to meet those needs. Each fall Uncle Martin – Martin Hass, her sister Emma's husband – drove in from their farm just outside Renfrew and the children would unload a winter's supply of wood, carrots and potatoes from his truck. While catalogues and the nearby stores offered alternatives to things homemade, Lena was by all accounts reluctant even to leave the house for the nearby shops, preferring to send one of the children. A "praying member" of the Catholic Women's League at St. Francis Xavier, she was a loner who took no active part in parish matters. She attended Mass on Sundays but expected her children to troop off to seven o'clock services seven days a week. With her husband away except for brief visits at Christmas and Easter, Lena Ryan was essentially a single mother, looking after the household and caring for her children, though early on the older girls took up their share of the women's work. Similarly, her eldest son Joe and his younger brother Frank (as William Francis was known in his younger days) began hauling in the wood as soon as they were able.

Young "Frank" Ryan was by all accounts an energetic and impulsive child. Before he was first packed off to school, he thought nothing of breaking through the screen of an upstairs window on a tedious rainy day so that he could get out to play with the leaves in the eavestrough. According to another family story, the young lad once accompanied his mother on a visit to her sister Mary's new house in Dacre where there was much discussion of the fire that had recently destroyed the old house. Sitting around after dinner, the two women smelled smoke – and it wasn't coming from the cookstove. As it turned out, all the talk had prompted young Frank to ponder the matter of fire, so he piled some dry leaves under a corner of the new house and set the pile ablaze.

No doubt Lena was glad when her second son's restless energy could be channelled in a more fruitful direction. For her, and for her husband, education was paramount. Neither had ever had a chance to get much formal schooling, so Lena made sure that education joined religion at centre stage in her household. Recalling those early days at what the family refers to as "Renfrew house," Joe Ryan made reference to a metaphorical "line" no fewer than four times. His mother kept her kids in line. You had to toe the line. "In a quiet sort of way she made sure we got out to church in the morning, kept our hands and feet clean, kept us in line. There's no doubt about that.... You had to measure up at school as well as at home. She was very anxious that we do well at school. She kept us in line."

School was just the thing for little Frank, who took seriously his mother's instruction that anything less than a first-place finish was unacceptable. The Ryan clan received its basic instruction from the Holy Cross Sisters who ran St. Francis Xavier School, and their rigorous approach certainly made its mark. Asked what he recalls of school, he replies immediately, "I got medals." This meant that the young fellow regularly placed first in the class. Such was his motivation that he felt it was "a great injustice" one time that he came second. It was also "unjust" when one of the teachers slapped him, although Frank would recall with some admiration that the nuns exercised "very good discipline" at their co-educational school. The principal was Sister St. Bernard, whom he described as "tough" – an adjective that he would use in later years to convey approval.

Early evidence of Ryan's single-mindedness came when, on his first day in primary school, he unilaterally decided to change his name. Going down the orderly rows of children, the teaching sister came to the dark-haired boy with the attentive look.

"And what is your name?" asked Sister Margarita.

"Billy Ryan!" came the quick response.

Scanning the carbon copy of her class list, she could find only a Francis Ryan and, although the surname was hardly uncommon in the Valley, there was no other Ryan to be found. She shrugged, figuring that Sister St. Bernard's office had made a mistake. She scratched out Francis and replaced it with William. Ryan would add Xavier when he took his Jesuit vows years later, and subsequently offered two explanations for becoming "Bill." On the one hand, he said that he admired his father and wanted to be known by his name. He also explained that he turned into Bill "because I consider Francis a girl's name." Whatever the case, he would henceforth be known as Frank (or, later, "Father Frank") to his family and Bill to the rest of the world.

Though Frank Ryan and Bill Ryan were not distinct characters, the name change provides an early clue to his personality. His family recalls a rambunctious, even impulsive boy driven to doing unpredictable things. Playing with matches is one thing, unilaterally changing your name at age six is, decidedly, another. Asked why he thought his younger brother did this, Joe Ryan made a quizzical gesture: "Who knows? With him, anything goes. He's his own man. What he says, goes.... He was different than the rest of us. If we said we were going this way, he went that way." His sister Helen described him as "kind of a renegade" and Bill himself would in later years claim, "I don't follow rules."

Yet, compared to his younger brother Bob (who died just as this book was going to press), Bill was a dutiful lad, fulfilling his mother's expectations to the letter. Bob bridled at his mother's great expectations. Though he rose early to serve as an altar boy at morning Mass, Bob attended church only until he was old enough to say "No." Bill was very attentive to his studies. He would return directly home from school, attend to his household duties and then do his homework. Like his brothers Joe and Jim, he would eventually enter the seminary. Bill would later describe Joe as "very different" from himself, "a good boy of duty, reliability and law and order." But it is hard to imagine young Bill, faithfully bringing home the first-place medals that his mother stored in a special little box, as any sort of renegade or even a nonconformist.

"My mum really wanted perfection. It was no good to come second. She expected the kids to go to church every morning," recalled Helen. Though Lena had been raised as a Lutheran, and may not have been thinking explicitly about what she wanted for her boys, "She was making priests out of them."

⇒➤●◄⇐

The Gatineau River drains Ottawa's cottage country hinterland, where rustic cabins have given way to architecturally designed chalets. The train that once hauled saw logs from the Gatineau watershed has become a curiosity, shuttling steam railway buffs and other tourists back and forth between Wakefield and Hull. The river itself, once jammed with pulpwood being boomed down to the E.B. Eddy mill in Hull, is now the preserve of kayakers and canoeists.

This is where Bill Ryan, Jr., spent his boyhood summers. Except for the one time that Father Quinn of St. Francis Xavier parish arranged for him and Joe to spend a few weeks at a Catholic boys' camp on Lake Clear on the Ontario side ("we thought of such vacations as suitable only for sissies," Bill later remembered), the entire family spent their summers in the Gatineau Hills. It was the only time his mother and father could live together in anything resembling close proximity. As foreman for logging and sawmilling operations, Bill Sr. was wedded to the woods, so each summer he would find a house as close as possible to the sawmill that he was running. Lena and her oldest daughter, Bernie, a take-charge young woman who came to be a sort of assistant superintendent of family logistics, would pack the entire family into McVeigh's taxi and head off from Renfrew to the Gatineau.

For the first few years, the rapidly growing family went to Masham, a village where Guy French had a sawmill right in the centre of town on Peche Creek. Exactly 143 steps took you up the steep hill from the gravel road that ran through town to the attic of the big house where the Ryans lived, built into the side of the hill. From there they could sit on the porch of a Sunday morning and watch families in their horse-drawn carriages heading for Mass at nearby Sainte-Cécile-de-Masham, where Father Filiatrault would warn the women to keep their arms and legs covered. Despite his familiarity with matters mechanical and his years as the boss at a steam-driven sawmill, Bill Ryan, Sr., never learned to drive a car and often employed as his chauffeur young Gérard Bertrand, whose family owned the general store next to the house on the hill. The Ryan children became friendly with the Renaud family, whose farm adjoined their house. Lena, however, did not want her children to mix with the Coderres, a poor, less respectable family down the hill. She worried that their children could well be dirty and would swear.

The early years at Masham gave young Bill Ryan an opportunity to spend time with his father. Bill Sr. would take his children fishing in the river and he helped out when Lena deployed the children to pick berries that she would be turning into the winter's supply of jam. In the early summer they foraged right at ground level for wild strawberries before moving on to raspberries and blueberries. In the mid-1930s the sawmill at Masham closed and operations shifted to a slightly more remote site at Gilbeau Lake. Since the mill was no longer in an actual village, the Ryans rented a house a few miles away and Bill Sr. remained at the lumber camp, sleeping in the office where he did rudimentary bookkeeping and looked after the payroll.

Like his wife, Bill Ryan, Sr., was quiet and reserved, devoting himself completely to work and family. But it was a family he rarely saw. If something had to be fixed at the mill on a summertime Sunday, he simply did the job himself, sometimes spending the day scraping the inside of a hot steam boiler or repairing a winch. His youngest daughter, Helen, reports that at age four she hid under the bed when he came home for one of his brief visits to Renfrew. "I never knew him very well... He was a stranger in our house, yet he was my dad." Even during the family's annual summertime migration to the Gatineau, after they left

Masham, Bill Ryan, Sr., would return to the family's rented house on Saturday evening, attend church on Sunday, have a noon meal and head back to camp.

If their father was an unfamiliar figure to the Ryan girls, his sons got to know him better in their early teens when each of them began to spend their summers in the lumber camp. Working shoulder to shoulder with gangs of French-speaking men who cut timber in the winter and ran the mill in the summer was not a job for sissies. Softwood or hardwood, pine or maple, logs and lumber are dense and heavy. It wasn't until after the Second World War that the forest industry introduced diesel-hydraulic power into the bush in the form of skidders and grapples. Before that, horses were still in widespread use. Although the steam mill where the Ryan boys worked featured a power jackladdder to hoist the logs out of the water and rudimentary conveyor belts to feed the saws, that was about it. A lot of the work was done by hand and the operation that Jack Argue took over from Guy French was not highly capitalized in the 1930s. Labour was cheap.

Bullwork was still very much the order of the day, and the boss's sons began to do their share at age twelve or thirteen. Looking back at that period, Joe Ryan doesn't see it as out of the ordinary that teenage boys would be putting in long days manhandling slabs of timber in a mill where the scream of the saw made it impossible to warn your fellow worker if something was going wrong. It was a hazardous workplace full of fast-moving wheels, belts and chains exposed to loose clothing or unwary fingers. Joe simply describes it as "heavy work." He and his younger brother spent many a hot summer day pulling heavy pieces of rough lumber, still wet from the millpond, off the sorting table and arranging them by grade and type so that the waiting teamster could load them onto his wagon. It was akin to assembly line work in that someone else – in this case the sawyer – set the pace. If you fell behind it was very difficult to catch up.

Bob Ryan, the youngest and the nonconformist among the Ryan boys, was the only one who became familiar with the culture of industrial labour, eventually taking up a working-class job at Ontario Hydro. (Bill and Jim became priests and Joe dropped out of the seminary to become a high school teacher.) Bob remembered the work as "very dangerous," particularly in comparison to his subsequent workplaces where safety regulations and precautions had taken hold. In his first year Bob found himself piling slabs, some of which were so heavy he couldn't lift them; when no one was looking he would let them pass. Like his brothers, he was able to "get to know what work is." And he too came to admire the knack his father had of running the operation and dealing with the men he had hired. Bob was sure that he would have heard the talk if there had been any ill feeling among the workers. "He never ever fired a man. He said, 'There's easier ways. You give him a job he doesn't like and he'll quit.'"

Although Bill Ryan, Sr., spoke no French, most men who worked for him were Quebecers from farms in the Outaouais. Many spoke little or no English, so it was a workplace like so many others in Quebec in those days: a unilingual English boss presided over a francophone workforce. They muddled through, most likely because some of the French workers spoke English. Joe says that they made themselves understood through "a mixture of French and English," although he admits to having only a few words of French when he arrived at a seminary in Montreal a few years later. According to Bob, the working language was English. Bill Jr. became familiar enough with French that he was able to get by when he studied in Belgium and France and wrote theses on Quebec topics during his years of Jesuit training.

The summers in Masham, Lake Guilbeau and later Lake Dumont were formative for Bill Jr. Not only did he get a taste of manual labour and pick up some basic handyman skills, but he also acquired an affinity for the natural world that would stay with him. The teenage boy spent long days working alone outside. Summer evenings in the wooded hills provided an opportunity for quiet contemplation once the machinery had shut down for the day, leaving only the sweet smell of freshly sawn wood and the lonesome call of the veery. This sort of solitary retreat to the woods was something that Bill Ryan would always value. He would also come to appreciate the risks of unregulated industrial labour, describing how he worked "dangerously." His older brother testified that young Bill "would start to think of other things rather than the saws" so that their father had to keep an eye on him. Today, Bill Jr. still has vivid memories of on-the-job hazards he faced. He once injured his shoulder when he was working under the mill and his clothing got caught in a moving belt. On another occasion he was attempting to break up a large pile of logs with a peavey. The sharp, pointed tool used for moving logs slipped and went through his hand just as a cascade of logs tumbled over his head. He was left with residual industrial stigmata and the impression that he had been lucky not to be killed.

His summers in the bush also left young Bill Ryan with an abiding respect for his father, whom he came to admire as a leader of men.

Describing Bill Sr. as a man of "absolute integrity," Bill Ryan recalled that he would never ask someone on the job to do work that he himself would not do. "In a place like Masham the French Canadians practically worshipped him. For all practical purposes, he was the mayor."

Even allowing for filial exuberance, there appears to be something to this claim. Bill Sr. was quiet and unassuming, someone who led by example, a manager who was effective because, having himself started working in the woods when he was very young, he was familiar with the operation from the ground up. He was also highly regarded because, during the Depression years, he was the source of scarce jobs in a region that had never been prosperous. Helen tells of the time when, some years after her father's death, she was in the market for a hedge. She saw an ad in the paper and when the man who supplied hedges arrived at her house in suburban Ottawa, she found that he was from Shawville (or *Shaw*-vul, as in shovel) on the Quebec side. When she remarked that her father had worked in those parts, they realized that he had worked for Bill Ryan.

"Your father had faith in me when nobody else did," said the hedge dealer. "He gave me a job, and turned my life around." Helen never received a bill and every year the former lumber worker returned to check the health of her hedge. Asked whether the fellow from Shawville, a town that is famously anglophone and rather Orange, was English or French, she recalled that he was "quite French."

Bill Ryan, Sr., was no doubt a valuable employee for Jack Argue of Shawville, and Bill Jr. describes his father as a "dutiful" worker. He was also a dutiful husband and father who faithfully passed his paycheque over to his wife, often entrusting it to a truck driver who would mail it to Renfrew. And although he was English-speaking, he was also a Catholic and a useful go-between for the Anglo-Protestant businessmen in their dealings with a French-speaking, devoutly Catholic workforce. Things like that still mattered in those days. According to Helen, who was born around the time that Bill Jr. started to work in the lumber camps, her older brother would go on to model himself after his father. "I think he thinks he's his dad's son. I guess he was." According to Bill Jr., his father was "always polite but never deferential. He was always able to mix with the big bosses and always stay himself."

Despite his father's lack of French, he apparently got on well with his subordinates, some of whom lacked formal education to the extent that they had trouble counting their money. He gladly helped them with that. The "French Canadians," Bill Jr. remembers, trusted their

English boss and he in turn worked well with them. In fact, he "loved them." This sort of workplace harmony was just the tonic for the times, at least according to official Catholic teaching. Quebec workers had been hearing this message from pulpits in Sainte-Cécile-de-Masham and across the province well before the Depression of the 1930s. With the arrival of the "Red Decade," Church warnings about the perils of class conflict and the necessity for on-the-job co-operation grew louder as priests attempted to curtail secular and socialist influence by backing a European-style Catholic unionism that emphasized harmony with the boss, the government and, of course, the Church. In 1931 Pope Pius XI had released the Jesuit-authored social encyclical *Quadragesimo Anno* to mark the fortieth anniversary of the Vatican's first attempt at Catholic social teaching. Condemning the excesses of both capitalism and socialism, the Depression-era document promoted the notion of an ordered society rooted in the medieval guild system and held that such a Vocational Order adhered to "natural law."[9]

As a future Jesuit, Bill Ryan, Jr., would eventually become familiar with the minutiae of the Church's social thought. But as the 1930s ended and the Wehrmacht prepared to surge across Europe, he was just beginning his high school years. The looming war would change his home town and transform the country at large, but it would have little immediate effect on the Ryan family.

————⟫•⟨————

When Bill Ryan, Jr., left St. Francis Xavier School, he and his family had three choices. He could, like many Catholic boys in the Ottawa Valley, enter the world of work and leave formal schooling behind. There being no Catholic high school for boys in Renfrew, he could go to Ottawa to attend one of the Catholic schools there, but that would involve paying for room, board and tuition. Or he could simply switch over to the public school system and Renfrew Collegiate Institute, the local high school. Given his parents' enthusiasm for education and their modest means (with Helen's birth in 1937 there were nine children under one roof), young Bill continued his education at "the Collegiate."

The divide that existed between Protestants and Catholics in the town did not spill over into the high school in any real way. The Catholics at the Collegiate were a small minority in which Bill stood out, placing first in each of his four years there and bringing home more of the shiny medals that his mother cherished.

Another top student, with whom Bill sometimes studied, was Harold Neil, a short fellow whose high school nickname became "Stubby." Neil was the son of a United Church minister who was posted to Renfrew in 1939. He recalls that, though the lines between the town's Protestants and Catholics weren't evident at the Collegiate, the kids at St. Francis Xavier sometimes took a run at him when he used their schoolyard as a shortcut. His friend Bill Ryan was considered to be a "brain." And although he was a good athlete as well as being at the head of the class, Bill was a quiet type, not someone who would stand out in a crowd: "Mentally and physically he was a tough guy. Tough in the sense of strong, muscular." His summers in the lumber camp stood Bill in good stead on the football field and the hockey rink. During one football game the ball carrier decided that, because the linebacker on the opposing team didn't look that big, the best way to deal with him was to run right over him. When he tried to bowl Ryan over by putting his head down, he bounced off and hit the ground hard and watched as the Renfrew player walked away. Bill's high school nickname was "Rock."

In the wintertime the Ryan children would turn the hose onto the side yard that their mother swept so meticulously in the summer. Rock Ryan had played enough shinny at home to realize that what he lacked in finesse on the hockey rink he could make up for with brute strength. And like many Canadian boys whose families couldn't afford equipment, his improvised shin pads consisted of magazines stuffed into his socks. "We were poor," he explains. It was a point he would make frequently as he looked back on his youth.

Poverty is, of course, a relative term. With nine children, the Ryan family certainly had to make do without the frills that a middle-class household of the day enjoyed. Lena Ryan was adept at making do, and despite her efforts to make much of what the family ate and wore, there is little doubt that the Ryans had to struggle to make ends meet. The family did, however, have a steady income during the hardest years of the 1930s, when many Canadian families faced destitution and depended on charity. Bill Ryan, Sr., was a trusted logging foreman whose job was probably as secure as it could be during that difficult time. In that sense, the Ryan family clearly had it better than those in Renfrew who spent the Depression years wondering when they might get a job and indeed when they might next get enough to eat.

When the war broke out, the first wave of enlistment from Renfrew was large. Young men who had had no steady work for years swarmed the recruiting office, some motivated by a sense of duty, others intrigued by the possibility of adventure. Those who didn't enlist got jobs at Renfrew Electric, whose plant on the edge of the Bonnechere had languished through the doldrums of the Depression but picked up when the wartime defence contracts began to flow. The military enjoyed pride of place in Renfrew, where the strains of a regimental pipe band were often heard on the streets. During the war, the traffic on the railway increased, with recruits going up the valley for training at Camp Petawawa and heading down to Montreal and Halifax for the voyage to Europe. The locals would often crowd the platform at the Renfrew station to wave at the troops leaning from crowded trains. "The war," said Stubby Neil, "was very real in Renfrew."

Neither Joe nor Bill Ryan succumbed to the temptation to enlist, devoting the war years to their education. Many Catholics dropped out of school after the elementary grades, so the student body at Renfrew Collegiate included only a handful of Catholic students. Sometimes they would chafe at uncomplimentary references to pope and Church in the history curriculum, but by and large there was little overt tension. During the 1920s, teaching in Canada had developed into a profession with higher standards and high school education had expanded, so that the quality of instruction was rigorous by the time Bill enrolled in the Collegiate. Miss O'Brien, the well-respected Latin teacher who was Catholic, kept an eye out for the Catholic students.

In spite of the clear religious divide – his mother apparently "indulged" him when he told her that he had a Protestant girlfriend – Bill Ryan recalls his last years in Renfrew fondly. He admired the high school principal, a large, overbearing man named Troop: "I felt there was some sort of primitive justice in him. The good got rewarded and the evil got punished. There was something straight about him." The courses were challenging and, when Joe moved on in 1940 to complete high school at St. Patrick's College in Ottawa, Bill took on more responsibility and became what he described as "the regular man of the house." The only family member in whom he confided in any intimate way was his older sister Bernie who, as time went by, increasingly assumed the role of woman of the house. Bill also took time off school to help with the timber operations in the Gatineau. His father would get his friend Paul Kluke, a farmer with an operation near the sawmill, to provide a letter requesting the labour of Bill Jr. Because they faced wartime labour shortages, farmers could do this. Although he did not work for Kluke, Bill thought that he was contributing to the war effort because Jack Argue was selling veneer logs to England and the aircraft industry. And as much as he enjoyed his studies, he relished the chance to spend some time – blackflies and all – in the lumber camp with his father. By this time the business upturn had prompted Argue to bankroll a new, larger sawmill at Lake Dumont. Bill Ryan, Jr., earned $1.33 a day.

Bill finished school in Renfrew in 1942. The local high school ended at grade twelve, so he had to follow Joe to Ottawa and the Oblate St. Patrick's College. His decision was made easier by a scholarship from the diocese of Pembroke. Officials of the diocese thought that he was a clever lad who would make a good recruit for the priesthood, and indeed, Bill had agreed to consider the idea, although he often told his friends vaguely that he was thinking about a career in engineering. He had also discussed the priesthood with the workers at the lumber camp, many of whom figured that Joe Ryan was the one headed for a clerical life. In any case, the small-town boy wearing his first suit left home at seventeen. He boarded the train for the city and moved into the dorm at St. Pat's, plunging into a new kind of life in which extracurricular activities took the place of family responsibilities. Bill found that Joe had left his mark; within weeks of arriving at the Oblate school, he found himself elected or appointed to several positions (such as business manager of the school paper and treasurer of the Sodality, a student association that organized religious and social events), apparently on the grounds that he was following his brother Joe.

Bill's reputation as Rock Ryan also followed him to Ottawa. "We played very hard hockey, sometimes brutal," he recalled. The competition was tougher in the city than it had been in Renfrew, but he managed to hold his own. Life at college offered new friendships and life in the city new distractions. Though he sometimes sneaked past the prefect's office for a night on the town, most of his socializing was more conventional. As president of the Ottawa Union Sodality, a grouping of a half-dozen sodalities from different Catholic schools, he helped to put on communion breakfasts and dances. Because the papal nuncio had forbidden the use of church property in Ottawa for school dances, Bill and his sodality friends held them at an Odd Fellows' Hall. No priest was willing to be seen on the premises, so Bill acted as chaperone. Ottawa Sodality also organized other events, on one occasion asking an up-and-coming cleric who was principal of St. Joseph's Catholic Teachers College in Montreal to speak. Emmett Carter, it turned out, was an engaging individual who regularly punctuated his remarks with an emphatic "Just as sure as God made little green apples."

In the spring of 1944 Bill Ryan felt the need to make a decision about his future. A serious young man who had just turned nineteen and was about to graduate from high school, he again had a number of choices. He could enlist in officer training for the air force. He could go to engineering school. Or he could follow Joe into the seminary. He decided to use prayer to help him figure out what to do. Perhaps God did want him to be a priest. Since St. Patrick's was an Oblate school, he spent three days at Holy Rosary, an Oblate formation house just east of Ottawa. In the end, his decision was final. A clerical life was not for him: "I was convinced that I should totally forget that idea and get on with my life."

A few weeks later Bill and a couple of other students were loung- ing around the dorm. The weather was warm, the windows were open and the talk gradually turned from the Canadians who were stalled in Normandy to the various priests they had encountered, at St. Pat's and elsewhere. The mood seemed to turn sour as the young men, each of whom had thought about donning the Roman collar, began grumbling about Father So-and-So and *Curé untel*. Then a fellow who had trans- ferred not long before from Regina's Campion College to St. Pat's came in and slouched onto one of the bunks.

"Ahh! You guys are always bitching," blurted Jim Connor. "If you want to be a priest you should join the Jesuits. I liked them. They're good priests."

Bill Ryan recalled that from that very moment he knew abso- lutely that he had been called to join the Society of Jesus, even though he was only dimly aware of what it was about. Asked to explain this mystery, he said he could not. "I've never had that happen before or since. But in Jesuit spirituality we learn that there is a time when the Lord deals with you directly. It's very unusual. Most of the time you have to struggle, work, learn, discern, think, pray. At that time I didn't. I just wish it would happen more often."

1   Fr. Paul Le Jeune, "Brief Relation of the Journey to New France, Made in the Month of April Last," in S.R. Mealing, ed., *The Jesuit Relations and Allied Docu- ments: A Selection* (Toronto: McClelland & Stewart, 1963), 19–20.

2   Interviewed in Kingston *Whig-Standard*, December 1, 2000.

3   Joan Finnigan, *Some of the Stories I Told You Were True* (Ottawa: Deneau, 1981), 134. Finnigan has compiled at least two dozen volumes of Valley lore.

4   C.C. Kennedy, *The Upper Ottawa Valley: A Glimpse of History* (Renfrew, ON: Renfrew County Council, 1970), 67.

5   Finnigan, *Some of the Stories*, 273.

6   *Tamarack* (Deep River, ON), 2 (May 1993).

7   Quoted in S. Evans, *Heart and Soul: Portraits of the Ottawa Valley* (Burnstown, ON: General Store Publishing, 1987), 154

8   Bernadette, 1916; Eileen, 1919; Katherine, 1921; Joseph, 1923; William Francis, 1925; James, 1928; Theresa, 1931; Robert, 1933; Helen, 1937.

9   See Phil Land, *Catholic Social Teaching: As I Have Lived, Loathed and Loved It* (Chicago: Loyola University Press, 1994), 4, 23–24.

Chapter 2

From Boot Camp to Harvard

Bill Ryan's *decision* to become a Jesuit was instantaneous, but the *process* of becoming a Jesuit would last twenty years. Jesuit training – or formation, as the order traditionally calls it – is famous for being thorough and extensive. Pedro Arrupe, who, as general of the Society in the 1960s and 1970s, became Ryan's mentor and inspirational leader, used to say of the Jesuits that "for the most part we're pretty ordinary men – but we do have good formation!"[1] Ryan's formation was drawn-out even by Jesuit standards. It would take him from Canada to the United States and Europe and back again, culminating in Cambridge, Massachusetts, with a Harvard Ph.D. The academic credentials he acquired, his experience of different cultures and the many contacts he made in the course of his travels would all serve him well in his subsequent career.

Implementing his decision had meant filling out a lot of papers and then going to Montreal for an interview with four Jesuits. He was accepted into the Upper Canada province by the socius, or assistant to the provincial, Father John Swain, like Ryan a native of the Ottawa Valley. With that hurdle out of the way, he packed his bags and set out for Guelph, a small city in the heart of Ontario's richest agricultural region some eighty kilometres west of Toronto. The Jesuit novitiate was located in an imposing building set on a working farm maintained by Jesuit brothers, just north of the city. It was here that Bill Ryan's long journey began in the fall of 1944.

The journey Ryan embarked on was not an uncommon one for young Catholics in that era. Of the 327 Jesuits in the Upper Canada province in 1943, there were 197 (just over 60 per cent) aged thirty-five and under.[2] People continued to join even though the program at the Guelph novitiate, like the early stages of pre–Vatican II Jesuit formation everywhere, was rigid and unimaginative. Father Brendan Cloran was in his first year as master of novices, and while he was respected as a "square shooter," in Ryan's words, he had no particular training or aptitude to serve as a spiritual guide to young men on the threshold of adulthood. Neil McKenty, a fellow novice of Ryan's who later left the Jesuits and became a radio talk show host, described the atmosphere in the novitiate:

> The maze of rules, regulations, traditions, and bells to stop this and start that (ringing thirty or forty times between our rising at 5:30 and lights-out at 9:30) was bound to produce a jumpy atmosphere in which one's nervous system itself became jittery.... One rule stipulated if we were ordered to stop what we were doing, even if we were writing a letter home, then we must stop immediately. One would likely interpret that to mean we should stop at the end of the word we were writing. Not so. Stopping your letter meant that if you were writing the letter "s" you should stop in the middle of it.[3]

Peter Larisey, who is four years younger than Ryan and entered the Society in 1952, says that the formation he experienced had its roots in a period when the Jesuits were trying to prove their orthodoxy after emerging from forty years in the wilderness of suppression (1773–1814), during which they had been cast into non-existence by papal decree. For Larisey, his formation was "characteristic of the nineteenth-century restored order, based on rules and military discipline. Being singular was looked down on. 'Particular friendships' were out, although they didn't talk about homosexuality."

Ryan acknowledges the rigidity but claims that he wasn't touched by it. To a certain extent, he survived because of the optimism and confidence that have been lifelong characteristics. Another reason was that, from the beginning, he did well as a Jesuit. McKenty describes the Bill Ryan he met as a "rough diamond who lacked finesse" but who was already recognized as a leader. Peter Larisey says, "The thing you have to understand about Bill is that he was always a success." The same could not be said of either McKenty or Larisey in the early years of their Jesuit formation – Larisey until he eventually found out while studying in

Montreal that his passion for the visual arts was not incompatible with his religious faith and that he could carry on his life's work of bringing together religion and modern art within the Society of Jesus.

Ryan also survived the rigours of the novitiate because, being close to the farm, he had access to an outlet that helped him through many difficult times: being outdoors and doing physical work. A special time of communion with nature was the thirty-day retreat, undertaken soon after he arrived in Guelph. The thirty-day retreat is based on the Spiritual Exercises developed by the founder of the Society of Jesus, St. Ignatius of Loyola, and remains a centrepiece of Jesuit formation. Ignatius, the story goes, was a soldier who, after being wounded in battle in 1521, experienced a religious conversion while recovering from his wounds. He set out on a pilgrimage, in the course of which he spent eleven months as a hermit near Manresa in northeastern Spain, taking stock of his life and the changes he had undergone. It was there that he sketched out a preliminary version of his Spiritual Exercises, which he continually revised in later years.

Although cast in terms that reflect Ignatius' own time – the Reign of Christ, the Standard of Christ and the Standard of Satan – the Exercises have proved an enduring contribution to spiritual life. Indeed, the early twentieth century saw a flowering of the Exercises, as they began to be offered to large numbers of lay people for the first time. Michael Higgins and Douglas Letson of St. Jerome's College in Waterloo, Ontario, prominent Canadian commentators on Catholic affairs whose books include one called *The Jesuit Mystique*, see the Spiritual Exercises as being the central element of the Jesuit identity. "Take the Exercises away and you just have a collection of professional men who happen to be bachelors and put 'SJ' after their name," says Higgins. "But if they're shaped and formed by the Exercises, then they're genuinely companions of the order."

Ignatius' text of the Exercises offers an imaginative entry into the life of Jesus, along with guidelines for discerning the "movement of spirits" that takes place during prayer. In this way, a person making the Exercises makes use of both intellect and imagination in an effort to become free – John English, a contemporary of Ryan's in the Upper Canada province who became a leader in the worldwide movement to revitalize the Exercises, entitled his book on the Exercises *Spiritual Freedom*. Specifically, a person seeks to become free of "disordered attachments" that stand in the way of their relationship with God. It is in such a state of freedom that a person is best able to make an important life decision. This is why the long period of Jesuit formation includes two thirty-day retreats, one near the beginning and the other near the end.

When Bill Ryan made the Exercises as a novice, they were given as a "preached retreat": the long periods of silent prayer were broken up four times a day by presentations from Father Cloran, which McKenty remembers as being "generally uninspired and uninspiring." But Ryan's memory of his first thirty-day retreat is mostly of being able to spend a lot of time outside, working on the farm and taking long hikes. "I really loved it," he says. "It was the first time I had ever prayed much. I didn't want the retreat to end." Indeed, he was so enamoured of the long periods of silence that the idea occurred to him that he might become a Trappist, although he soon thought better of it.

In his second year in the novitiate, Ryan had a turn at being admonitor, a kind of foreman of the novices. It was the admonitor's job to enforce the myriad of rules that governed the novices' lives. Here again McKenty's memory and Ryan's are different: McKenty remembers Ryan's regime as admonitor as being "fair, but on the rigid side," while Ryan remembers trying to change the rules. Another highlight of the second year was a visit from his father, who made the journey to Guelph and spent a day and a half walking and talking with Bill. Although they hardly spoke of how Bill Jr. felt about the decision he had made, he felt confirmed in his life choice by the fact of his father's visit. Then, after taking vows of poverty, chastity and obedience, he moved on to the next stage of Jesuit formation, the juniorate, also in Guelph. Again he was appointed to a leadership position for a time, that of beadle, where he says he "learned a lot about house politics and how to get things done without causing people to be upset." And once more he "stayed sane" through the program of English and classics that made up the juniorate by spending as much time as he could working on the farm, hiking and playing sports.

The next stage of Jesuit formation, the three-year philosophy program, was given at Regis College in Toronto, then located in an old building by a railway track on a site where the offices of the Toronto *Globe and Mail* now stand. Ryan did not take well to the move from the farm at Guelph to the urban desert of this part of west-central Toronto. Nor was he much engaged by his philosophical studies, based on St. Thomas Aquinas' *Summa Theologica*. Philosophy was taught by the thesis method, with theses stated and proved and counter-arguments disposed of. As Neil McKenty remembers it, "The adversaries were always the same suspects, Descartes, Hume, Kant, Spinoza, Hegel and Locke....

We just lined up these 'pagan' philosophers like decoys, then constructed our own syllogisms and proofs based on St. Thomas and shot all our adversaries dead every time."[4]

Ryan suffered a "small crisis in obedience" because he had a hard time accepting that many of the proofs actually proved the propositions in question. His relationship with his professors became increasingly strained, and he remembers that the rector, Fred Lynch, "eventually thought I was crazy." To restore his sanity, he asked to be sent to Guelph to shovel manure for three weeks, and his request was granted.

———————————

What he would do after he finished the philosophy program was not clear. He had asked to be sent to Darjeeling in northern India, where the Upper Canada province had established a mission, and his superiors had agreed, but they were also putting pressure on him to do further study in philosophy. He wasn't averse to more study, but philosophy did not interest him. Instead, he wanted to study economics. John Swain, who had been promoted to provincial, supported his choice, and in the fall of 1951 he began a master's program in economics at Saint Louis University – a turn in his life almost as decisive as his decision to join the Jesuits seven years earlier.

Studying such a worldly subject as economics was not exactly an expected course for a Jesuit in formation. And yet it had its roots in Catholic and Jesuit tradition. From 1891, when Pope Leo XIII issued his landmark encyclical *Rerum Novarum* ("The Condition of Labour"), the Church had sought to regain the fading allegiance of a European working class more intrigued by socialists preaching the gospel according to Marx than by clerics denouncing democracy and modernity. Towards this end it had sketched out its own approach to modern industrial society, separate from both capitalism and socialism. The Church condemned the exploitation and human misery that were conspicuous results of capitalism, but it could not abide the notion of class struggle advocated by socialists. While supporting the formation of trade unions, it insisted that those unions should strive for class collaboration rather than conflict.

These ideas, elaborated in a series of encyclicals and other Church documents, became known as "the social teaching of the Church." Jesuits were active in formulating and promoting the social teaching, and one of the most important social encyclicals, Pius XI's *Quadragesimo Anno* (1931), was largely written by a German Jesuit,

Oswald von Nell-Breuning. It was in *Quadragesimo Anno* that a crucial and controversial idea of Catholic social teaching was developed: the promotion of corporatism as a "third way" between capitalism and communism. Society was to be organized into "corporations" along vocational lines, transcending class divisions. In this way, class collaboration would replace class struggle, social peace would be achieved, the moral evils of capitalism would be mitigated, and social justice would be promoted. In a world ravaged by the Depression, corporatism had considerable appeal, but its association with Mussolini's Italy and other fascist and authoritarian states in Europe and Latin America made it suspect – even *Quadragesimo Anno*'s author, the Jesuit Nell-Breuning, was appalled by the uses to which it was put.[5] Corporatism also had avid supporters in Quebec, notably among the Jesuits of the École Sociale Populaire in Montreal, who in 1933 made it the basis of their *Programme de restauration sociale*.

At the same time, social issues were becoming an increasingly prominent concern of the Society of Jesus itself. In the spring of 1938 the Society's 28th General Congregation, held in the shadow of the German invasion of Austria and looming war in Europe, endorsed the kind of social-apostolic work advocated by *Rerum Novarum* and *Quadragesimo Anno* as being among the most important ministries of our age. It called for the establishment of centres for social research staffed by Jesuits with graduate training in economic and social questions. The 29th General Congregation in 1946 made the social apostolate the subject of a specific decree for the first time.

This congregation also elected as general superior of the order Father Jean-Baptiste Janssens of Belgium, who three years later addressed an "Instruction on the Social Apostolate" to all Jesuits. In the Instruction, Father Janssens noted that the social policies of the 28th and 29th General Congregations had not been implemented "in an orderly and persevering manner" as a result of the Second World War. Now, he said, centres for research and social action should be set up "to teach the theoretical and practical social doctrine to others, especially to priests, educated laymen, and the better educated working men, and to help them by counsel and advice." He urged Jesuits to become "trained in that sincere and active charity which today is called 'a social attitude' or 'social-mindedness.'"[6]

At the time, Bill Ryan was only vaguely aware of these developments, which were not emphasized in his formation. His interest in economics had its roots not in Rome but in the Ottawa Valley and the lumber camps where he had spent his summers in his youth. He had observed the region's dependence on the industry as well as the dangerous conditions that went along with the jobs the industry provided. He wanted to deepen his understanding of how all this worked, and studying economics was a way to reach that goal.

This stage of his education took place in surroundings that were very different from the novitiate at Guelph and Regis College in Toronto. He was now at a full-fledged university – indeed, the second-oldest Jesuit university in the United States and the oldest university of any kind west of the Mississippi River – located in a black neighbourhood of downtown St. Louis that had already begun to decay. Catholic social teaching was a particular focus of Saint Louis University, and an Institute of Social Order had been formed, housed at the university but separate from it, which Ryan would later see as a precursor of the Center of Concern in Washington that he headed in the 1970s.

One of the professors at the university who was also associated with the institute took a particular liking to the young Canadian Jesuit. Phil Land was himself a native of Canada, having been born in Montreal to American parents in 1911. His family moved to Vancouver when he was a young boy and then across the border to Washington State. Unlike Bill Ryan, Phil was an indifferent student, frequently playing hooky, until he joined the Jesuits at eighteen. While he threw himself into religious life with zeal, he never lost his independent spirit. Catholic social teaching soon became a particular interest of his, and he did graduate work in economics at Saint Louis and at Columbia University in New York, writing his doctoral dissertation on the social ideas of *Quadragesimo Anno*.

Land was Ryan's teacher in his intermediate economics course. "Phil wasn't the best teacher," Ryan says. "He saw too many things." The two became close, and one night Land showed up in Ryan's room and made an unorthodox request: would Ryan help him set the exam? Ryan suggested a number of questions, and four of them turned up on the exam, along with two others that Land had chosen himself. Land's path and Ryan's would cross frequently in subsequent years. Later in the 1950s, while Ryan was a theology student in Louvain, Belgium, Land was called to Rome to teach at the Gregorian University. On his way to his new post, he stopped at Louvain, where he told Ryan of his misgivings about living and teaching in Rome. He would stay in Rome almost two decades, but his departure would be clouded by a disagreement with the

Vatican on the issue of birth control. He would then accept an invitation from Bill Ryan to join the staff of the Center of Concern.

At Saint Louis, Land was also involved in encouraging Ryan to choose a Canadian subject for his thesis. There were two choices: Social Credit, and the Catholic trade unions in Quebec. Ryan was not interested in Social Credit and so, with Land as his thesis adviser, he embarked on a study of the Catholic trade unions. It was an exciting subject to be exploring in 1952. The Catholic unions had been founded under the influence of Catholic social teaching in the early part of the century, and had been organized into a federation, the Canadian and Catholic Confederation of Labour (CCCL), in 1921. Their hallmark in the early years was their advocacy of class collaboration and corporatism, in contrast to the more militant stance of the U.S.-based unions affiliated with the American Federation of Labor that had branches in Quebec. But in the 1940s, under dynamic new leaders and in response to the rapid industrialization of Quebec, the Catholic unions became much stronger advocates of the interests of workers, and in 1949 they fought a bitter strike in the asbestos mining towns of eastern Quebec that became a turning point in the province's history. Ryan interviewed many of those new leaders, including Jean Marchand and Gérard Pelletier, who later joined Pierre Elliott Trudeau in becoming federal members of Parliament and the vanguard of a new generation of Quebecers in Ottawa. Ryan later wrote:

> The biggest help, however, came from a Jesuit, Jacques Cousineau, the national chaplain of the unions at the time of the historic Asbestos strike in 1949. Like Archbishop Joseph Charbonneau of Montreal, Jacques was banished from his post for siding with the workers in that long ugly strike. I found him, silenced on this issue, teaching classics at Collège Garnier in Quebec City. Without comment, he entrusted to me his personal files – and I had my thesis![7]

His thesis was a straightforward and sympathetic exposition of the history of the Catholic trade union movement in Quebec. Addressing American readers for whom the whole idea of Catholic trade unionism was something of an anomaly, he traced the cultural and philosophical sources of the movement's orientation in its early years – clerical, corporatist, emphasizing social peace, disdainful of militancy and the strike weapon. In particular, he devoted considerable space to explaining Quebec's extraordinary Collective Agreement Act of 1934, passed at the urging of the CCCL.[8] Under this act, a collective agreement adopted by a particular union and employer could be extended by decree to an entire sector. Administration of this provision was entrusted to sectoral "parity committees," which some saw as an embryo of corporatist organization in Quebec. While such legislation could be used to improve wages and working conditions and provide stability and predictability in labour relations, it was also open to abuse by employers, who could use it to promote monopolies and hinder the growth of unionism. It also placed substantial power in the hands of the state; under an anti-labour government such as that of Premier Maurice Duplessis, in office from 1936 to 1939 and again after 1944, this power could be used against the workers.

Even while he tried to counter prevailing prejudices against Catholic unionism – and against French Quebec – in dealing with the CCCL's early years, Ryan's sympathies clearly lay with the more militant orientation the movement adopted in the 1940s. He described Gérard Picard, elected president of the CCCL on a platform of reform in 1946, as "a brilliant, energetic young lawyer and journalist" who is "a very well-informed and versatile labor leader" and "the most competent labour leader in Quebec today," and spoke in equally glowing terms of Picard's chief lieutenant, general secretary Jean Marchand.[9] Ryan observed that, with these leaders and its new orientation, the CCCL "promises to be the union of the future in the French Catholic province of Quebec."[10] He noted that, while the CCCL continued to be inspired by the social teaching of the Church, and remained faithful to its corporatist roots in promoting the new ideal of "co-management," it had begun to downplay its Catholic connections and there was talk of dropping the word "Catholic" from its name.[11] These observations proved prescient, as the Canadian and Catholic Confederation of Labour would change its name to the Confederation of National Trade Unions (CNTU) in 1960 and become the most dynamic element in the Quebec labour movement in the heady 1960s and early 1970s. Even in its new secular guise, however, the CNTU would be notable for the extent to which it advocated an overall vision of society and not just material gains for its members.

<hr>

Ryan's thesis was well received, and his professors suggested that he could receive a doctorate if he did a further year of studies at Saint Louis. But he had not enjoyed living in the city and felt that he did not have much more to learn at the university. For Ryan, restless as ever, it was time to move on. Theological studies, a central part of Jesuit formation, were still to come. But Jesuits in formation were being pressed into service to teach in Jesuit high schools because of a shortage of teachers, and so first Ryan spent a year teaching mathematics and economic geography at St. Paul's high school in Winnipeg. Fighting was common among the school's adolescent male students; as Ryan remembers, "I became Rock Ryan again," breaking up the occasional schoolyard fight. He turned down an offer to remain at St. Paul's to coach the football team, and left to begin his theological studies in Europe in the fall of 1954. The plan was for him to spend a year at Heythrop College in Oxfordshire, England, and then three years at Enghien in France.

The physical surroundings at Heythrop – a 16-hectare sheep farm with a garden – nourished Ryan's love of the outdoors. He enjoyed chopping down trees to make clearing routes through the surrounding forest. The British Jesuits were congenial and easy to live with. On the door of the old house they lived in was a sign they had obtained that evoked an earlier era in Protestant–Catholic relations in England: "Fifty pounds for the head of a Jesuit, living or dead." The intellectual atmosphere, however, was stifling.

The Tridentine Church that had been forged in the Counter-Reformation of the sixteenth century, the time when the Society of Jesus had been formed, was in its last decade. A new epoch would open in the 1960s, as the institutional Church began to forge a new relationship with its own faithful and with the modern world at the Second Vatican Council. The ideas that would gain the favour of the bishops at the Council were being developed and discussed in restricted circles in the 1950s. The French Jesuit paleontologist Pierre Teilhard de Chardin had made it his life's work to create a broad synthesis of Christianity and Darwin's theory of evolution. Also in France, theologians such as the Dominicans Marie-Dominique Chenu and Yves Congar and the Jesuit Henri de Lubac were recovering and reinterpreting earlier currents of Christian thought and applying them to the modern situation. De Lubac looked for insight in writers ranging from Origen in the third century to St. Bernard in the twelfth, as well as more recent philosophical and literary texts. His contention that no human formulation could capture the totality of revealed truth challenged the primacy of St. Thomas Aquinas that was then a central element in Catholic theology. In the United States, another Jesuit, John Courtney Murray, was advocating a more sympathetic attitude towards religious freedom than was then allowed in official Catholic teaching.[12]

But all of these thinkers operated under varying degrees of official Vatican disapproval, and generally received at best lukewarm support from their own religious orders. Teilhard de Chardin's major works could never be published in his lifetime. In 1950 Pope Pius XII issued a highly technical condemnation of the ideas of the French theologians in his encyclical *Humani Generis*, and their opportunities to teach were restricted. Murray was prevented from writing on the subjects he cared most about. Students at most Catholic seminaries and other academic institutions were barred from having any contact with the new ideas. Heythrop, where in 1954–55 books that challenged the prevailing orthodoxy were kept in a locked room commonly referred to as "Hell," was no exception.

Ryan's next step did not proceed according to plan. It turned out that there was no room for him at Enghien. He did not want to stay at Heythrop. Then a place opened up for him at Collège Saint-Albert, a Jesuit college on the outskirts of the Belgian town of Louvain, home of the oldest Catholic university in the world. Louvain was also one of the few places where the new ideas that were officially disapproved of in Rome circulated with relative freedom. The books that were consigned to "Hell" just across the North Sea at Heythrop were read with great excitement at Louvain.

Among Jesuits of Ryan's generation – those who were trained before the Second Vatican Council but were to spend most of their working lives in the wake of that epochal event – an experience that took them outside the rigid certainties of the standard Jesuit formation of the time is a common theme. For Peter Larisey, it was his discovery of the possible synthesis of art and religion in Montreal. For John English, it was his studies at St. Beuno's in Wales, where a British Jesuit named Paul Kennedy was developing a new framework for the Spiritual Exercises. While Bill Ryan had already stepped gingerly outside the box with his graduate studies in economics, his three years at Louvain would expand his horizons in a much more radical way.

In his first meeting with Ryan, the dean of studies at Collège Saint-Albert, Léo Malevez SJ, asked the Canadian to explain his main theological interest. Ryan said that he was primarily interested in the way theology related to economic and social institutions. Malevez went to his shelf and brought down two books, de Lubac's *Le surnaturel* and Teilhard de Chardin's *Le phénomène humain*. Both were forbidden to seminary students at the time.

Teilhard in particular would be a lifelong influence on Ryan – someone who worked with him some four decades after Father Malevez gave him *Le phénomène humain* to read would describe him as a "Teilhardian." *Le phénomène humain* – the title is mistranslated into English as *The Phenomenon of Man* – is the book in which Teilhard developed his ideas most fully. Vatican censorship prevented its publication until the year of his death, 1955 (the same year Ryan arrived in Louvain), when it was finally released by a secular publisher in Paris, Éditions du Seuil. While Teilhard insisted that *Le phénomène humain* be regarded as a scientific treatise, not as a work of philosophy or theology, his inclusive approach made scientists as well as Church officials uneasy, especially at a time when the gulf between science and religion seemed to be unbridgeable. In particular, Teilhard argued that consciousness, "the within of things," needed to be considered a scientific phenomenon, present in the universe from the beginning although only fully realized in human beings.[13]

Teilhard traced a continuous path from inanimate matter through the emergence and increasing complexity of life to conscious human beings. Just as the earth contains a sphere of inanimate matter (the lithosphere) and a sphere of life (the biosphere), he posited, it also contains a sphere of consciousness, which he called the noosphere. He believed that the noosphere was tending towards a kind of unity of human consciousness, which to him also meant that it was tending towards Christ. The underlying principle of his whole system was evolution, which was still held in suspicion by most Christian thinkers of the time. And despite the deeply Christian nature of his synthesis, his emphasis on progress rather than on fallen humanity in need of redemption also placed him outside the mainstream of Christian thought. But the breadth of the paleontologist's vision immediately appealed to Ryan. As the priest and ecologist Thomas Berry later characterized Teilhard's contribution, "He told the story of the universe in an integral manner, perhaps for the first time."[14]

Father Malevez himself, who introduced Ryan to a phenomenological approach to theology,[15] was also a significant influence on him, as were other Jesuit professors at Louvain, notably René Carpentier, whose work involved weaving together moral theology, dogmatic theology and spirituality. Early in his stay at Louvain (while recuperating from a broken ankle incurred in playing basketball), Ryan wrote a paper on justice that Carpentier criticized because it did not deal with poverty. Ryan had seen justice and poverty as being entirely separate matters, but from Carpentier he learned to approach theology in a more holistic way.

A student of Carpentier's, Gérard Gilleman SJ, had written a book called *Le primat de la charité en théologie morale* in which he shifted the emphasis of moral theology from the avoidance of sin to the positive practice of virtue. Carpentier wanted the book, which reflected his own thinking, to reach English-speaking readers, and he persuaded Ryan and a French-Canadian Jesuit, André Vachon, to translate it.[16] It was a painstaking process, as the two Jesuits struggled through the arcane text at a rate of a page a day. Vachon would produce a literal translation while Ryan would refine the way Gilleman's concepts were expressed. When they ran into trouble, Carpentier was always able to help them interpret Gilleman's thinking – Gilleman himself had been posted to India and was unavailable for consultation. If the work was difficult, it was also rewarding for Ryan, since Gilleman's book contributed to his developing sense that Christian faith was to be lived out through action in the world.

This was the theme he took for his major research paper at Louvain, in which he laid out a theological basis for being active in the temporal world. Since such "temporal engagement" includes most of the things people actually do in their lives, from working on an assembly line to making scientific discoveries, it might not seem to require much justification. But there is a Christian tradition of "detachment" that has often been taken to mean withdrawal from the affairs of the world. In this tradition, the Christian's place is not to build up the world but to await humbly the kingdom of God, which will come or not come regardless of what human beings do. "Is all our scientific and industrial work relevant to the coming of the kingdom?" Ryan asked. "Or might we not just as well weave and unweave baskets, as did monks of past times?"[17]

Ryan's exposition was based on traditional sources – Scripture, the Church Fathers, St. Thomas Aquinas – along with the new influences he had encountered at Louvain. His citations included Teilhard, de Lubac, Chenu, Congar and Murray as well as Malevez, Carpentier and Gilleman. Not surprisingly, he concluded that there were better things to do than weave and unweave baskets. Detachment did not mean withdrawal, he argued; rather, it "consists in making not self, but Christ the centre of the material world." And since all human beings are members of Christ, "attachment to Christ already includes devotedness towards all His members." Furthermore, human beings are bodies as well as souls, so that "charity towards them will inevitably engage Christians in temporal action."[18] But this temporal action will take on a particular character. In the case of a Christian investor, for example, "wages, working conditions, methods of advertising, prices, product standards, etc. are all major preoccupations." This idealized investor "will do his utmost to avoid unjust and even uncharitable actions towards workers and consumers alike.... Any sound plan to include workers among the stockholders merits his wholehearted support."[19]

In addition to the professors, the other students at Louvain, who came from twenty-four different countries, also helped to broaden Ryan's horizons. Among these was a Uruguayan Jesuit named Juan Luis Segundo, whom Ryan remembers as being bored with theology and spending much of his time reading novels. Back in his home country, Segundo became a leader in developing a new constellation of ideas known as liberation theology that would set the agenda for much of the Latin American Church in the late 1960s and 1970s and have worldwide influence. But despite the intellectual excitement at Louvain, in one important respect life was less congenial for Ryan than it had been in England. The setting of the college was much more institutional than Heythrop, the way of life was more impersonal and the physical surroundings were drab. The students lived in a large nondescript building built in the 1930s and life in Belgium still had an atmosphere of postwar austerity.

In his spare time Ryan got out of Louvain and travelled around Europe, learning about social movements in the places he visited. One of his trips, however, got him into trouble. He went to Rome to study communism, but Jesuits were not supposed to enter Rome without the permission of the general. Father Janssens was on vacation at the time, and an English Jesuit, Father Bolland, was temporarily in charge. Ryan tried to make an appointment to meet with Bolland to share what he had learned on his visit. Bolland refused to see him because he did not have permission to be in Rome, and a heated correspondence followed in which Bolland accused Ryan of not being a good Jesuit. Ryan's difficulties could have been serious had it not been for a freak occurrence: in the midst of the controversy Father Bolland was killed in a streetcar accident and the matter faded away.

Towards the end of his stay at Louvain, in August 1957, Ryan was ordained a priest. The ceremony was the occasion for a rare visit from three of his sisters – the rest of the family would have to wait until he returned to Canada and his ordination was celebrated again with a party in Renfrew in May 1959. Although he had not given priesthood much thought before ordination, and did not regard himself as having reached a long-sought goal, he felt comfortable with his new status, and confirmed in his Jesuit identity. He was now ready for what is generally the final year of Jesuit formation: tertianship, a time for a Jesuit to rediscover his interior self and re-establish his relationship with God after all the years of acquiring intellectual knowledge. Ryan spent that year at Paray-le-Monial in east-central France, under an ascetic and somewhat stern Jesuit named Father Goussault.

The centrepiece of the tertianship year is a second round of the full thirty-day Spiritual Exercises – according to Michael Higgins, it was this retreat that traditionally created fully formed Jesuits. For Ryan, it helped create a sense of spiritual, intellectual and apostolic groundedness. In one respect, this retreat was very much like his first one fourteen years earlier: he spent much of it outdoors to "keep sane." There was a very large tree stump in the courtyard at Paray, and he broke it up using wedges, giving other retreatants lessons in how a Canadian lumberjack cuts up trees. Pastoral work is also part of the tertianship experience, and Ryan spent a good part of the year ministering to Canadian and American military bases in France and Germany. Before coming to Paray he spent several weeks as chaplain to a house for asthmatic children in the Swiss Alps, where he did his first real mountain climbing. He also discovered that care of asthmatic children was not the only activity going on at the sanatorium. The director was in jail for spying, and his wife offered Ryan some watches to sell at a suspiciously low price. Although there was a strong possibility that the watches were smuggled, he decided to give her the benefit of the doubt.

In the summer of 1959, Ryan was back in Canada, but his education was still not complete. There was still the matter of the doctorate in economics that had been left hanging when he left Saint Louis six years earlier. The provincial, Gordon George, agreed that Ryan should pursue a doctorate in economics, and wanted him to do it in Canada – he had been out of the country long enough. Ryan, however, had his eye on Harvard; he got George to agree, and his application to Harvard was the only one he submitted. It was not until later that he found out that Harvard admitted only one out of every fifteen applicants. But Ryan's background of successful study in Canada, the United States and Europe made his application stand out, and he was accepted.

While Ryan's inclination for being part of the forces of change, a consistent characteristic of his later career, had been nurtured at Louvain, his decision to go to Harvard showed his equally ingrained affinity for the centres of power. The lines of communication between Cambridge, Massachusetts, and Washington, D.C., have always been active, and never more so than during the time Ryan was a student at Harvard. In the fall of 1960, John F. Kennedy was elected president of the United States. The Irish Catholic Kennedys had achieved respectability largely by sending their sons to Harvard, and now JFK turned to his alma mater to fill many of the senior posts in his administration. Cambridge supplied the new president with "the best and the brightest" who would bring Camelot to Washington (and, with some honourable exceptions, destruction to the rice paddies of Vietnam). Historian Arthur Schlesinger, Jr., became a White House aide, economist John Kenneth Galbraith was sent to India as ambassador, and McGeorge Bundy, dean of Harvard College, became national security adviser. Bundy's deputy, Walt W. Rostow, came from the Massachusetts Institute of Technology, a few blocks east along Massachusetts Avenue. As the Harvard historian Samuel Eliot Morison wrote, "The newspapers were inquiring, 'Who is left in Cambridge to teach the students?'"[20] One of those students was Ryan, whose initial thesis adviser, David Bell, was called to Washington to head the Bureau of the Budget (he later became director of the Agency for International Development).

As a Catholic priest in his mid-thirties, Ryan was an unusual student, and he commanded respect. Professors addressed him as "Father Ryan" and stood when he entered their offices. But his years in Europe had accustomed him to studying a very different discipline in a different milieu, and mostly in a different language. During his first semester he struggled to keep up, and his health suffered as a result. Both his grades and his health improved, however, as he became more acclimatized to the Harvard way of doing things, and he would eventually rank Harvard as being among the best educational experiences of his long career as a student – matched only by his time at Renfrew Collegiate Institute.

With his competitive streak, Ryan thrived in the cut-and-thrust of the Harvard seminar. He still remembers how he once "shredded" a paper by one of his professors, a Russian émigré named Alexander Gershenkron, in front of Gershenkron's thesis candidates. On another occasion Ryan challenged Gershenkron to explain why he taught economic history the way he did, eliciting a three-hour response. Ryan and

Gershenkron developed a close relationship, and when David Bell left for Washington, Gershenkron became his thesis adviser. It was also at Harvard that Ryan first met Barbara Ward, then a visiting professor. A British Catholic of upper-class background and a former foreign editor of *The Economist*, Ward was a liberal critic of the international "development" enterprise then just gearing up. Ryan would meet Ward again at a World Council of Churches (WCC) meeting in Geneva in 1966, and they would subsequently work together and become friends.

Development was one of the buzzwords of the era, and the disillusionment and cynicism that would later cling to the effort to improve the lot of what were then known as the underdeveloped countries had not yet set in. There was broad agreement on the idea that the countries of Asia, Africa and Latin America, many of which were then just gaining formal independence from colonial rule, could and should be brought to the same economic level as the West. For western governments, this was a way of keeping these countries out of the hands of the communist enemy in the Cold War, then at its height. The leading theorist of this approach was MIT's Walt Rostow, who entitled his influential book on the subject *The Stages of Economic Growth: A Non-Communist Manifesto*.[21] Rostow proposed that each society moved from underdevelopment to development through a period of rapid economic growth that he called the "take-off." The goal was to help the underdeveloped countries reach the take-off point.

Gershenkron and other professors were interested in the role of religion in the development process, and they encouraged Ryan to structure his thesis around that theme. In particular, how had the Catholic Church affected development in areas where it was influential? This was a subject that sparked Ryan's interest – he would still be studying the relationship between religion and development in the 1990s. For a case study, Ryan once again turned to Quebec. Rostow had already identified the "take-off" period in Quebec, as in Canada as a whole, as being the years between 1896 and 1914. Rather than study his native Ottawa Valley, Ryan looked at the watersheds of two other western tributaries of the St. Lawrence that had undergone rapid forest-based economic growth during that period, the Saint-Maurice and the Saguenay.

The notion that the Catholic Church in Quebec had consistently opposed industrialization was well entrenched and served a number of agendas. At a popular level, English Canadians believed that if Quebec was behind the rest of Canada economically it was the Quebecers' own fault, and so the idea of a church that "held the people back" was a staple of English-Canadian stereotypes about Quebec. This stereotype was supported by a considerable body of academic work. For example, the prominent University of Toronto sociologist S.D. Clark wrote that in Canada "the promotion of the religious interest in itself has involved a weakening of the economic interest, because of the fundamental antagonism of the one for the other."[22] French-Canadian modernizers, who led an increasingly vigorous opposition to the Duplessis provincial government and the traditional Quebec it stood for in the 1950s and gained the upper hand with the election of the Liberals under Jean Lesage in 1960, had their own reasons for emphasizing the backward-looking aspects of clerical influence. In the new Quebec they envisioned, the Church's role would be greatly reduced, and so these writers – whether neo-nationalists such as Michel Brunet or anti-nationalists such as Pierre Elliott Trudeau – cast an unfavourable light on what they saw as the clerical shackles that Quebec was casting off.[23]

Ryan was thus proposing to walk into something of a minefield, and his Jesuit superiors in Canada were not happy. Gordon George and his consultants feared that Ryan's thesis could harm the Church in Quebec and complicate relations between their Upper Canada province and the French-Canadian Jesuit province. One of the consultants said that it wasn't even an economic thesis, and George asked Ryan to drop his line of research. Ryan, whose conception of Jesuit obedience did not involve automatic acquiescence, argued strongly in defence of the thesis proposal. He wrote to George expressing his surprise that the provincial and the consultants seemed to know the conclusions of his thesis when he didn't know the conclusions himself. The professors at Harvard, he noted, thought that what he was proposing was an economic thesis. George kept up the argument a while longer but ultimately gave Ryan permission to proceed.

Ryan spent the better part of a year poring through diocesan and parish archives and other historical records in the Saint-Maurice Valley and the Saguenay–Lac Saint-Jean region. As had been the case when he was researching his master's thesis, Quebec Jesuits and their files proved a useful source. In addition, he gained the confidence of Mgr. Albert Tessier, custodian of Church archives in the Saint-Maurice Valley, and his counterpart in the Saguenay, Mgr. Victor Tremblay. Both Tessier and Tremblay gave him access to numerous private documents in addition to the ones in the official archives. The picture that Ryan pieced together from these documents did not correspond to the stereotypes. The intellectual clerics may have railed against industrialization, but in diocese after diocese, parish after parish, Ryan found that the bishops and especially the curés were deeply concerned with the economic welfare of the people and welcomed the new industries that would give them jobs.

Clerical enthusiasm for industry was at its highest in those rare instances where the mills were in the hands of French-Canadian entrepreneurs. In the bustling city of Chicoutimi on the Saguenay, there was "unprecedented harmony and co-operation between the Church and the French Canadian Chicoutimi Pulp Company. The occasion of the solemn blessing of their second mill, in November 1903, was a combined religious and civic holiday and provided the theme of local and Quebec newspapers for days on end."[24] At the request of Bishop M.-T. Labrecque of Chicoutimi, the owner of the company, Alfred Dubuc, received a papal knighthood in 1904. But industrialists did not have to be French Canadian to work harmoniously with the clergy. At Grand'Mère on the Saint-Maurice, the Laurentide Pulp Company mill was owned by American and English-Canadian interests. The American manager of the mill, George Chahoon, later described his relationship with the local curé, Father Louis-R. Laflèche: "He smiled, and putting his hand on my shoulder, said, 'Mr. Chahoon, you and I are partners – I look after the spiritual welfare of my people while you are responsible for their bodily well-being.' The partnership was never dissolved."[25]

On the basis of local circumstances such as these, as well as the Church's broader role in promoting education, agriculture and new settlement, Ryan concluded that "the Church's role in economic development in the pre-war spurt was, on balance, positive, without being either decisive or determining."[26] But if French-Canadian economic inferiority and the paucity of French-Canadian entrepreneurs were not due to clerical opposition to industry, what was their cause? Ryan's answer to this question was remarkable in its appreciation, rare among English-Canadian writers, for the Quebec nationalist understanding of history:

> It would be to miss completely the heart of the problem of why the French Canadians were in an inferior economic position if one failed to realize fully that, from the time of the conquest until the middle of the last century, they, the earliest Canadians, were usually considered in practice, if not in official policy, as "outsiders," whom the British hoped eventually to assimilate.... While English and American entrepreneurs, capitalists, skilled workmen, as well as their technical publications and trade jour-

nals, all rallied to build the new English Canadian economic world, the minimum entrance fee to this world for the French Canadians was to become bilingual – no small task in a young country where education was still very rudimentary![27]

The depth of his research and the freshness of his point of view, particularly coming from an anglophone, made Ryan's thesis a work of lasting importance. It was published as a book by Les Presses de l'Université Laval in 1966 under the title *The Clergy and Economic Growth in Quebec (1896–1914)* and attracted the attention of Quebec's most eminent nationalist historian, eighty-nine-year-old Canon Lionel Groulx. In a review that he published shortly before he died in 1967 in his historical journal, the *Revue d'histoire de l'Amérique française*, Groulx praised *The Clergy and Economic Growth* as "a book that should attract attention":

> It can be concluded from Mr. Ryan's brilliant study that, if the Quebec church has not always played an active, determining role in the economic field, and has more often played a rather marginal role, its actions have never been negative, let alone harmful…. His work is a work of candour, a search for truth. In this chapter in the history of the Quebec clergy, he has not hidden the errors and omissions. He will not make all the prejudices disappear. He will make some of them disappear. For a historian, that in itself is a lot.[28]

In the late 1970s, one of the authors of this book, working on a study of Quebec's relations with the United States,[29] came across a copy of *The Clergy and Economic Growth in Quebec* in a library. It led to a revision of some simplistic ideas about the antagonistic relationship between Quebec's clerical nationalists and American capital. For someone who had no previous acquaintance with Bill Ryan or any other Jesuits, the existence of such a book by an English-Canadian Jesuit came as no small surprise.

—⇒●⇐—

One Harvard graduate has noted that the value of her degree increases in proportion to the distance from Cambridge. When Bill Ryan returned to Canada with his Ph.D., almost forty and ready for his first real job, he was in possession of a valuable commodity indeed, and the label "Harvard-trained economist" would cling to him throughout his career. He landed first at Loyola College, an English-language Jesuit post-secondary institution in Montreal (now part of Concordia University), where he taught economics. It was clear from the start, however, that he was destined for bigger things. John English, who was with Ryan at Loyola at the time, remembers that there was some resentment that after so much Jesuit money and effort had been invested in Ryan's education, a Jesuit institution in his home province would not benefit from it.

Two possibilities emerged for Ryan. One was to go to the Gregorian University in Rome, where his friend and mentor from Saint Louis, Phil Land, was teaching economics and Catholic social thought. The other was to work at the Ottawa office of the newly invigorated Canadian Catholic Conference (CCC), the umbrella organization of Canada's bishops. Wherever he went, it would be in the context of a rapidly changing Church. While Ryan had been studying at Harvard, the world's Catholic bishops had begun meeting in Rome in an epochal council. Henri de Lubac, Yves Congar and other theologians whose works Ryan had tasted as forbidden pleasures while at Louvain were now advisers to the bishops. The Church would now not simply proclaim eternal truths; it would read the "signs of the times" – a favourite phrase of Pope John XXIII's that would also become a favourite phrase of Ryan's. As the Dominican theologian Marie-Dominique Chenu explained it in an article in the *Nouvelle revue théologique*, the journal of the Jesuit professors at Louvain, the phrase meant that Christians needed to pay attention to the movement of history. The signs of the times were those historical events that were not only important in themselves but also brought about changes in human consciousness. In the 1960s, there were many such signs to be seen:

> It falls to Christians to recognize and receive those values which, having become autonomous, are the common capital of believers and nonbelievers. In their faith, they listen assiduously to the modern world, now having no place for the doctrinaire and paternalistic attitude of someone who, autonomously and in advance, has all the answers to every question. They become able to recognize moral norms whose current appearance in history has not come from the Church, even if it was the Gospel that took the radical step of initially proposing these norms. So it is with freedom. So it is with the emergence of feminine values. So it is with respect for the child as a human person. So it is with peace among human beings.[30]

A Church that was attentive to history, that worked with non-Christians, that did not claim to have all the answers – all that seemed possible in the mid-1960s. The changes would have as profound an effect on the Society of Jesus as on any other segment of the Church, and the Society would live out the changes in its own way, with its own dramas, in which Bill Ryan would be a significant player.

Jean-Baptiste Janssens died in 1964, and a general congregation, the 31st (or GC31 in Jesuit shorthand), met the next year to choose a new general. The congregation's choice was Pedro Arrupe, the first Basque since Ignatius to head the Society. Arrupe had been a medical student in Madrid before joining the Society at the age of twenty in 1927. After the Jesuits were expelled from Spain by the Republican government in 1932, he lived in Belgium, Holland and the United States before being granted his wish to be sent as a missionary to Japan. He arrived in Japan, following in the footsteps of his hero Francis Xavier (Ignatius' friend and fellow Basque), in 1938, and became a pastor in the southern city of Yamaguchi. After the Japanese bombed Pearl Harbor in 1941, he was arrested on suspicion of being a foreign spy and held in jail for a month before being released. The next year he was appointed master of novices and transferred to the novitiate at Nagatsuka, on the outskirts of Hiroshima. He had just entered his study on the morning of August 6, 1945, when he saw a blinding flash of light, heard a deafening explosion, and was thrown across the room by a blast of hot air. With his medical training, he tended to the victims of the first atomic bomb ever used in war.[31] In subsequent years, he wrote and lectured extensively about his Hiroshima experience. He also became provincial of Japan in 1954, a position he held until he was elected general.

The spirit of GC31 was one of change: "Our whole training in spirituality and studies...must be changed;...the very spiritual heritage of our Institute, containing both new and old elements, is to be purified and enriched anew according to the necessities of our times."[32] The atmosphere was as heady in the austere Jesuit curia on Borgo Santo Spirito as it was at the more opulent setting of the nearby Council. According to Jean-Yves Calvez, a French delegate to GC31 who would become one of Arrupe's closest advisers, "spirits were bubbling over" at the time, the spirit of opening up, of John XXIII's *aggiornamento* affecting the Jesuits in the same way it was the entire Church.[33]

It was, as befits a gathering of men famous for their learned and serious comportment, a serious affair. Delegates had to make their way through some nineteen hundred *postulata*, or recommendations from Jesuits around the world. Still, one sign of the times was an event unparalleled in Jesuit congregations, a lighthearted evening entertainment staged on the roof of the curia, complete with skits, songs and a parody in arcane Latin of every cliché being used in the great *aula*, or congregation hall, downstairs. The new general rendered two tenor solos, one in his native Basque, the other in Japanese.

Once elected, Arrupe threw himself into the modern world, travelling more in his first two years than any Jesuit general had ever done, giving press conferences, being interviewed on television. Pope Paul VI, who succeeded John XXIII in 1963, had reminded GC31 that the Jesuits had to commit themselves to the struggle against atheism, and in light of their special fourth vow of obedience to the pope, they did so. For Pedro Arrupe, however, atheism could be rather broadly defined: "The battle against atheism can be identified, at least in part, with the battle against poverty, since poverty was one of the reasons that the working classes have abandoned the Church."[34] At a press conference only a few weeks after his election, Arrupe made the first public statement ever by a Jesuit general in support of the work of Pierre Teilhard de Chardin. Although Teilhard's fame and influence had grown steadily in the decade since his death, his work was still under a warning, a *Monitum*, from the Vatican's Holy Office. "His vision of the world exerts a very beneficial influence in scientific circles, Christian and non-Christian," Arrupe said. "Father Teilhard is one of the great masters of contemporary thought and his success is not surprising…. We cannot ignore the richness of Father Teilhard's message for our times."[35]

Warm, open, optimistic, charismatic and trusting, Arrupe inspired fierce loyalty in most of the Jesuits who served under him, although he also had his detractors in the Society ("One Basque founded the Society, another is destroying it"). He said that he preferred the simplicity of the dove to the cunning of the serpent, and this was both his strength and his weakness.[36] Change would not come easily. It would take another general congregation before the Society of Jesus clearly moved in the direction Arrupe wanted to take it: towards greater emphasis on serving the poor and promoting social justice.

Among the Jesuits who were inspired by Arrupe was Bill Ryan. For a Jesuit who believed that Christian faith was something to be *done*, to be lived out in positive action in the world, there would be much work in the years and decades ahead. For the next few years that work would be done in Ottawa. In his long career as an international Jesuit, Ryan would never live in Rome. After his twenty-year journey, he came to roost barely a hundred kilometres from where he was born.

1 Quoted in introduction to Peter-Hans Kolvenbach SJ, *New Vigor for the Church: Conversations on the Global Challenges of Our Time* (Toronto: Compass: A Jesuit Journal, 1993), v.

2 William F. Ryan SJ, *Update: Our Way of Proceeding in the '80s* (Toronto: Society of Jesus, Upper Canada Province, 1983), n. 15.

3 Neil McKenty, *The Inside Story: Journey of a Former Jesuit Priest and Talk Show Host towards Self-Discovery* (Sainte-Anne-de-Bellevue, QC: Shoreline, 1997), 53.

4 McKenty, *The Inside Story*, 70.

5 See Charles Fernandes, "Corporatism and Its Fascist Friends," *Compass*, March/April 1993, 16–18.

6 Quoted in Michael Czerny SJ, and Paolo Foglizzo SJ, "A Jubilee of a Hundred Years: The Social Apostolate in the Twentieth Century," in *Jesuits: Yearbook of the Society of Jesus 2000* (Rome: General Curia of the Society of Jesus, 1999), 102.

7 William F. Ryan SJ, "My Life Between the Two Solitudes," *Compass*, January/February 1997, 12–13.

8 William F. Ryan SJ, "An Experiment in Catholic Syndicalism: A Brief History of the Origins, Growth, and Ideological Evolution of the Canadian and Catholic Confederation of Labor," Unpublished master's thesis, Saint Louis University, 1953, 84–104.

9 Ibid., 129–31.

10 Ibid., 6.

11 Ibid., 153, 163–72.

12 See Pierre Vallin, "French Theolgians' Time of Trial," *Compass*, March/April 1995, 13–14; Thomas O'Meara, "Raid on the Dominicans," *America*, February 5, 1994; Ignacio Echániz SJ, *Passion and Glory: A Flesh-and-Blood History of the Society of Jesus*, vol. 4, *Second Spring: 1814–1965–1999* (Anand, Gujarat, India: Gujarat Sahitya Prakash, 2000), 244–63, 271–78.

13 Pierre Teilhard de Chardin, *The Phenomenon of Man*, tr. Bernard Wall (1959; London: Collins, Fontana Books, 1965), 58–63.

14 In a 1987 interview with Jane Blewett, in *Teilhard de Chardin in the Age of Ecology* (film), filmed and produced by Lou Niznik, 1988.

15 Malevez's critique of Teilhard de Chardin from a phenomenological point of view, "La méthode du P. Teilhard de Chardin et la Phénoménologie," is contained in the journal of the Jesuit faculty at Louvain, the *Nouvelle Revue Théologique*, June 1957, 579–99.

16 The translation was published as *The Primacy of Charity in Moral Theology* (Westminster, MD: Newman Press, 1961).

17 William F. Ryan SJ, "Detachment vs Temporal Engagement: A Modern Christian Dilemma," unpublished paper, Collège St. Albert, Eegenhoven, Louvain, Belgium, 1958, p. 4.

18 Ibid., 25–26.

19 Ibid., 61.

20 Samuel Eliot Morison, *The Oxford History of the American People* (New York: Oxford University Press, 1965), 1111.

21 Cambridge, U.K.: Cambridge University Press, 1960.

22   S.D. Clark, "The Religious Factor in Canadian Economic Development," *Journal of Economic History*, supplement, vol. 7 (1947), 94–95, cited in William F. Ryan SJ, *The Clergy and Economic Growth in Quebec (1896–1914)* (Quebec City: Les Presses de l'Université Laval, 1966), 5.

23   See Michel Brunet, "Trois dominantes de la pensée canadienne-française: l'agriculturalisme, l'anti-étatisme, et le messianisme: essai d'histoire intellectuel," *Écrits du Canada français*, vol. 3 (1957), 33–117; Pierre Elliott Trudeau, "The Province of Quebec at the Time of the Strike," in Pierre Elliott Trudeau, ed., *The Asbestos Strike*, tr. James Boake (Toronto: James Lewis and Samuel, 1974), 1–81.

24   Ryan, *The Clergy and Economic Growth*, 158.

25   George Chahoon, "A Speech on Labor Relations," given probably in 1943, cited in Ryan, *The Clergy and Economic Growth*, 67.

26   Ryan, *The Clergy and Economic Growth*, 296.

27   Ibid., 291.

28   *Revue d'histoire de l'Amérique française*, vol. 20, no. 4 (March 1967), 641–44.

29   Robert Chodos and Eric Hamovitch, *Quebec and the American Dream* (Toronto: Between the Lines, 1991).

30   M.-D. Chenu, O.P., "Les signes des temps," *Nouvelle revue théologique*, January 1965, 39.

31   George Bishop, *Pedro Arrupe SJ: Twenty-eighth General of the Society of Jesus* (Anand, Gujarat, India: Gujarat Sahitya Prakash, 2000), is a recent account of Arrupe's life with emphasis on his experiences at Hiroshima.

32   Quoted in John W. Padberg SJ, "The General Congregations of the Twentieth Century," in *Jesuits: Yearbook of the Society of Jesus 2000*, 14.

33   Jean-Yves Calvez, *Faith and Justice: The Social Dimension of Evangelization* (St. Louis, MO: Institute of Jesuit Sources, 1991), 25.

34   Quoted in Manfred Barthel, *The Jesuits: History and Legend of the Society of Jesus*, tr. M. Howson (New York: William Morrow, 1984), 281.

35   Quoted in Echániz, *Passion and Glory*, vol. 4, 254.

36   Ibid., vol. 4, 341, 343.

Chapter 3

Kairos

It was an odd sort of living arrangement, unlike anything the priests had experienced at the seminary or the rectory. It wasn't quite an arrangement like the ones where the students of the day were beginning to share the joys and challenges ("Whose turn is it to...?") of co-op living. Nor was the way they found themselves living exactly akin to a handful of bachelor executives in bachelor apartments. But it had elements of each. It was, like so much else in those days, new, different, stimulating.

In 1966 a group of priests rented a wing of the ninth floor of the Bayshore apartments in west-end Ottawa. Each was a staff member of the Canadian Catholic Conference (CCC) and each had his own small apartment, except for the two Jesuits, Bill Ryan and Gordon George, who stayed together. And most evenings they all dined as a group. There was no reason to go out to eat because the food was better at home. Everett MacNeil, the assistant general secretary of the CCC, had hired a skilled cook and Mrs. Munroe's table soon became a magnet for out-of-town visitors including bishops and officials of Protestant churches, their newly minted "ecumenical partners." Bishop Alexander Carter of Sault Sainte-Marie was a frequent guest.

The lively conversations over dinner ranged from the latest gossip about Vatican politics to the state of English–French relations, both at the Conference and on the wider political landscape, where the new Quebec nationalism was questioning Confederation and ushering in changes that transformed the Church in that province. After dinner the priests would wander off to their own places to read or catch up on some work before reassembling in the big apartment that doubled as chapel and common room. Madame Munroe had looked after the dishes and the group would sit around the black and white television to watch the eleven o'clock news. The latest war news from Saigon or the tensions within John Diefenbaker's Tories over the proposed "two nations" policy kindled boisterous debates.

Things were also bubbling at the CCC offices on Parent Avenue, where the men at the Bayshore worked. The Conference had been founded in 1943 to deal with issues from Catholic education and hospitals to social action and immigration. It was, for its first two decades, a modest operation that essentially reflected the way the Church as a whole worked. Meetings of the Canadian bishops were top-down affairs run by lavishly costumed cardinals and the leading archbishops of the day. "A scowl from a cardinal," noted the Conference's official history, "could kill a motion before it was even seconded."[1]

The bishops were in many ways courtiers – hardly surprising for a Church headed by an infallible sovereign and run on monarchical lines, an institution that routinely referred to its leadership as the "hierarchy," often with a capital "H." Everett MacNeil, the organizer of the unorthodox living arrangement at the Bayshore apartments and the Conference's general secretary from 1968 on, bluntly describes that institution in its early years: "Undemocratic."

All this was changing when Bill Ryan took up his new post at the social action department of the CCC in the fall of 1964. The Second Vatican Council was in full swing and Canada's bishops (one of the few hierarchies to set up its own office in Rome during the council) found themselves meeting with their fellows from around the world for three months a year, soaking up the atmosphere in what quickly became a hothouse of Church reform. Back at their Ottawa office, the Canadian bishops were beginning to put wheels on the ideas that were taking shape in Rome. In 1964 the CCC's board decided that a modern, forward-looking episcopal organization needed "a dynamic, top-quality general secretariat" equipped with the research skills that would allow them to understand rapid social change and analyse "all problems of interest to the Church."[2]

Jack Shea, a diocesan priest from northern Ontario who had recently joined the secretariat as director of social action, had heard about the up-and-coming Jesuit with a Harvard Ph.D. in economics who was teaching at Loyola College, and wanted him for the Ottawa office. Shea went to Montreal and met with Ryan, who quickly agreed to join the team.

The CCC's treasurer was Bishop Alex Carter of Sault Sainte-Marie, one of the leading reformers in the Canadian Church. By 1967, Carter was reporting that the CCC's expenditures had risen more than sixfold in a mere four years. No task seemed too daunting for the new generation of clerical officials, Ryan and his contemporaries, who set the tone at Parent Street. They had a heady mandate and the wind at their backs. Though they had grown up in a world apart from their "separated brethren" – Catholics in Ryan's hometown used to shut their windows when the Orangemen marched down Main Street – ecumenical initiatives now abounded. Bill Ryan became the first Canadian Catholic official to attend a meeting of the World Council of Churches.

Though the proceedings of the Vatican Council had been carried out in ecclesiastical Latin that many bishops scarcely understood, the liturgy at home had changed. When Ryan began returning to Renfrew each Christmas to celebrate mass at St. Francis Xavier, he faced the congregation and spoke in a language that they could understand – though the edge of his distinct Ottawa Valley accent had been filed away by his years in other parts of Canada, the United States and Europe. A Church that had related to the non-European world in a way that the Jesuit theologian Karl Rahner described as "an export firm which exported a European religion as a commodity it did not want to change" was slowly gaining respect for cultures it once considered inferior.[3]

Though their social teaching had once blended sombre, finger-wagging admonitions about sobriety and restraint with warnings of the perils of communism, the Canadian bishops had by 1966 started to emphasize social justice, looking beyond symptoms to the causes of poverty. Their 1966 Labour Day Statement, penned by Bill Ryan, would rely on the brand new Vatican II document *Gaudium et Spes* ("Pastoral Constitution on the Church in the Modern World") to make the point that "social justice requires that all men work together to eliminate those social conditions that foster poverty and deprivation."[4]

In 1960, anticipating the winds of change that would be generated by Vatican II, the Swiss theologian Hans Küng had written that while recognizing the good that there is in the Church, the Christian should also see it as an institution worth criticizing, in need of criticism. "He knows too," said Küng, "that every thing and every act, even every reforming and renewing act, has its *kairos*, its 'due time.'"[5] When Bill

Ryan began his first real job at the CCC, it was indeed an auspicious time for a priest with ambitions and ideas to finally get his feet wet. Ryan was, to say the least, energetic. He took to running up and down nine flights of stairs at the Bayshore apartment to get some exercise.

"One of the fellows in the office used to say, 'We have a man in the air at all times,'" recalled Father Dennis Murphy, who began working on Catholic education at the Conference in 1966. "We were all incredibly enthusiastic about what we were doing. New vistas were opening up before us in the Church."

———————◦———————

One of the changes wrought by Vatican II was in the area of social action, social teaching and what soon became known as "social justice" – which involved an openness to the political left. One only has to look at the character of the CCC's social apostolate as late as the early 1960s and contrast it to what was being done later in the decade to get a sense of the dramatic turnaround that took place within a few short years.

As Vatican II got underway, the priests who worked as social action directors for Canada's bishops had for some time been publishing documents that they judged relevant to their flock under the banner *Social Thought*. In 1960, for instance, one of these "selections of social significance" was an article by a Catholic social worker. An activist in the Christian Family Movement, he took up the issue of husband-wife relations, decrying any notion of democracy or equality within the family and declaring that "false" equality had "debased" women. "It takes little imagination to see what this means to our concept of the husband as head and the wife as the heart."[6] That same year *Social Thought* reprinted the musings of one of the major Canadian banks as set forth in its "commercial letter."

In 1962 the social action department organized a regional social life conference in Windsor, Ontario, sponsored by auto firms, brewers and distillers. This was one of a series of large social life conferences, modelled on Quebec's Jesuit-inspired *Semaines Sociales*. The conferences typically brought together hundreds of people and were designed to let concerned lay people know that the Church was concerned with their temporal as well as spiritual welfare – that because social problems are moral problems, they were of concern to the Church, which had a body of social teaching dating back to 1891 and *Rerum Novarum*. The Windsor conference's general chairman was Emmett Carter, then auxiliary bishop of London. To welcome delegates the organizers published a pamphlet featuring backlit photos of Carter and his superior, Bishop John Cody, both dressed in full magenta-and-lace regalia. In an address on the Christian and social progress, the bishop of Nelson, British Columbia, W.E. Doyle, reminded the delegates of the traditional Catholic emphasis on a corporatist social order in which harmony could be achieved through the co-operation of government, industry and responsible unions. Though every labour contract in the heavily unionized Windsor auto plants contained a strict management-rights clause, Bishop Doyle asserted that owners and managers had no greater or lesser rights or duties than any other member of the community. As for the Christian working man, he had a duty to be "competent, honest and loyal," and the "pagan, whatever his qualifications…is the most incompetent member of society." Doyle quoted a Jesuit named Richard Lombardi, who asked, apparently rhetorically, "How can an unbeliever solve a social problem?"[7]

The Church is, however, a big tent. It sheltered a growing number who did not share this perspective, or at least its most corporatist variants. Although the first director of social action for the CCC, Francis Marrocco, held to the corporatist line regarding worker-management co-operation, he also shared the Catholic adult-education perspective that emerged from Father Moses Coady's Antigonish movement and emphasized the value of unions and co-operatives. Later, looking back on his career from his position as bishop of Peterborough, he employed the band-aid metaphor favoured ever since the 1960s by critics of the charity-based approach to tackling poverty. It was better, he said, to get at the roots of "exploitation and persecution…. My concept of social action was far removed from adhesive tape medication of the socially disadvantaged."[8]

Within a few months of joining the bishops' conference as co-director of social action in 1964, Bill Ryan found himself in Montreal at a planning meeting for the next national social life conference, slated for that city the following year. He urged a change of course from the old way of proceeding with such meetings, recommending a keynote speech that would stress "the new theology abroad." Ryan was uneasy about the Conference's exclusively Catholic orientation in those ecumenical times. He also told his fellow officials about the need to get away from the Church's association with what he called "this rural concept." Fresh from a doctoral thesis that attempted to rebut the notion of a hidebound Quebec church resisting urbanization and industrialization, Ryan added that "many of the fears that we had years ago about cities and industry crushing people stemmed from the fact that we were depending too much on laissez-faire thinking." It would be better to rely on a co-operative form of "economic planning" – and better not to have a social life conference dominated by clergy who could get "carried away with theology." Displaying a slight technocratic bent, Ryan felt that "experts" should be invited to speak. He pushed for discussions of poverty, medicare and "population development."[9] As it turned out, the 1965 meeting *was* the last of the big social life conferences that had taken up much staff time (plans for another one to mark Canada's centennial would come to naught). The bishops paid heed to modernizers like Ryan and Jack Shea who wanted the bishops to work ecumenically, developing solid research and engaging the laity.

The Montreal social life conference, held at Loyola College, did include non-Catholic resource people. It also reflected several issues percolating away in the country at large and among its Catholic citizens. The workshop on international affairs concerned itself with the link between poverty and population growth, noting optimistically that the Church was "seriously studying" its stand on contraception and urging it to move quickly to clarify its position on this issue.[10] Cardinal Paul-Émile Léger, archbishop of Montreal and a high-profile reformer at Vatican II, gave the keynote address at the Windsor Hotel. Léger said that the Church was engaged in "an often agonizing effort to understand itself better" in a rapidly changing world. He warned that the "technological democracy" of the day – there was much talk of cybernetics abroad in the land – could lead to "exaggerated reverence for the expert." Amazingly, one of the country's pre-eminent Catholics was moved to point out to a cosmopolitan Canadian audience something that his time at the Vatican Council (then about to begin its fourth and final session) had shown him was not all that obvious to the Roman curia: "We live in a...democracy, not a feudal system. It matters little whether we may think the latter is a better system, it is not in fact the one in which we live. This means that if the Church tries to conduct her affairs as though she were living in a feudal society, the attitude will prove unworkable." In closing, the influential prelate sounded a warning note about the limitations of Church teaching. Presumably the popes "actually mean to be taken seriously when they issue encyclicals." But, he continued, "the whole history of the encyclicals on the Church's social teaching shows this does not happen." What was written down on high was "rarely preached" (let alone, one assumes, practised). "There is not enough serious effort made to pass on the contents of the encyclicals to the laity," Léger concluded.[11]

The Montreal archbishop was obviously concerned about whether the spirit of the Vatican Council would filter down to the people in the pew. He knew that the Council was embroiled in a tug-of-war between men who wanted to issue a few documents and condemn assorted errors and those who wanted something more. The sides were clearly drawn: doctrinal conservatives in the Vatican curia and their allies who formed a distinct minority among the assembled bishops versus reformers who took John XXIII at his word and wanted to embrace the modern world at last. Arriving at the first session in 1962, Léger and the rest of the delegates had been confronted by a preparatory commission that attempted to finesse the process with a time-honoured ploy familiar to reforming politicians faced with civil servants wedded to the status quo. If you want to stall change, simply produce paper in volumes sufficient to immobilize the reformers – in this case, background materials comprising 2,000 folio-size pages written in a language that most bishops had left behind at the seminary. Dominican Yves Congar, whose work would soon underpin the Council's breakthrough *Unitatis redintegratio* ("Decree on Ecumenism"), looked back at the beginning of the Council and noted dryly that "in the preparatory work absence of unity has been manifested in a plethora of documents."[12]

Along with Léger, Cardinal Jozef Suenens of Brussels, an influential intellectual who would have the ear of John's successor, Paul VI, in preventing the curia from deflecting the Council's momentum, made an important intervention as the first session drew to a close. It conveys the spirit of the Council that so infected priests like Bill Ryan:

> This Council should aim at making the Church the real light of nations…. We must say something about the very life of the human person, the inviolability of that life, its procreation, its extension in what is called the population explosion. The Church must speak on social justice. The moralists have written volume after volume on the Sixth Commandment [the commandment against adultery] but have been practically silent when it comes to determining the social responsibility of private ownership. What is the theological and practical duty of rich nations towards the Tiers-Monde of the nations who suffer from hunger. The Church must speak about bringing the Gospel to the poor and some of the conditions the Church must meet to make the Gospel relevant to them. The Church must speak about inter-

national peace and war in a way that can help enlighten the world.[13]

Suenens' remarks are credited with helping to pave the way for the Council's 1965 *Gaudium et Spes*. They also represent the sort of socially concerned message that Cardinal Léger worried was not reaching the laity. After the Montreal social life conference, Bill Ryan and Jack Shea headed to a cottage in the Gatineaus to prepare an intervention in support of *Gaudium et Spes* for Archbishop Anthony Jordan of Edmonton, who chaired the CCC's social action committee at the time. Ryan found a Jesuit who could translate Jordan's support of the reform document into Latin. The Edmonton bishop told his colleagues in Rome that the Church didn't have all the answers to society's problems and that it had to be more humble, learning from the world. It was his only speech at Vatican II.

When the Council ended in 1965, an enthusiastic Jack Shea returned from Rome along with the Canadian bishops, most of whom also felt energized by what they had gone through. At Anglican headquarters, Ted Scott, who would become Anglican primate and emerge as one of Canada's most influential Church leaders, had just begun a two-year stint with that Church's Council for Social Concern. Along with Shea and Bill Ryan and their counterparts at the United Church, Scott helped to launch the politically engaged wing of the Canadian ecumenical movement. Scott recalls someone back then asking a young bishop named Remi De Roo, a key Catholic reformer who had attended all four sessions in Rome, the basic difference in the Catholic Church after the Council:

> He said, "The pre-Vatican II emphasis was the building up of people loyal to the institution." He said the fundamental change that Vatican II points to – whether it will be carried through is another matter – is the development of committed Christians, which meant an open relationship and discussion with other groups and not the closed kind of pattern.

Scott, a veteran of innumerable international Church gatherings and ecumenical meetings in Canada, added that "the thing we forget about an event like Vatican II, which opens up so many things, is that when you go through an event like that there's no way you can bring home to other people who've not been part of the event the totality of what you've experienced." That did not stop the socially conscious clerics who had become influential in the CCC both at the staff level and among the bishops, from trying. After the Council ended,

Shea and Ryan hit the road, criss-crossing the country to telegraph to diocesan priests the news that the Church was going to attempt to engage with the modern world. It was a world where things were happening fast. Technology was on the march. The anovulant pill had already been approved, giving women new-found freedom to participate in controlling conception. Napalm was being deployed in Vietnam, marijuana and LSD on campus. With the foundations of the welfare state in place, Lester Pearson's Liberal government was attempting to erect the superstructure. Participation, a keyword at Vatican II and in the subsequent social teaching of the Canadian bishops, was very much in the air.

Bill Ryan and Jack Shea complemented each other. Shea had a graduate degree in sociology, Ryan his Harvard doctorate. The Jesuit talked about the "practical" side of things, peace and justice issues and economics, while Shea dealt with the theology of the recent developments at the Vatican. As they sat down to spread the word about *Gaudium et Spes* to parish priests in Moncton, Calgary and more than a dozen other Canadian centres, it became apparent that Cardinal Léger had been right. "It was news to the pastors of the parishes," recalls Shea, himself a former diocesan priest in Sault Sainte-Marie. "They weren't thinking in terms of changing social life or changing society. They were dealing more with the sacraments."

Shea had less experience with Church social teachings than Ryan, whose stint at Louvain had prepared him for this sort of work. In his eight years in the seminary in London, Shea hadn't heard much about a worldly Church: "I had to study social questions and encyclicals by myself, on the side. It wasn't taught. So a generation of priests were not equipped to appreciate *Gaudium et Spes* when it came along." On the other hand, Shea had not only been a pastor; he also knew about the nuts and bolts of the Church and politics, having worked as a labour educator during northern Ontario's bitter interunion battles in which the Church, along with the RCMP and most of the rest of official Canada, helped the United Steelworkers raid the left-wing Mine-Mill union. For Bill Ryan, the trip across Canada talking to local priests was a learning experience. His experience in English Canada had been limited to Ottawa and the Valley, the sequestered world of Jesuit formation in Guelph and Toronto, and his brief period as a high school teacher in Winnipeg.

Although Ryan had not attended the Council, he was pleased to work in an environment so conducive to his energetic temperament and his reform inclinations. He brought to play the analytical skills of a trained economist, a background shared by few Church officials of his generation. Ryan was the first to insist that the bishops' teaching be backed not simply by moral exhortation but also by a solid body of research that would give their voices more resonance in secular (particularly government) circles. "Perhaps the most profound change that has taken place in the Canadian Bishops' National Conference since Vatican II," he told a gathering of American social action Catholics at the time, "has been the growing tendency to study more and to consult the experts for help to read the 'signs of the times' before moving into action."[14] Although Ryan was overstating his case (the democratization of the Conference that gave voice to all bishops instead of a handful of big-city cardinals was a more important development), the shift foretold a new political role for the Church. Instead of a quiet call from cardinals to cabinet ministers, Church representations to government would soon be taking the form of copiously footnoted briefs by ecumenical coalitions.

Ryan's Jesuit training also served him well. The Society of Jesus has always had a reputation as an order well versed in the arts of diplomacy, whether advising popes or working the back stairs as counsellors and confessors to kings. From Vienna during the Thirty Years' War, when the Holy Roman emperor's Jesuit confessor, Father Lamormaini, served as his chief adviser and gatekeeper, to Rome under Mussolini, when the pope's go-between with Il Duce was Father Tacchi-Venturi SJ, the Jesuits had been more concerned with worldly affairs and matters institutional than any other religious order. Though Bill Ryan never concerned himself with affairs of state at the highest levels, like many Jesuits before him he made it a point to get to know people with power both inside the Church and in the world at large – the "top people," as he invariably called them.

In the Canadian Church of the mid- to late 1960s, this meant working closely with a keen group of bishops and their clerical and lay officials who found themselves thrown together at 90 Parent Street. The CCC office was in the backyard of Ottawa's grand Notre Dame Cathedral and the archbishop's sumptuous residence, and just down the street from Parliament Hill where politicians and their advisers were busily attempting to erect the edifice of the country's welfare state. A can-do spirit was abroad in the stodgy old capital – public pensions, public health care, a new flag, the centennial celebrations. And though Pearson advisers like Tom Kent always had to contend with hard-bitten reactionaries on the opposition benches, in the civil service, in the press and within the governing party itself, there seemed to be little to stand in the way of the reforming Catholics. "Everything was upbeat," chuckled Grant Maxwell, who arrived at Parent Street in 1968 as one of the CCC's first lay officials. "It looked like the new Jerusalem was just around the corner."

According to the people who worked at the CCC at the time and were soon to lead it, the social action office was a particularly busy place. There was a blizzard of documents from both the Vatican and the Protestant World Council of Churches. Dennis Murphy, who later became general secretary of the CCC, explained that the social action office at the bishops' conference "has always been a bit of a gadfly.... They were always a bit to the left of where the Conference was. They pricked its conscience."

Everett MacNeil arrived in Ottawa in 1966 from the socially engaged diocese of Antigonish. He took up the post of assistant general secretary and soon succeeded Gordon George as general secretary after Bill Ryan came across his fellow Jesuit and boss suffering a severe heart attack at the Bayshore apartment they shared. MacNeil, a plain-talking priest and veteran Catholic troubleshooter, recalled "wonderfully heady times in terms of the Church. Renewal. Openness. Everything was possible." MacNeil called the episcopal brain trust of priests who came to work at the Conference after the Council "thoroughbred racehorses – somehow you have to keep them on the track. Jack Shea and Bill Ryan grabbed the Church documents, especially 'The Church in the Modern World,' and really started to run with them.... When *Populorum Progressio* came out [in 1967], Jack Shea just about went nuts. Another great document to whip out across the country."

The social action job also gave Bill Ryan a chance to try his hand at writing Church documents himself. He drafted the 1966 Labour Day Statement, a message concerning poverty that differed radically from the missives of the past. There was none of the old tone that his fellow Jesuit Ed Sheridan (provincial from 1969 until he was called to Rome in 1972 to be an adviser to Pedro Arrupe) described as "exhortatory and moralizing."[15] Indeed, Ryan gave less space to the pope than he did to the influential Protestant theologian Karl Barth, who said that the government had a particular responsibility for the weakest members of society and "equality before the law" was too often a "cloak" masking unequal treatment of rich and poor, bosses and workers, at the hands of the state. No corporatism here. Ryan relied on *Gaudium et Spes*, and the only time he cited the Gospel was when he made a passing mention of Matthew 26:11 – "You have the poor with you always." Ryan used this old saw to urge a break in "the vicious circle of poverty that enchains so many of our citizens." And, for the first time, Ryan was able to get statistics into a Church statement. He culled some data on poverty (nearly a quarter of Canadian families were officially poor) from the Prime Minister's Office. The 1966 statement was a sea change, foreshadowing an increasingly radical approach to economic analysis by the conference.

A new cadre of reform bishops was pulling its weight at the Conference. Montreal native Alex Carter, bishop of Sault Sainte-Marie, was a key player. His father had been fired for his lonely attempt to organize the typographers at the Montreal *Daily Star* into a union. Never as well known, especially outside Catholic circles, as his more ambitious and competitive brother Emmett, the future archbishop of Toronto, Alex was, according to Emmett's biographers, "a genuinely liberal Church leader."[16] As bishop at the Sault, he initiated the first Native diaconate program and a non-ordained Order of Women. The renewal of the CCC would not have proceeded without Carter, who served as president from 1967 to 1969. Along with Archbishops George Flahiff of Winnipeg and Philip Pocock of Toronto, he had been among the Canadians appointed by John XXIII to the Vatican II preparatory commissions.

This trio, along with Emmett Carter and Joseph-Aurèle Plourde of Ottawa, did much to drive the post-conciliar reform impulse at the CCC. When Everett MacNeil took to the road in 1966 in his new job as assistant general secretary, he detected some rumblings of discontent in local dioceses. Some bishops and priests felt that things were moving too fast. A "clique" was running the show. For many, the proposed changes wrought by Vatican II were hard to swallow and the Church, being a large, complex organization that included so many different people and factions, would not be an organization easy to transform – or even, in the parlance of the day, "renew" (the standard metaphor of turning a supertanker around is perhaps most appropriate). MacNeil defended the reformist "clique" as hard-working, bilingual and not afraid to speak out. "They could take an issue and move it," he explained. For this career Church official, renewal meant "levelling" an institution that had become too centralized, and "recognizing and trying to empower the baptized, the laity: educating them and bringing them along and showing them that the Church is not the hierarchy, that bishops, priests and deacons are servants. But we don't project that image."

Dennis Murphy, who was studying in Rome during the Council, often heard the latest scuttlebutt (priests being as avid gossips as just about anyone) from the Carter brothers over dinner. Murphy recalls hearing Alex Carter questioning the traditional role of bishops even before the Council. When he was elected president of the CCC in 1967, Alex Carter was only the second non-archbishop to hold that position. For Carter, a bishop was not just a branch manager. He felt a direct responsibility for the laity (from the Greek *laos* or "people") that did not simply spring from head office and the men who appointed him. "It was not just something that he fulfilled in terms of edicts from Rome but in light of the peculiar circumstances of those people. He was singing a different song than what I had traditionally heard," said Murphy. "He's the one who brought that episcopal conference to maturity in the sense of saying that this is a group of bishops that have rediscovered the role of the bishop in ways that had become diminished after Vatican I." The changes of the 1960s largely reversed the thrust that Pius IX, whose papacy spanned fully one third of the nineteenth century, had given the Church at the First Vatican Council (1869–70). He presided over the Church during a period of tremendous change in society, with the consolidation of capitalism accompanied by a growing agitation for personal and political freedom – of speech, religion and association. Pius IX's papacy, ferociously anti-modern and anti-democratic, opposed them all. His Vatican I consolidated the pope's authority at the expense of the bishops.

———➤•◗———

Ryan's first task on arrival at the CCC in 1964 was to digest Justice Emmett Hall's 900-page report on the possibility of introducing a national medicare program in Canada. In November 1963 Justice Hall had received a letter from his insurance company telling him that his private health insurance was being terminated because he had just turned sixty-five. The Saskatchewan judge was, however, a long way from retirement. He was just putting the final touches on his medicare report, and Hall knew that nearly a third of Canadians could not afford private health insurance, particularly once they stopped working. Should the country adopt a universal, publicly funded health-care plan?

The Hall Royal Commission report, released in early 1964, urged the Pearson Liberals to proceed with medicare, basing its recommendations on "social principles and the co-operation and participation of society as a whole."[17] But the question was still far from resolved. The Canadian Medical Association (CMA) denounced the proposal for a universal plan as monopolistic and heavy-handed. The insurance industry was clearly opposed. The tone of the business opposition recalled the recent struggle in Saskatchewan where the doctors had gone on strike after the province's social-democratic government introduced medicare. Charges of state monopoly and grandiose government schemes flew once again. "Next you'll be proposing grocerycare," scoffed Alberta Premier Ernest Manning at a federal-provincial meeting.

While right-wing Liberals like Mitchell Sharp had always been lukewarm to medicare, the prime minister seemed committed to keeping a promise that the Liberals had campaigned on in 1962 and 1963. But Pearson also wanted a majority government. He delayed medicare legislation until after the election of November 1965 that would, he hoped, give him that majority. When the Liberals wound up with another minority, the blame fell on the shoulders of Finance Minister Walter Gordon, the leading cabinet left-winger, who had urged Pearson to call the election. Pearson reluctantly accepted Gordon's resignation from cabinet, and Sharp took over the key finance portfolio. The future of medicare seemed cloudy. "The government was dispirited. Mike was very dispirited indeed," recalled Pearson's chief adviser, Tom Kent, a member of the special Privy Council committee on medicare. "Whether medicare would be implemented and when was thrown into doubt. At that point a public expression of desire for it was needed to strengthen the government's sinews."

It so happened that organized support for medicare was growing. Shortly after starting work at the CCC, Bill Ryan had received an invitation to a Canadian Labour Congress meeting in Niagara Falls, where he discussed the plans for medicare with Congress President Claude Jodoin and Joe Morris, who would later lead the union federation. Would Father Ryan help to secure the backing of the bishops and possibly the main Protestant denominations? Ryan got the green light from the CCC to talk to Ted Scott, his opposite number at the Anglican Church, and they engaged other Church officials in a series of ecumenical social action discussions in Toronto.

Three weeks after the election that so disappointed the governing Liberals, a Health Services Convention took place at Ottawa's Château Laurier Hotel, sponsored by twenty-one organizations[18] and chaired by Claude Ryan, a Catholic activist who had become publisher of the Montreal newspaper *Le Devoir*. The tone was careful. Pro-medicare doctors as well as CMA representatives were invited to give their views along with keynote speaker Emmett Hall, who told the 225 delegates that though he thought medicare was important, Canada really needed a broader "health charter" to protect all its citizens. Hall, a Catholic whose mother said the rosary and led her family in prayer, had quoted John XXIII in his report. He had also been a guest speaker earlier that year at the Montreal social life conference.

At the Château Laurier, a Saskatchewan physician testified that not only was public medicare affordable, but administering it would be cheaper than having the private sector look after health insurance. A Catholic social philosopher from Quebec captured the new, socially engaged spirit within the churches that emphasized expanded popular participation and the need for a "one for all, all for one" ethic. Father Jean-Marie Lafontaine told the teach-in-style meeting, similar to those being organized on university campuses, that Hall's proposals posed a "moral issue" for Canadians. "To meet the really human want is not to guarantee the possession of such and such an object, it is to assure its universality," he continued. "Such a perspective is not mere Utopia. The industrial society gives us the real possibility to make it effective."[19] Coverage was mixed: the Liberal Toronto *Star* reported the meeting on its front page while the Conservative *Globe and Mail* found room on page 41 under the comics, focusing on the CMA's reservations.[20]

In the end, of course, medicare was an idea whose time had come. It was working in Saskatchewan. The insurance industry and the physician lobby, along with the right wing of the Liberal Party, succeeded in delaying implementation until 1968. But public sentiment as evidenced by events like the Château Laurier conference provided a provided a counterweight that tipped the balance. With the labour movement, the mainstream churches, liberal editorial opinion, the New Democratic Party, part of the governing Liberal Party and – perhaps most significantly – public opinion backing public health insurance, widespread support for medicare could not be denied. A reflection of the "can-do" times, this constant pressure would give rise to what may have been the most important underpinning of Canada's new welfare state. "The sense of public support and desire for medicare was definitely very important in keeping the thing on course," said Tom Kent. "There was a danger of a counterattack – reformation and counterreformation to put it in Catholic terms – and that sort of conference would have been evidence of public opinion within an organization like the Catholic Church."

———➤●◀———

While Catholics were discussing medicare with their allies and ecumenical partners in Ottawa, the last session of the Vatican Council was wrapping up in Rome. And few bishops faced such daunting challenges on their return home than did those of Canada's most Catholic province. Many liberalizing and secularizing changes that had unfolded gradually in other industrial societies were telescoped into a decade of frenetic activity in Quebec. The most common English-Canadian perception is that, during the course of the Quiet Revolution, Quebec finally threw off the shackles of a clerical domination that had inhibited progress in fields from industrialization to education, at last emerging as a modern society. The reality, as Bill Ryan's Ph.D. thesis showed, was somewhat more complex.

There can be no doubt that the Quebec Church had taken profoundly reactionary positions, from its condemnation of voting Liberal as a mortal sin in the 1870s to its denunciations of communism and socialism in the 1930s and beyond. The Church banned books, fired teachers who stepped out of line, and preached allegiance to French bosses in politics and English bosses on the job. It was an enemy of modernity, liberalism and all the other dangers identified in the famous *Syllabus of Errors* of 1864, Pope Pius IX's wildly ambitious (and notoriously out of step with the times) denunciation of science, materialism, democracy and freedom of speech. The Quebec Church toed this reactionary line well into the twentieth century, yet the situation was paradoxical. The Church was a bulwark of Quebec nationalism, espousing an ideology that, while anachronistic, also preserved and maintained the national identity that did so much to fire the Quiet Revolution and the new, modernizing nationalism of the 1960s. At the same time, much to the consternation of the hierarchy, Catholic clerics and lay activists played important roles in watershed events such as the Asbestos Strike and were among the fiercest critics of the hidebound Duplessis regime.

It was against this background that Bill Ryan and Jack Shea travelled in 1966 to Montreal to discuss plans for a joint Semaine Sociale/ Social Life Conference to mark Canada's hundredth birthday. The city embodied the Church's paradoxical position. Though one of the biggest boulevards was (and still is) named after Pius IX, by the mid-1960s Catholic activists were busy in community organizing efforts promoting tenant rights, better public health and, in many cases, the establishment of a independent, socialist Quebec. When Ryan and Shea sat down with their opposite numbers on the Quebec side, it was obvious that the idea of celebrating Confederation with a joint social conference was a non-starter. Father Richard Arès, a Jesuit intellectual who headed the Semaine Sociale organization, was a clerical nationalist of the old, corporatist school. He had written part of the 1956 report of Judge Thomas Tremblay's Royal Commission on Constitutional Problems, a landmark statement of Quebec's argument for provincial autonomy, and was moral counsellor to Quebec's leading traditional nationalist organization, the Saint-Jean-Baptiste Society. Arès told Ryan and Shea that the Semaine Sociale had "lost its popular appeal" of late. It would be very hard to get even fifty Quebec delegates "of the right quality" to attend. Linking it to Confederation would "do much harm to the Church in the eyes of many French Canadians," to which Shea and Ryan admitted that it would be "quite impossible to disassociate in the English-Canadian mind such a joint conference taking place in 1967 from the birthday of Confederation."[21] The plan died aborning.

Aside from the state of Catholic social action work in Quebec at the time, two interesting points emerge from this encounter. One is that at this time the Semaine Sociale was already an organization at arm's length from the Quebec bishops, who had only one member on its board. This foreshadowed developments within the social action work of the English-Canadian Church, for when the new Canadian Catholic Organization for Development and Peace (CCODP) was set up in 1967 by left-leaning Catholics like Ryan, not only was it at arm's length from the Vatican's official development effort, Caritas, but it was an organization led by lay people.

The second point is that in 1966 Ryan and Shea had the sense that Quebec's resistance to a joint meeting was a function of the symbolism of the centennial celebrations, and so they believed that the idea should be postponed rather than dropped altogether: "The dangers foreseen would, we presume, not exist in any other year than 1967."[22] As it happened, the joint project did not unfold, and English Catholic social action work sponsored by the Canadian bishops gradually took on a more ecumenical cast. As social action became social justice, Quebec largely went its own way.

Since its founding, the CCC had been a uniquely Canadian institution in that, unlike most "national" organizations, it had attempted to accommodate the binational character of the country. Most other pan-Canadian institutions are really either English Canadian only or uneasy coalitions that do not reproduce the complexities of English–French relations. The CCC (after 1977 the CCCB) has maintained a bilingual Ottawa office and had both anglophone and francophone general secretaries. For many years, its social action office also had French and English co-ordinators. And its presidency has resolutely alternated between French- and English-speaking bishops.

In 1967 the CCC was faced with the delicate task of cobbling together a centennial statement. Quebec's bishops were keenly aware of the rising nationalism at home. As long-time CCC staffer Bernard Daly recalled, "The bishops were really caught on this because the CCC is bilingual and bicultural. They had to say something to celebrate Confederation and the Quebec bishops were saying, 'Well, our people are asking, what's to celebrate?'"

As it turned out, a typically Canadian compromise was hashed out, the fine points brokered by Alex Carter and Paul-Émile Léger who well understood that calling Quebec a "nation" raised thorny issues and that "mere words can improve good relations or destroy them." The statement said that there was "no concealing the fact that the chief malady" affecting Canadian society was "the deep discontent felt by a growing number of French Canadians." At the same time, the words were carefully chosen, concentrating not on Quebec as such but on Canada's French-speaking "community" that "so easily sees itself as a nation."[23] Looking back, Ryan felt that the 1967 statement "doesn't seem to say much." He added that in matters that touched social issues or international affairs (on which the CCC was starting to say things), there was usually considerable agreement among the bishops during the 1960s. But though they always managed a compromise, things were different "when something touched the inside of Quebec."

As a senior staff member, Bill Ryan played a role in massaging the statement, which received more scrutiny than anything else that the bishops published at the time except for their position on Pope Paul VI's controversial encyclical on birth control. As an Ottawa Valley native who had grown up among French-speaking people and done intensive academic research in Quebec, Ryan was an anglophone well placed to understand what was happening in Quebec during the busy years of the 1960s. He felt that his work on Quebec gave him credibility in intellectual and clerical circles there, what he described as "access." He had also developed close relationships with Quebec priests, particularly the Jesuit intellectual Julien Harvey, who became his window on Quebec – a window most English-Canadian Jesuits and indeed most of the English Catholic hierarchy did not have.

Ryan had met Julien Harvey during his brief stint teaching economics at Loyola in 1963. The two immediately hit it off. Ryan had just spent time in the Saguenay working on his doctorate; Harvey hailed from Chicoutimi. Harvey had played a lot of hockey and so had Ryan. Ryan was an outdoorsman, a hiker and mountain climber; Harvey was a keen canoeist. Ryan had a Ph.D. in economics; Harvey's doctorate was in biblical studies. Ryan also found Harvey a stimulating conversationalist and simply fun to be with. In 1963 the Quiet Revolution was at its height and Harvey could explain all the frenzied goings-on to Ryan, who had been out of the country for so long. And, of course, both were Jesuits.

Aside from his CCC work, Ryan attended scholarly meetings to give papers on his research on the role of the Church in Quebec's economic development, continuing to criticize the widely held notion that the clergy had uniformly opposed industrialization and instead supported an agriculturalist option for their people. Indeed, Ryan always seemed comfortable with Quebec nationalism, at least as espoused by his friends Julien Harvey and, later, Bishop Bernard Hubert of Saint-Jean–Longueuil. "Both of them were separatists at least at some level," he asserted later. "But that never bothered me." Harvey's separatism, Ryan sensed, was tempered by his social concern: "He would put a socially just society before separatism if he was convinced that separatism would not produce such a society." Nor was Harvey's nationalism like that of Richard Arès, his fellow Jesuit and predecessor as editor of the Jesuit journal *Relations*, who opposed the nationalization of electricity and defended the old order.

Ryan also evinced great admiration for Archbishop Maurice Roy of Quebec, whom he described as "always the Canadian." Roy, an early backer of the CCODP, was also president of the Pontifical Commission on Justice and Peace. Although Paul-Émile Léger had a much higher profile, Ryan, always aware of the institutional politics of any situation, described Roy as "the person you negotiated with."

It was during this period that Ryan began to manifest a skill that was to serve him well throughout the rest of his career. Although this was his first institutional job, he already had a sense of organizational politics, how to move things forward or, to put it more precisely, move them in the direction he felt they should be moved. He had an apparently God-given ability to read a situation and detect where there was room to move. It is something that, if bottled, could be sold by the gross to MBA programs where they try to translate organizational theory into practical management skills. But such skills are not easily taught; they are more of an inherent aptitude. For Ryan, it is something he would often in later years describe with a question: "Where's the energy?" This means that in a meeting or a broader organizational context one gets a sense of who is supplying the energy and – just as importantly – who is detracting from it. It is a way of reading, not the signs of the times, but the signs of a particular moment in time.

Ryan explains that you do this emotionally and spiritually as well as analytically, remaining open to all possibilities rather than feeling obliged to choose one path or another. "Your strength is your freedom." Part of this strength he acquired from his Jesuit training and his experience with the Spiritual Exercises. Those making the Exercises pray by themselves, summoning inner resources, strengths that emerge from their relationship with God. "I put it in terms of energy," Ryan says. "Where is it coming from? What's happening?" He recalls the endless hours wandering the fields and paths of the Jesuit property in Guelph, deep in contemplation: "A lot of the time you're just out of yourself, floating…. It opens the social imagination. Often the box we live in is so small. But once you start thinking of the whole of creation, all the peoples of the world, the wonder of it all, the world is so beautiful." Jesuit spirituality, married to the mysterious process called discernment, contributes to the practical, worldly character of the order. And it allowed Ryan to fine-tune his antennae and gauge the energies around him, among individual people, inside institutions and in the world at large. It helped to develop his ability to read a particular situation, watching for nuances of body language and inflection, identifying the people who would determine the result. He learned that if he couldn't resolve an issue by himself, it was best to take it to someone else – often but not always a fellow Jesuit. He had already learned about the process with respect to prayer: "Staying free."

All of this served him well in his years at the CCC. He was, of course, fortunate to arrive at a time when so much seemed possible, when the energetic reform clerics whom his new friend Everett MacNeil identified as "The Clique" were poised to translate the changes that Vatican II seemed to promise into action. He was able to get the bishops to publish whatever he felt appropriate in their *Social Thought* periodical. He moved the new-style Labour Day statements he had drafted through the social affairs commission and the CCC's administrative board with relative ease. He plugged into the momentum that was there when he arrived and the bishops trusted the high-achieving staffer with the doctorate in economics from Harvard; Ryan pronounced it "doctor*ate*," with a long "a," and mentioned it often, both out of pride in his accomplishment and as a means of enhancing the credibility that he knew would advance his agenda.

"Bill could work inside just about any structure," observed MacNeil, explaining that the Jesuit would always make sure he had the backing of those bishops who swung the most weight at the CCC. "He knows what buttons to push, what chasms to avoid and he has a pleasant way with him."

It was that background, together with his curiosity about the world at large, that led Ryan during this period into the world of international meetings where the big issues of the day came under scrutiny. It was a world that he took to easily, enjoying the company of the Top People who met one another at conferences organized by the Catholic Church and other churches, governments, the United Nations and multilateral bodies. Ryan was already well travelled, having lived in the United States, England, France and Belgium, so that the then-new jet-age prospect of taking off to spend a few days in Geneva was nothing out of the ordinary and was, indeed, quite welcome. If the joke around 90 Parent Street was that the CCC had a man in the air at all times, that man was, likely as not, Bill Ryan, a priest who was more at home at a high-level international get-together than a planning session to organize citizens around local issues.

One of the first and most significant of the dozens of global gatherings Ryan would attend was a two-week "Church and Society" meeting that took place in Geneva in 1966 under the banner of the WCC. Msgr. Joe Gremillion, director of the new Pontifical Commission for Justice and Peace in Rome, had befriended Ryan, inviting him to international meetings of the WCC and of his commission, which included Barbara Ward. Coinciding with the wave of decolonization that had abolished European rule in Asia and had just crested in Africa, it was the first major World Council of Churches meeting where representatives from the Third World outnumbered Christians from Europe and North America. It also marked the first time Catholics were officially delegated to come to such a WCC conference. And for Ryan, as for the other delegates from the industrial world, it was apparently something of an eye-opener. As he put it to a leftist Student Christian Movement (SCM) audience a few months later: "For the delegates from the so-called Christian West and especially for the self-righteous North Americans, it proved to be a trying experience to be forced into the 'furnace of doubt,' as one after another of their values was questioned, not by 'atheistic Communists' but by Christian leaders of other countries and cultures around the world – not by their enemies but by their friends in Christ."

Among the messages that the northern delegates heard from their southern counterparts were, reported Ryan, that their countries and churches were not spiritual leaders but hypocritical, materialistic and power-seeking; that the Vietnam War was a cynical capitalist affair to keep the yellow race in its place; that automation and cybernetics were but ways of preventing poor people from expressing themselves; that much foreign aid was a desperate attempt by the rich to preserve the friends of capitalism in the Third World; that rich economies had achieved wealth by exploiting their own poor as well as those in their former colonies; and that the world economy was laden with Western value-assumptions, its trade system rigged against the poor. What's more, Ryan told his student audience at Fredericton, "my own Church…has loved the past too long." Looking back to a Jesuit whose work had been suppressed by his order and his Church but whom he had long admired, Ryan suggested that the WCC and the Vatican Council were now in step with Teilhard de Chardin's belief that Christian churches had had to identify themselves "closely with modern man in his struggle to build a better world."

As was his custom when making speeches, Ryan peppered his formal presentation to the SCM with longish quotations, as if reading a paper at a scholarly conference. Clearly inspired by the meeting in Geneva, he regaled the students with quotes from a fellow Jesuit, Father Tucci of *La Civiltà Cattolica*, who had recently asserted confidently that the Church was "courageously open for dialogue." And then, much to the surprise of the meeting's organizers, who had hoped to spark fireworks by putting Father Ryan on the same podium as radical community organizer Saul Alinsky, he closed with a flourish: "The French Communist, Roger Garaudy, has suggested that dialogue between Christians and Communists will permit the world to survive due to what Teilhard de Chardin called 'the common front of all those who believe that the universe is moving forward, and that it is our task to make it move forward.'"[24] *Social Thought*, where Ryan's remarks were reprinted, had come a fair distance in the seven years since it had reprinted bank newsletters and paternalistic homilies of laymen worried about the breakdown of family values.

It was at the WCC meeting in Geneva that Ryan came to know Barbara Ward, who had been at Harvard during his time there. Her bona fides as an economist and her charismatic presence made her a popular speaker at a time when many activist Christians were quickly coming to terms with the realization that the end of formal colonialism did not mean an end to what they called "a world broken by unshared bread." In Canada this group included Bill Ryan and Protestant counterparts who saw similarly that the post-war boom and the welfare state had left millions of Canadians behind in poverty. Ryan's 1966 Labour Day message for the CCC had made the point. It was an example of the steady increase in social justice activity that in turn was part of an unprecedented wave of co-operation between Catholics and Protestants.

As Dennis Murphy put it in bit of wry understatement, "Before the Vatican Council the Roman Catholic Church was not particularly famous for its ecumenical endeavours." But in the mid- to late 1960s, much of the historical suspicion and isolation had melted away, particularly when it came to work on poverty and what was at the time referred to as "development." Ryan's CCC job description included regular trips to Toronto, where the Presbyterian, Anglican, United and Lutheran churches had their offices, as did another CCC, the Canadian Council of Churches, umbrella organization for the large Protestant denominations.

The reform wing of the United Church (an organization that had sprung in part from the Social Gospel in the early twentieth century) and its earlier Methodist incarnation had long been a seedbed for socialists and socialist ideology in Canada, with Salem Bland preaching the Social Gospel in the Ottawa Valley back when Bill Ryan's father was a boy. Bland criticized competitive individualism and Protestant otherworldliness while promoting the co-operative commonwealth and industrial democracy. Such ideas sparked controversies within his Church and led to his dismissal from Winnipeg's Wesley College. Bland was not alone. As Canada industrialized after 1900 and its economy grew, most workers remained destitute. The rising tide did not lift all boats. Socially engaged Protestants, including the radical Student Christian Movement, pointed out that it lifted primarily the yachts of the rich.[25]

The "new" industrialism of the 1960s was also coupled with the economic growth of the post-war boom, and it prompted a new generation of socially concerned Church officials to deploy their institutional resources to engage more vigorously with society at large. For Ted Scott, who worked for the Anglican Council for Social Concern at Church House in Toronto from 1964 to 1966, the key was to understand the links among poverty, human rights and broader cultural issues. "The Church was tending to become much more of a ghetto within a wider cultural situation that it was not affecting very deeply," he recalled, adding that he and United Church staff in Toronto shared common concerns with Bill Ryan and Jack Shea at the Catholic office in Ottawa:

> We got very much concerned about the whole relationship between religion and culture...all the issues of cybernetics and automation and the move to a more technologically based culture. The whole context of the culture was changing. Everywhere in the world we were moving to an urban industrial culture and that focused largely with the American publicity and television that has spread since then. Wherever you lived you were under the impact of an urban industrial culture that focused on the production of goods. There was less concern about the environment and more concern about the bottom line. We saw this as a real challenge to the Christian faith.

Pat Kerans, Ryan's successor at the CCC, put it more bluntly: "People were discovering that poverty still existed. It was a real scandal given the ideology of the rising tide raising all boats. The rediscovery of so much poverty was a real slap in the face with a wet mackerel."

By the late 1960s, ecumenical work on social justice had started to gel. After the 1965 conference in support of medicare came the WCC meeting in Geneva in 1966 and then another one in Beirut in early 1968. A National Committee on the Church in Industrial Society, reflecting Ted Scott's concerns, provided an important forum where Church leaders and staff people in their social action offices could meet and exchange ideas. Friendships resulted in joint actions that in turn gave way to institutional adjustments as this group concentrated on what United Church theologian Roger Hutchison called "the 'ripest' and 'hottest' social issues of the day."[26]

⫸◦⫷

A French revolution that almost was. Russian tanks in Prague. The Tet offensive in Vietnam. Martin Luther King's assassination, followed by massive urban riots. More riots at Chicago's Democratic convention. Rioting in Montreal before the election victory of new Liberal leader Pierre Trudeau. In a decade remembered not just for images of violent confrontation but also for radical rethinking of the way institutions work, 1968 was a momentous year. "Participation" was a watchword as students and many others put forward a proposition that wasn't all that radical, just democratic – that those affected by decisions should have a voice in making those decisions. Debates over participation also marked a watershed year in the life of the Catholic Church.

The Second Vatican Council had set a new tone for the Church, but it had not probed the links between the struggle for social justice and the Church's evangelizing mission. In 1968 Latin American bishops meeting in Medellín, Colombia, signalled a dramatic shift in a Church traditionally aligned with the dominant classes. The Medellín meeting outlined a "preferential option for the poor," decried the institutionalized violence of poverty and gave rise to the thousands of Catholic *communidades de base* (base communities) that allowed the continent's peasantry and working classes to participate in new structures designed to give them a say in decisions that affected their lives. According to Jean-Yves Calvez, a general assistant to the new Jesuit general, the need for "radical change" asserted itself: "It can be said that at this moment an awareness of the injustices from which its people suffered crystallized in the general consciousness of the Church on the continent that contained the largest number of Catholics."[27]

For Bill Ryan and his fellow Canadian Church leaders, 1968 brought an event that was a prism through which the ecumenical and social justice optimism of the decade was reflected. Their "Christian Conscience and Poverty" meeting in Montreal brought together delegates from across the country in May, just as the revolutionary upsurge in France ("everything is political!") was coming to a head. The organizers succeeded in securing the support of the federal government along with six provinces, twelve denominations including the Salvation Army, the Pentecostals and the Baptists, and a list of corporations such as IBM, Bell Canada, Dominion Stores and General Foods.

The meeting, a far cry from the more pious social action meetings in the not-too-distant past, attracted much press attention. The plenary sessions featured an international roster of high-profile speakers including Bill Ryan's new friend Barbara Ward and Archbishop Helder Camara of Recife in Brazil's poverty-stricken northeast, a Church leader whom the Montreal *Star* described as "known for his hard support of socialist radicals." The University of Montreal's social centre where Camara spoke was decorated with posters of Ho Chi Minh and Mao Tsetung. Ward (teaching at Columbia University, then besieged by radical students) told the 500 delegates that the rich nations enjoyed living standards twelve times the level of the poor and predicted that if nothing was done the gap would grow to eighteen times by century's end.

Archbishop Camara was forthright, saying that the Latin American Church had accepted African slavery for three centuries and after that accepted the "national slavery" that was colonialism. "The Christians in South America have always been aligned with the land-owning classes," said the soft-spoken, strong-willed priest. "And what did we Christians give to the masses? A passive half-magic religion and a fatalistic outlook." Camara had already endured threats from death squads.

The conference organizers, aware of the need for a broadly representative gathering, had invited poor people to participate in the meeting (reports vary; between 10 and 20 per cent of the delegates qualified as such) along with lay Church people, academics, social workers and activists. One of the conference chairs was Pauline Vanier, widow of the former governor general. By all accounts Madame Vanier handled the situation well when a group of demonstrators representing Montreal's poor arrived to say their piece. Representing the citizens' committees that were then doing community organizing in the city's extensive slums (they had been responsible for the *"Visitez les slums!"* graffiti adorning hoardings erected to protect tourist sensibilities at Expo '67 a year before), the demonstrators had their say and, after initial hesitation from surprised delegates, were welcomed to stay on. But their message to the assembled Christians was clear enough. "Enough talk, let's act – and now," admonished the citizens from the Mile End district. "We protest that the numbers of working-class people taking part in the conference are far too few."[28]

Bill Ryan had been a key player in conceiving and organizing the conference, describing it as the biggest thing he did in his years on the social action desk at the CCC. It was the first major ecumenical effort on poverty in Canada, laying the groundwork for coalition work in subsequent decades. Along with Walter McLean (later a Conservative MP), Ryan wrote the follow-up report for the conference. It was rather obliquely titled *Pussy Cat Purr or Tiger Roar;* apparently an impatient delegate had expressed disappointment to the closing plenary, "I thought we'd unleash a tiger, but wound up instead with a fat, toothless, gutless pussycat!"[29]

Ryan, rarely impatient or disappointed, saw things differently. For him, it was a big step on a long road. The Catholic Church and a wide spectrum of Protestants had mended some fences and seemed poised to take on hot social justice issues. Top People had shown up for the Montreal meeting. Barbara Ward was a member of the newly minted Pontifical Commission on Justice and Peace and Cardinal Roy, who also attended, was its president. The Catholic bishops, English and French, were onside. Anti-poverty activists had been well received. As he and McLean pointed out in their wrap-up report, its title page adorned with a union bug, "This bilingual bicultural enterprise was unquestionably the most dramatic and potentially the most significant inter-church venture up to this time in Canada, and possibly in the world."[30]

Their *Pussy Cat Purr* document was surely a sign of the times, a sign of the way socially engaged Catholics were thinking. Ryan and the rest sounded optimistic and resolute, certain of the need to heed the conference message about the need for a new era of interchurch co-operation on education and political pressure for "justice and development." As the report put it:

> Possibly the most significant feature of this conference was that it clearly revealed the undercurrent of dissatisfaction beneath the surface placidity of society and the churches. This dissatisfaction is felt by many good Christians who are asking the church to be the social conscience of our society by her teaching and example.... To be effective the churches must try to evolve a more comprehensive and articulate strategy for action. Vague pronouncements, scattered action, and limitless devotion will no longer serve.[31]

The stage was apparently set for reformers like Bill Ryan to move in lockstep with the times that were, as the song went, a-changin'. In the summer of 1968, however, Canada's bishops and their staffers at 90 Parent Street had their hands full with a looming pronouncement that was anything but vague.

Vatican II had not dealt directly with the issue of birth control, Pope Paul VI having unilaterally removed it from the agenda. But he had already tipped his hand in 1965 when he warned the United Nations against artificial contraception, which would be "irrational" and would "diminish the number of guests at the banquet of life."[32] By 1968, the Vatican was ready with an official papal encyclical on birth control. When Alex Carter began circulating advance copies of the encyclical, it was quickly apparent that the Church was out of step not only with the times but with virtually all of its allies on the social justice front. Ignoring the advice of various commissions of theologians and lay advisers, *Humanae Vitae* reiterated the traditional injunctions against contraception. Many Catholic women, intrigued by the now-practical possibility of participating in decisions about their reproductive lives, could read much into *Humanae Vitae's* tone as well as its substance: "The Church, calling men back to the observance of natural law...."[33]

The document was the subject of difficult discussions around Mrs. Munroe's table at the Bayshore Apartments. The Canadians knew that Rome had placed their Church, and particularly parish priests, in a quandary. How to formulate a response that would be helpful for pastors? They knew that most Catholic women, aware of the debilitating effects of compulsory annual pregnancies, would simply ignore Rome's stern admonitions to obey "natural law."

"I was surprised and disappointed by the tone of it," recalled Dennis Murphy. "We all wrote various papers and circulated them to one another." Finally Ed Sheridan came up with a position paper for the bishops' upcoming meeting in Winnipeg where, under Alex Carter's leadership, they managed to make the best of the situation, balancing the realities of the society in which they lived with the controversial head office *diktat*. Parliament had already moved to change Canada's antiquated ban on contraception (sale of contraceptive devices was illegal until 1969), and while the pope's various commissions were pondering the morality of birth control, the CCC had skilfully used Vatican II's teachings on the Church and the modern world in its communications with the laity and its submission to the parliamentary committee studying the matter. It had even appended a large swath of the text of *Gaudium et Spes* to its brief.

In Winnipeg, the bishops approved a statement, largely drafted by Alex Carter's brother Emmett, that reaffirmed the encyclical's teaching but sought to ensure that those who in good conscience could not follow it would not feel cut off from the Church.[34] Pope Paul, in communications with several Canadian bishops, expressed his approval of the statement. But Emmett Carter's role in crafting the Winnipeg statement would earn him the undying enmity of the Church's most conservative elements. Bill Ryan recalls: "At that time, the atmosphere of freedom at the CCC was such that the professional staff articulated a consensus view – along the lines of the final bishops' statement – and shared it with the bishops. Cardinal, then bishop, Emmett Carter questioned the initiative but not the position proposed by the professional staff. Most bishops were glad to get any help they could get from any source. It was a good test of freedom in the church after Vatican II."

Ryan, putting the best possible face on the situation, was by now a keen student of Church intrigues. He knew that politics consists famously of the art of the possible and that the reform bishops of the time had gone as far as they could. And, of course, the imperative of institutional loyalty prevented him and his CCC friends like Dennis Murphy and Everett MacNeil from pushing things further, at least in public. These priests, however, were also aware that bishops from the United States to Brazil to the Philippines to France were saying much the same thing. Only the Dutch Church, where independent thinking would eventually result in a rancorous split with the next long-serving pope, John Paul II, said what so many were thinking: "The encyclical's total rejection of contraceptive methods is not convincing on the basis of the arguments put forward."[35] In another development that foreshadowed things to come, young Jesuit seminarians in Europe turned their backs on Father Gustave Martelet SJ when he returned from Rome to teach moral theology. They knew from fellow Jesuits that he had co-authored *Humanae Vitae* and refused to take his classes. Many would soon leave the priesthood.

In the meantime, Ryan could take heart from more encouraging developments elsewhere. Just before Canada's bishops met at Winnipeg, their Latin American counterparts had concluded their historic gathering at Medellín. The tone was passionate and angry. The bishops were divided between those who (supported by the young technocrats on the staff of the continental episcopal conference, or CELAM) were leaning towards what would soon become known as liberation theology and a hard core of conservatives centred in Colombia. But the bishops who occupied the moderate middle ground listened to Helder Camara – one of the leaders who made it his business to disseminate the ideas of Vatican II in Latin America – and took several steps to the left. The Medellín documents held that the poor were oppressed by "institutionalized violence," that the continent was dominated by unjust structures that "seeking unbounded profits, foment an economic dictatorship and the international imperialism of money."

As at the World Council of Churches meeting in Geneva two years previously, where Ryan had seen a shift from a Cold War, East-versus-West mindset to one that viewed the world through a north/south, rich/poor lens, the Medellín meeting rejected both communism and capitalism as systems that "affront the dignity of the human being." The Latin Americans rejected trickle-down notions about the economy, denouncing the "developmentalists" from whom Ryan had heard so much at Harvard. "Placing more emphasis on economic progress than on the social well-being of the people" was, for them, absurd. The two key concepts that sprung forth from Medellín were liberation and participation.[36]

In 1969 Bill Ryan took the first of many trips to the Third World. Like many of the Canadians who went south in the 1960s as backpack tourists or as volunteers for Canadian University Service Overseas (CUSO) – and whose political energies were galvanized by the experience – he wasn't prepared for what he saw. "I'd seen poverty as a kid but I'd never understood," he recalled. "It was the first time in my life I had that sense of anger that something has to be done."

He first visited Colombia. Arriving late in Bogotá, the inexperienced traveller asked the taxi driver to take him to a modest hotel. He found himself on a mat on an earthen floor. The next morning he called the Jesuit provincial and within twenty minutes found himself in a well-appointed suite overlooking the cathedral square and the presidential palace. The country that had just sponsored the bishops' meeting had also been home to Camillo Torres, a priest who had been radicalized by his studies in sociology at Louvain and the desperate situation of the Colombian peasantry. Torres took to the hills, joining the guerrillas, and was killed in his first skirmish with the army in 1966. On the whole, the Colombian Church was extremely conservative, having raised the sole dissenting voice at Medellín.

By contrast, in the next country he visited, Brazil, liberal papal nuncios of the 1950s had transformed the hierarchy by promoting the appointment of left-leaning bishops and many Catholic bishops, priests and lay people were on the leading edge of social criticism and social action. The "economic miracle" that followed the military ouster of President João Goulart in 1964 – the coup had been assisted by the Central Intelligence Agency (CIA) on account of Goulart's talk of land reform – had not trickled down. When Ryan visited the country it was both a laboratory for Marxist critics of development theory, who began writing about the "development of underdevelopment," and a testing ground for the brutal national security states that were soon to come in neighbouring countries. His host, Archbishop Helder Camara, whose walls were scarred with bullet holes, said that he was called a Christian when he fed the poor but a communist when he questioned the reason for their hunger. Camara had been threatened, his associates jailed, tortured and murdered. "Why should the Church be surprised that it is persecuted?" asked the soft-spoken prelate. "Did the Lord's warnings refer only to the first centuries of the Church?"[37]

Ryan's experiences in the lumber camps of the Gatineau and the pulp towns of the Saguenay and the Saint-Maurice Valley had left him unprepared for what he witnessed when he visited the squalid settlements where Camara's followers lived in flimsy houses built on stilts over the water. "They'd offer you coffee and it tasted like pee. But you didn't say anything. I came back to Canada that summer and I was angry. I just realized I could kill."

Violence was much on his mind. The liberation theologians talked of the institutionalized violence of poverty. But just as Latin America's radical Catholics rejected the top-down model of state socialism, they also felt that lasting change could be propelled only from the bottom up, with the participation of the most marginalized and destitute. So they invested massive organizational energy in base communities that, unlike mixed parishes, were locally generated, socially cohesive bodies in which the sacraments cemented mutual aid and assistance. Often oriented to consciousness-raising and social action, they were (and are) tightly knit groups reminiscent of early Christian communities.

While Bill Ryan shared the goals of the liberation theologians, his main community was the Jesuit order and his main strategy for influencing society was classically Jesuit. As former Jesuit Pat Kerans, who succeeded Ryan at the social action office of the CCC, put it, "Looking back, I see him as fulfilling the stereotype of the Jesuit. You figure out who's got the power and you try to influence them." In 1969 Ryan was concentrating his energy on helping Canada's Church-based social justice efforts and developing the informal social justice coalition that had had its origins in the medicare conference of 1965 and come together with the bilingual Montreal anti-poverty conference in 1968. At the end of that year, the CCC and the principal Protestant denominations had decided that the next step would be a "Coalition for Development," an ecumenical anti-poverty initiative that would again move things forward. Ryan and Grant Maxwell drafted the coalition's manifesto on a train from Halifax to Ottawa. Following the same optimistic logic as the *Pussy Cat Purr* document, it appeared in May 1969, outlining an ambitious agenda covering everything from tax reform to foreign aid. It declared that the Church coalition would be a "radical questioner of the status quo" and a "lobby for the dispossessed."

"We were going to revolutionize Canadian society with all of these volunteer groups," recalled Maxwell, "but it never happened." As it did happen, several of the people involved in the coalition, including

Bill Ryan, would soon move on to other jobs. A key challenge that fell naturally to the Catholics was to maintain strong working links with Quebec, something that was difficult during this period of the founding of the Parti Québécois and the October Crisis when those Quebecers most keenly interested in social justice tended to be just as interested in independence. It was an issue that would dog the Canadian left for the next several decades, especially during the debates over free trade in the late 1980s in which Tony Clarke, one of Ryan's successors behind the social action desk at 90 Parent, played an important role. Still, the changes of the 1960s gave way to engaged interchurch coalitions whose work in English-speaking Canada would call the status quo into question, often in a radical way.

———➤•◄———

After six years in Ottawa, Bill Ryan was ready for a change. For most of this period, the general secretaries of the CCC, his immediate bosses, had been fellow Jesuit Gordon George and Everett MacNeil, with whom he had established what would be a lifetime friendship. The bishops themselves were a varied lot, and Ryan cut his organizational teeth among them, figuring out who the key players were and building the appropriate alliances. Once the conference had become more democratic, no longer dominated by an elite group of big-city cardinals and archbishops, it became important for staff to develop support for their ideas before bringing them forward. Ryan learned how to do this during what MacNeil called those "high and wonderful times." He developed a close relationship with Alex Carter, and as soon as Pat Kerans arrived at the social action department in 1970, the first thing Ryan did was drive up to North Bay with him to spend a day with Carter. Kerans, who would leave the Jesuits in 1973, recalled that along with Carter and the French general secretary, Charles Mathieu, Ryan was a moving force at the CCC during this period: "He was one of the people who really gave it the kick."

Ryan also developed other leadership skills, gaining a stronger sense of how to work with people, bringing them along, instilling confidence by allowing his own quiet self-confidence to spill over. Grant Maxwell, a veteran newspaper reporter who came to the conference from a stint as a lay Catholic official, described Ryan as "a shrewd appraiser of people. He really sized people up, figured out their strengths and weaknesses.... He sometimes knew better than the person himself, myself included: 'You can do this. Because I expect you to do it.' I surprised myself at what I did get done.... He made me believe more in myself."

Ryan had limited classroom experience, but the Society of Jesus has always been known for turning out good teachers. In addition, his organizational instincts, combined with his apparent ability to inspire the people with whom he was working, clearly made him leadership material. Given all of this, along with Ryan's academic qualifications, it is not surprising that he would be in line for a job in Rome, whether it was a teaching position or an administrative one. His fellow economist Phil Land, who knew Ryan from Saint Louis, wanted him to come to Rome where Land was teaching at the Gregorian University and promoting social justice in whatever way he could. Pedro Arrupe apparently felt that the Canadian should be doing something different, but vetoed the idea of having Ryan head up a new joint Vatican–World Council of Churches centre in Geneva called SODEPAX (Society for Development and Peace). The Jesuit general felt that the job was too political for a Jesuit at that time. In the end, Ryan landed in Washington, D.C.

Unlike the rigidly hierarchical structures of the Catholic Church as a whole, the Jesuits had by this time developed a system that lent itself more to a consensual style of leadership. Of course, the vows of obedience and the quasi-military structure remained, but provincials and the general himself were surrounded by a group of consultors mandated to discuss major decisions, advise and file regular state-of-affairs reports. In his 1969 notes for a presentation to an informal study group where Ottawa priests mulled over the changes that were shaking up both Church and society, Ryan laid out a perspective that reflects his reading of the signs of those times: "Today's priest must be a team-man above all; one who serves in the total community of both the Church and the world; one who leads more as a selfless brother than as an authoritative father."[38]

The 1960s were drawing to a close when Ryan headed for Washington. He and the friends he had made among the CCC staff, children of the Depression, did not suspect the kinds of images that the 1960s would later conjure up. As Ryan dismantled the bookcases he had fashioned from bricks and boards, he packed away his copy of *The Council, Reform and Reunion* by Hans Küng, published at the beginning of the decade. Küng's measured optimism about reform and renewal having its *kairos*, its due time, was still very much in the air in 1969. Ryan's Anglican friend Ted Scott, poised to take over the leadership of his Church and usher in reforms that would bring women into the priesthood, reflected that "you only reach *kairos* points when there's been an educational focus, so the possibilities of a move forward are there. If you move forward too quickly, you just lose support." There would be times in the coming decades when it would appear that Ryan and his fellow reformers in the Church had indeed moved too quickly. But during the next period of his life, his eight-year sojourn in Washington, the forward thrust would continue.

[1]   Bernard Daly, *Remembering for Tomorrow: A History of the Canadian Conference of Catholic Bishops 1943–1993* (Ottawa: CCCB, 1995), 104.

[2]   CCC Administrative Board Meeting, April 16, 1964, in Daly, *Remembering for Tomorrow*, 104.

[3]   Karl Rahner SJ, "Toward a Fundamental Theological Interpretation of Vatican II," *Theological Studies*, vol. 40, no. 4, 717, quoted in Edward F. Sheridan SJ, ed., *Do Justice! The Social Teaching of the Canadian Catholic Bishops* (Sherbrooke, QC: Éditions Paulines, 1987), 19–20.

[4]   Canadian Bishops, "Labour Day Message 1966: Poverty in Canada," in Sheridan, ed., *Do Justice!*, 118.

[5]   Hans Küng, *The Council, Reform and Reunion* (New York: Sheed and Ward, 1961), 44.

[6]   CCCB Archives, Series1,1, item 61,1, box 53.

[7]   Most Rev. W.E. Doyle, "The Christian and Social Progress," Regional Catholic Social Life Conference, September 14–16, 1960, CCCB Archives, box 53.

[8]   Letter from Francis Marrocco to Grant Maxwell, July 16, 1973, quoted in Daly, *Remembering for Tomorrow*, 31–32.

[9]   "Minutes of the Planning Meeting for the 1965 Social Life Conference Montreal, October 16–17, 1964," CCCB Archives, box 53.

[10] "Report of Seven Basic Groups: International Life," 11th National Social Life Conference, 1965, CCCB Archives.

[11] Paul-Émile Cardinal Léger, "The Christian and the Community," Address to the 11th National Social Life Conference, May 29, 1965, CCCB Archives.

[12] Yves Congar, *Report from Rome: The First Session of the Vatican Council* (London: Geoffrey Chapman, 1963), 88.

[13] Quoted in Robert Kaiser, *Inside the Council: The Story of Vatican II* (London: Burns & Oates, 1963), 218.

[14] William F. Ryan SJ, "A Developing World, a Developing Church," address to the 11th annual convention of the National Catholic Social Action Conference, August 24, 1967, reprinted in *Social Thought*, October 1967, 11.

[15] Edward F. Sheridan SJ, "Introduction," in Sheridan, ed., *Do Justice!*, 36.

[16] Michael Higgins and Douglas Letson, *My Father's Business: A Biography of His Eminence G. Emmett Cardinal Carter* (Toronto: Macmillan, 1990), 14.

[17] Quoted in Dennis Gruending, *Emmett Hall: Establishment Radical* (Toronto: Macmillan, 1985), 94.

[18] The sponsors included the main Christian churches, the Canadian Jewish Congress, the Canadian Labour Congress, the Confederation of National Trade Unions, several women's organizations, farm and co-operative organizations and, oddly enough, the Chamber of Commerce (Daly, *Remembering for Tomorrow*, 181–82).

[19] Ottawa *Citizen*, December 1, 1965.

[20] Toronto *Star*, November 29, 1965; Toronto *Globe and Mail*, November 30, 1965.

[21] Minutes of a meeting concerning proposed joint conference, January 26, 1966, in CCCB Archives, box 55.

[22] Ibid.

[23] Assembly, Canadian Catholic Conference, "On the Occasion of the Hundredth Year of Confederation," in Sheridan, ed., *Do Justice!* 127.

[24] William F. Ryan SJ, "Values in Contemporary Society," address to the Atlantic Region Student Christian Movement, Fredericton, NB, January 20–22, 1967, reprinted in *Social Thought*, January 1967.

[25] See Richard Allen, *The Social Passion: Religion and Social Reform in Canada, 1914–28* (Toronto: University of Toronto Press, 1971).

[26] Roger Hutchison, "Ecumenical Witness in Canada: Social Action Coalitions," *International Review of Mission*, vol. 71 (1982), 345.

[27] Jean-Yves Calvez, *Faith and Justice: The Social Dimension of Evangelization* (St. Louis, MO: Institute of Jesuit Sources, 1991), 15.

[28] *Le Devoir*, May 25, 27 and 28, 1968; Montreal *Star*, May 27, 28, 29 and 30, 1968.

[29] Montreal *Star*, May 30, 1968.

[30] Walter McLean, ed., *Pussy Cat Purr or Tiger Roar: The Report of the Canadian Conference on Church and Society* (Hamilton, ON: Canadian Conference on Church and Society, 1969), 8.

[31] Ibid., 15, 37.

[32] Quoted in Paul Blanshard, *Paul Blanshard on Vatican II* (Boston: Beacon, 1966), 237.

[33] Paul VI, *Of Human Life (Humanae Vitae)*, n. 6, quoted in Garry Wills, *Papal Sin: Structures of Deceit* (New York: Doubleday, 2000), 95.

[34] Higgins and Letson, *My Father's Business*, 101–13.

[35] Quoted in Wills, *Papal Sin*, 96.

[36] Penny Lernoux, *Cry of the People: The Struggle for Human Rights in Latin America – The Catholic Church in Conflict with U.S. Policy* (New York: Penguin, 1991), 37–47.

[37] Ibid., 14.

[38] William F. Ryan SJ, "Notes on the Hyphenated Priest," mimeo, February 12, 1969, 5.

Chapter 4

Belly of the Beast

Rome. Autumn, 1971. The Vatican Council was long since over, but the halls of Vatican City still reverberated with the sort of talk that had galvanized the assembled bishops six years previously. The tone was, if anything, more urgent, as a smaller group of bishops met in synod to discuss the problem of social injustice.

"The time has come," declared one Canadian cardinal, "to ask ourselves whether or not much of the official support, especially financial, given to the Church by bourgeois society" was intended as a mere "social band-aid." George Flahiff of Winnipeg worried that his Church was confined to a "marginal role of consoling the victims of the system." This was not good enough. Christians had to follow the example of Ralph Nader, digging out the facts to make the case for an attack on "social sin." Flahiff's colleague Alex Carter told the assembled bishops that corporate power was eclipsing the power of nation-states. Carter already had some facts. Nigeria was smaller economically than Ford or General Motors. "Multinational corporations" accountable to a handful of shareholders were on a global march, while military spending accounted for 7 per cent of world production. "Good men are enslaved to inhuman systems."[1] Alex Carter later described the synod as a "great pivotal moment.... It would not be an exaggeration to say that our efforts caused a minor sensation." Equally memorable for Carter was being kissed by Barbara Ward, who exclaimed, "I love the Canadian bishops!"[2]

The author of these declarations by the Canadian bishops, Bill Ryan, had reason to be optimistic as the International Synod of Bishops worked its way towards a toughly worded statement that would be called "Justice and the World." Both Flahiff and Carter were influential Church leaders who had been appointed to Vatican II preparatory commissions and were active reformers during Ryan's time at the CCC. Both had been keen to have Ryan act as *peritus*, or adviser, to the Canadian delegates attending the synod, itself a deliberative body that seemed to foreshadow a new, more collegial phase in Church history. Ryan, by this time a seasoned participant in international gatherings, was keen to attend. Perhaps these synods would become permanent, democratic assemblies that would reflect the much-discussed need for popular participation in the world outside the Vatican walls. Moreover, some of Ryan's friends were also in Rome for the synod, working to move things along: Barbara Ward, Julien Harvey, Phil Land.

Ryan would later call the 1971 synod "crucial," its work a "magna carta" for the Washington-based social justice centre he was organizing at the time. His optimism was well founded. "Justice in the World" was clear – the promotion of justice was fundamental to the Gospel tradition: "Action on behalf of justice and participation in the transformation of the world fully appear to us as a constitutive dimension of the preaching of the Gospel."[3]

The key word here was *constitutive*. For a small but active group of Catholic priests, a socially engaged Church could not avoid central issues of social justice – war and peace, inequality among and within nations, the absurdity of trickle-down economics. They had read the signs of the times and, for them, Christian love of neighbour was inseparable from action against injustice. Words were no longer enough. What's more, an official Church assembly of cardinals and bishops had, with the blessing of Pope Paul VI, clearly endorsed the centrality of this notion to the Gospel message. No section of the final document got less than 94 per cent approval.

The 1971 synod was also clear on another lofty goal. It was one that would prove just as thorny as achieving world peace and global equality. Bill Ryan's former teacher Phil Land, now a professor at the Gregorian University and an adviser to the new Pontifical Commission for Justice and Peace, had helped to write much of the synod's material. The impish American, who was fond of trying to insert the word "liberation" into official Vatican pronouncements, was attending a pre-synod planning meeting in Rome where he presented the draft documents to some "big people." It was the kind of gathering where one could easily be ripped apart for merely speaking out of turn. Land read a paragraph that he felt was crucial to the credibility of a Church preaching about social justice: "I said to them that the Church should not speak about injustice unless it is willing to recognize its own injustice." Cardinal Pericle Felici, a veteran Vatican official, replied, "The Church does not have any injustices." A long silence followed before Land summoned up his courage. "Your Eminence, I really believe if we cannot say that the Church has injustices, we should not have a document."[4]

This apparently broke the ice and the discussion continued with the result that the paragraph was approved with only Cardinal Felici voting against it. The new social justice imperative was clear enough. But if the Church wanted this message to have real traction in the outside world, it had to be just itself, in its own internal life.

⟫―•―⟪

The 1971 synod took place only a few weeks after a Washington-based organization called the Center of Concern had opened its doors with four full-time staff, three of them Jesuits. Bill Ryan, its director, had nearly found himself at the Jesuit-run Gregorian University in Rome, but a series of events that he never regretted intervened. The years that followed were to be the most challenging and rewarding of his life.

By the late 1960s, Bill Ryan had become a much-sought-after commodity in Roman circles. His qualifications as an economist, an energetic Jesuit who was quickly developing a network of international contacts, made him particularly attractive to clerical officials anxious to further the Church's social justice mandate. Yet despite all the talk of opening up and letting light in, Rome could be a lonely place for energetic reformers. Phil Land wanted Ryan to come to teach at "the Greg" and start a new social justice centre that would work in conjunction with the Pontifical Commission for Justice and Peace, headed by the American Father Joe Gremillion. According to Ryan, he seemed "destined" to spend the next few years in Rome.

Gremillion had also been discussing the idea of setting up an American-based organization to promote the Catholic social justice agenda with his friend and fellow Louisiana Cajun Msgr. Marvin Bordelon. Both men had backed the civil rights movement in the deep south and were beginning to realize that, unless the message of global equality got through to the power brokers in Washington, any work in

Rome, Geneva or elsewhere would be next to futile. Bordelon, who had just gone to work on international matters for the American bishops (the U.S. Catholic Conference, or USCC), was an energetic clerical entrepreneur with an aptitude for fundraising. He adapted well to the high-energy world of Washington politics. Among the people he got to know was World Bank economist Irving Friedman, whom he managed to interest in the idea of a Washington-based social justice organization. At that time, as Bordelon recalls it, he soon learned that the American bishops were far more interested in building new Catholic schools than in justice and peace issues – least of all an agency "outside the bishops that was more free to call a spade a spade." But a new general secretary, Joseph Bernardin (who would go on to become archbishop of Chicago and one of the most respected American Catholic leaders of the 1980s and 1990s), was much more open to initiatives like the one Bordelon had in mind. Msgr. Bordelon headed for Rome, where he and Joe Gremillion met with Vincent O'Keefe, the savvy American who was one of Pedro Arrupe's principal advisers and a key Jesuit modernizer. "Vinnie" O'Keefe immediately warmed to the idea and arranged a meeting with Arrupe. After trading jokes about how Basques and Cajuns were similarly hard-headed, Bordelon floated the idea of a U.S.-based organization. He would raise the money while the Jesuits would provide one of "theirs" to kick-start the new agency. Or, as Bordelon put it, that Jesuit "would be seconded to me."

In late 1969 Bill Ryan had arrived in Washington at the invitation of Joe Gremillion. He was open to the idea that he might not, after all, go to Rome, but he made no commitment to Gremillion and Bordelon. Ryan's recollection is that it was at this point that the two Americans decided that Washington was the weak spot in the justice and peace network; Bordelon remembered coming to this conclusion earlier. Whatever the case, the USCC asked Arrupe if the Jesuits would help with the project and within a few months Bill Ryan arrived in Washington to conduct a feasibility study for what became known by the unwieldy name of "A Center of Concern – Focus: Toward a World that is Human." With temporary quarters at the USCC offices on Massachusetts Avenue, the organization seemed headed for a smooth start. It had the formal joint sponsorship of the U.S. bishops and the Society of Jesus. By February 1971, Eileen Olsen, a young midwesterner whom Ryan had hired as the Center's sole employee, was typing up Ryan's optimistic prospectus for an organization with "potential global influence." Turning this vision into reality, concluded the upbeat document, "deserves the active assistance of all men." The budget for the first eighteen months was $151,200. Although the attached letters of support from Pedro Arrupe and Joe Bernardin were full of strong endorsements, they contained no firm funding commitments to a "fresh, unfettered, flexible, fearless structure" that would be ecumenical, global and autonomous.[5]

The financial uncertainty did not stop things from proceeding apace. Ryan began planning for the formal opening of the new Center at the United Nations, which he hoped would be a main focus of its activities. Within three months he had arranged for Pedro Arrupe to travel to New York for this event. A young priest named John Myers who was doing an internship for Ryan issued a press release promising effective representation of the world's oppressed on the Center's staff and board and a "radical questioning" of society: "Can churches or any corporation earn money from militarism, racism and other kinds of exploitation without hypocrisy?"[6]

When Arrupe arrived at the UN with Francisco Ivern, his newly appointed social justice adviser, he shook hands with UN Secretary General U Thant in the company of a dozen men in Roman collars. The American Jesuits were represented by John O'Connor, head of their Conference of Major Superiors, and Jim Connor, provincial of Maryland, while Joe Bernardin and Marvin Bordelon represented the American bishops. It was a strictly Catholic affair, with none of the ecumenism Ryan had been hoping for. But the UN setting and the presence of someone of the stature of the secretary general indicated that though the Center would be based in Washington, its focus would be global.

As for its autonomy, that was still an open question. The fledgling Center had a bank loan and a board of directors cobbled together by Marvin Bordelon. It was obvious from the start, however, that the Jesuit who had been "seconded" to the USCC staffer had his own ideas about the Center. Although the scheme had been hatched by Bordelon and Gremillion, once Bill Ryan and the Jesuits arrived on the scene, things became more complex. Ryan was anxious that the Center be an independent outfit, but the American bishops were a cautious lot, unlikely to put money into something that they did not control. And while the USCC's president, Cardinal John Dearden, and its general secretary, Joe Bernardin, were both sympathetic to the initiative, others in the hierarchy were less supportive. Within days of the formal launch of the Center at the UN, Ryan found himself in Mexico, where he had a nasty blow-up with Cardinal John Krol, the conservative archbishop of Philadelphia who would succeed Dearden as USCC president. The occasion was a meeting to prepare for the 1971 "Justice in the World" synod. Ryan had helped write a preparatory document for the meeting of bishops from the Americas that would inform their work in Rome that fall. Not wishing to be seen carrying the ball on social justice after the Medellín meeting, the Latin American bishops provided background on the ministerial priesthood, the other subject of the upcoming synod. Galvanized by the poverty he had seen in Latin America, Ryan developed a strongly worded argument (prepared with the help of Pat Kerans and Grant Maxwell and co-authored with American theologian Father Joe Komonchak) inspired by liberation theology. The usual quotes from papal pronouncements and official Vatican II documents were accompanied by extracts from the work of Barbara Ward and Dom Helder Camara and even a radical Canadian magazine called the *Last Post*. Ryan and Komonchak criticized donor countries' practice of requiring aid recipients to purchase goods and services from them ("tied aid") and political meddling in Latin America by northern corporations and the U.S. government. With an eye to proposals for a "New International Economic Order" then emerging at the United Nations, their paper promoted fairer trade and a better deal for Third World commodity producers. And they provided a virtual menu of discontents at home – expressing the pervasive feeling that "something has gone wrong" in North America, where "older generations" were puzzled by disgust with racism, poverty, illiteracy, the alienation of youth, the urban crisis and environmental degradation. "There is much surprise, resentment and fear," observed *The Liberation of Men and Nations*, "at seeing the 'American experiment' radically called into question."[7]

Cardinal Krol was one American who was surprised, resentful and fearful. Arriving in Mexico City on the eve the preparatory meeting, Ryan found himself seated at a table with Krol and Joseph Bernardin. He also found himself arguing with Krol. Realizing that this might be impolitic given that Alex Carter and the CCC president, Archbishop Joseph-Aurèle Plourde of Ottawa, had to present his paper the next day, he started to retreat but Bernardin nudged him on. The discussion was amiable enough, but Ryan's final remark was, "If you believe that, you are not a Christian."

The next day, the twenty-two bishops generally agreed with the text of the preparatory document and discussion proceeded quietly until Cardinal Krol, who had remained silent, asked for a point of privilege and was granted the final fifteen minutes. "He demolished what we had prepared," said Archbishop Plourde. "I was furious." Ryan used the word "shredded" to describe Krol's commentary on his paper. Although Plourde gave a speech the next day refuting Krol's critique and the document went forward, Ryan had blotted his copybook with an influential member of the U.S. hierarchy.

Aside from this, Marvin Bordelon, who had envisioned the new social justice centre as something akin to the other major Washington lobby groups emerging at the time, was not able to shepherd the plan through the Conference. He was assuming more responsibilities at the USCC's Massachusetts Avenue headquarters and recalled that he soon began to "lose footing" with the bishops. Even before that happened, however, he and Ryan, both strong personalities, had had differences over who was in charge of the initiative. Finally, while the Canadian Jesuit was never in doubt about his vocation, the American monsignor may have been pondering his future. He would soon leave the priesthood.

The original sponsoring committee melted away and no conventional board was ever established, though Bordelon's friend Irving Friedman continued his association with the project. Friedman was clearly an establishment figure, economic adviser to the president of the World Bank and influential at both the bank and the International Monetary Fund. Although Bordelon and Ryan were different in many ways, they shared the tactician's appreciation of the need for legitimacy, and Bordelon had made friends with Friedman soon after coming to Washington. A warm friendship also developed between Friedman and Ryan soon after the Canadian arrived in the U.S. capital. Both were economists and Friedman, who held fellowships at Yale and Oxford, was impressed by Ryan's Harvard pedigree. Friedman was a faithful Presbyterian, Ryan an ecumenically minded Catholic priest. Friedman's orthodoxy (how could anyone but a resolutely mainstream economist rise to the top of the World Bank at that time?) was not particularly ideological. Both men liked to talk, and for Ryan – always one who liked to have the ear of the people close to the top – exchanging ideas with Friedman would always be a pleasure. Peter Henriot, a Jesuit who would be one of the Center of Concern's first staffers and its second leader, knew both men well. His description of Friedman's role in Washington could just as easily be applied to the way his friend Bill Ryan worked within the Church: "He was a true 'insider' in Washington, but never put 'outside' those who were trying to do something good in the mix of things."

Bill Ryan's new Center of Concern (the name was coined by Friedman) could not survive just on its friends in high places. Though it would always proceed on a modest budget, in mid-1971 the Center had no budget at all. What it did have were a few desks and typewriters as well as a $20,000 debt and plenty of that elusive accounting category called "good will." When Eileen Olsen made her last entry in the new ledger and escaped the oppressive heat of the Washington summer for her first holiday, it was clear that her new employer was in financial trouble. When she returned a few weeks later she was stunned to find a wad of cash on her desk along with a bundle of cheques and pledge sheets.

"That was a riot," laughed Olsen, who would spend the next seven years at the Center, parlaying this experience and night-school courses into a degree in accountancy. "It gave us freedom. The Board didn't get the money. The bankers didn't find the money. The USCC didn't find the money and the Jesuits didn't find the money."

Bill Ryan found the money – and was just as surprised as Eileen Olsen to find it. He had begun to get discouraged about his new job amounting to anything. He had already recruited two other Jesuits but was not looking forward to the prospect of telling Friedman that perhaps he would have to go to Rome after all. Just before he was to meet with Friedman, Ryan travelled to Atlanta and a meeting of the Leadership Conference of Women Religious, where he had been asked to conduct a four-day workshop on poverty with a hundred women representing nuns from across the United States.

Two important things happened at the meeting. Ryan bumped into Cardinal Flahiff of Winnipeg who asked him to attend the upcoming synod in Rome as an adviser to the Canadian bishops. And at the end of the workshop he happened to mention that the new Center of Concern was floundering. Mary Catherine Hunt, superior of the Sisters of Divine Providence in Covington, Kentucky, immediately began talking to other superiors and collecting cash and pledges on the floor of the meeting. Within ten minutes Ryan was assured of $16,000. That night he returned to Washington to meet with a discouraged Friedman, who was as pleasantly surprised to receive Ryan's news as the Jesuit had been to get the support of the nuns. They agreed that Friedman would be the "chair" of the Center's ostensible board. As it turned out, the World Bank economist continued to be an ardent supporter of the Center, adding legitimacy by lending his name to funding proposals.

Even more important, however, was the backing of the American women religious, something that neither Ryan nor Bordelon nor Gremillion nor the Jesuits (who matched the nuns' pledges) had planned on. Not surprisingly, these priests assumed that the hierarchy's higher-ups would take care of things. The women religious, who had in large measure built the American Church through their work as teachers and nurses, had long been part of the ecclesiastical wallpaper. They went about their work and had had no presence, let alone voice, in the upper echelons of the institution. Like many others, Bill Ryan was learning not to take the women of the Church for granted. Paradoxically, by maintaining a rigidly patriarchal structure for so many centuries, the Church had countenanced the development of a vast network of semi-autonomous organizations run by women. With Vatican II and all the talk of opening up and justice, it was not surprising that these faithful Christians took the Church at its word. And, given the feminist wave that was such a crucial element of those tempestuous times, neither was it any surprise that many women religious would begin to raise the issue of justice within the Church itself. Phil Land was not alone in arguing that the Church had to get its own house in order if it wanted to have credibility when it proclaimed the need for equality on the world or national stage.

Once the Center of Concern received the crucial seed money, Ryan and his two new Jesuit colleagues were ready to get on with the task at hand. Ryan scrapped what he called the "earlier grandiose plans" and decided that the Center's autonomy meant two things. First, it would have to have independent sources of income. In "granting" parlance, this means sporadic "project funding" as opposed to the more reliable "core" or "program" funding that often comes with strings attached. It also meant that the new Center would never be lavishly funded. Indeed, its director came to enjoy proclaiming that "we were poor but independent. It was the best thing that ever happened to us."

The Center had a big advantage over other new groups that might have found themselves in the same straitened circumstances. Jesuit labour came cheap. Because there was lots of Jesuit labour around in those days and because Ryan shared his order's long-standing skill in talent-spotting, he had come up with a small team that would have made any public or private sector administrator envious – two energetic men who had passed through the rigorous Jesuit formation and gone on to excel in academic studies.

When Ryan contacted him, Pete Henriot was immersed in anti-war activity while doing postdoctoral studies at Harvard, having completed his Ph.D. in political science at the University of Chicago. An incisive, highly organized thinker (colleagues remarked on his uncanny ability to reduce any problem or issue to three essential points) who had just been ordained a priest, Henriot was intending to teach at Seattle University when he was called to Washington. He did not hesitate. It was the height of the struggle against the Vietnam war and the corrupt Nixon regime, a time when the American civil rights movement was still very much alive and into its militant phase, when the beginnings of the feminist upsurge coincided with a growing sensitivity to poverty on a global level: "Well, this is 1971. Sounds great! But what is this Center of Concern? Such a funny name. I immediately learned the first lesson about Bill Ryan. He is a great persuader, even when the idea is very unclear. His personal zeal and commitment are contagious. His vision is lofty, even if it's difficult to pin down."

The other Jesuit recruit tempted by his Canadian colleague's enthusiasm for the as-yet-undefined task at hand was Bill Callahan. Nicknamed "The Hammer" in the conservative New England province, he was the chief organizer of a plan for democratic reform of the province's structures. Ryan stumbled across the tall, charismatic priest with a doctorate in nuclear physics, an intense gaze and the irrepressible desire to see justice done while visiting the New England provincial. He had intended to enlist the provincial's chief assistant but, like many others, this man was in the process of leaving the priesthood. After spending a few minutes over coffee with Callahan, Ryan immediately offered him the job.

Callahan's assessment of Ryan and his enthusiasm for the new project mirrored Henriot's: "He's a dreamer himself; he projects that and recognizes it in others." Callahan was well acquainted with dreaming big dreams. He would go on to start an independent, Washington-based group of his own, naming it the Quixote Center.

The Center of Concern's first step towards independence was to move out of the USCC's downtown headquarters with the huge statue of Jesus out front. Its new location was symbolic of its relation to the Church, close to but not part of official Catholicism. The office in the northeastern Washington neighbourhood of Brookland was at 13th and Otis, across a small valley from the sprawling campus of the Catholic University of America. There was a residence for Jesuit seminarians just down the hill on Otis and the frame house itself was rented on the cheap from the Viatorians. Their adjacent seminary had so few students that the order had no need of the modest clapboard dwelling, so they let it out to the trio of Jesuits and their office manager. The house sat on a large treed lot and had a sun porch that Bill Ryan took over as a workplace.

The place was furnished as a residence, but there were enough small student desks for Henriot and Callahan. The two Jesuits briefly lived upstairs before the Center's rapid expansion forced them into the unfinished attic. (Ryan stayed at the big downtown Jesuit residence where he had lived when he first moved to Washington.) Eileen Olsen set up the main office in the dining room and put the photocopier in a living room that doubled as a meeting space.

The Center ran on a quasi-consensual basis, which meant that there were frequent meetings. Sometimes a neighbour would drop in to chat with Olsen, asking, "Are they meeting again? When do they ever get any work done?" Olsen said that "they met and they met and they met and then Bill made the decision." Although Ryan was not a conventional boss, he was still the one in charge. "He was the one who started it," she explained, adding that Ryan would refer constantly to "process."

A former staff member recalled that Ryan would say with a laugh that he practised management-by-walking, paying regular visits to the offices of colleagues to catch up on things. Lifestyle was important. The people who worked at the Center made a point of assembling every day for a simple lunch of soup, crackers and peanut butter. In fact, the group seemed to wear its frugality as a badge of honour, regularly mentioning modest salaries and tight budgets in its early reports. Ryan stressed that they tried to make sure everyone received the same pay, with special provision for dependants. Clearly uneasy about the frequent disconnect between the Church's preachings and its practices, the Center was hopeful that its work would help bring about a turnaround in the Church and the world at large. The spirit of the place was reflected by an early publication ("printed on ecology paper, 50% reclaimed waste") featuring a sketch of Don Quixote and his squire Sancho Panza. The personal, as the saying of the times went, was political. And the signs of the times meant a response that integrated the personal and the scriptural: "Since our past teaching focused on personal morality, we are actually developing a new religious process for our own lives, translating our faith into a present-day way of life. This is a perennial call beginning with Jesus and the Scriptures, but it has been specially invoked in recent years by the Council, Pope John and Pope Paul, the 1971 Synod, and by the words and witness of a growing number of U.S. and Canadian bishops, religious and lay persons."[8]

The 1971 Justice in the World synod was a high point in Bill Ryan's career. He had already developed a taste for high-level international gatherings in Beirut or Geneva. Here he was, a Canadian working in Washington, going to a meeting in Rome for which he had prepared in Mexico. Many bishops he was meeting and advising in those days shared his vision of a reforming – and reformed – Church, its teachings buoyed by a social message that was not just an aside. Social justice could not be separated from spirituality and salvation. This was the message of the Latin American bishops and their advisers at CELAM, the bishops' conference that had organized the landmark meeting at Medellín three years previously. Unjust structures controlled by the rich were perpetuating the "development of underdevelopment." Ryan had reason to be optimistic about changing these structures in his new job in Washington, the belly of the beast. His friend and fellow economist Barbara Ward, with whom he worked in Rome to push the 1971 synod in a more radical direction, had recently written that a "lopsided" old system in which 80 per cent of the world's resources were reserved for 20 per cent of its people could not long endure. She held up the hopeful example of a small group of Christians who had helped to abolish the slave trade some two hundred years previously: "Their methods could be a model to any groups – Christian, liberal, humane, radical – who believe today that grinding but remediable poverty is the contemporary form of slavery endured by a large part of the human race."[9]

The synod was the context for everything the new Center of Concern did during its formative stage. Ryan returned from Rome in the fall of 1971 convinced that the Center needed a two-pronged strategy to promote the synod's vision. The international arena was crucial and the Center would soon gain official consultative status at the United Nations. This was an important step for Ryan, who longed for legitimacy and the influence that he felt it would bring. The small team working out of the house in 13th Street would also spend considerable time and energy carrying the message to the Church in the United States. The people most receptive were women religious. Not only had they come up with crucial seed money for the Center, but American orders of nuns from Des Moines, Iowa, to Encino, California, were also eager to learn more about social justice from the Jesuit fathers who arrived from the Center of Concern. These priests' casual attire differed from conventional clerical garb just as their presentations about the unjust nature of international trade departed from the usual pastoral homilies about individual salvation. Within a month of his return from Rome,

Ryan was conducting a workshop at a convent in Seattle for the Sisters of Charity of the Blessed Virgin Mary. The pace continued. There were few weekends when Center of Concern staff were not on the road.

It seemed to Ryan, Callahan and Henriot that the Catholic Church was emerging from its long conservative past and that the women of the Church would be in the vanguard of that transformation. At that time there were some 180,000 women religious in the United States. But there were very few social justice organizations to provide the framework and legitimacy that would assist in making common sense of social doctrine and propagating it widely. "The women religious were the backbone of the early days of the Center of Concern," said Bill Callahan. "The backbone of the funding, the backbone of the commitment to the ideas of social justice that we were proclaiming."

Of course, it was no easy task to work at transforming the Church along these lines, particularly when it came to women, even at the apogee of reform that was the 1971 synod. At that meeting, the bishops had prepared a text on the role of women and society. When the document made it onto the floor, the section dealing with women was gone. Archbishop Plourde of Ottawa described what happened: "I went to Bishop Rubin, who was the Secretary of the Synod, and said, 'What happened to our text?' He said, 'Members of the curia read that and did not agree.'" Clearly, there was a long road ahead in sensitizing the Church to the position of women in the world at large and within its own walls. It was a road on which even the Center of Concern had some distance to go, as indicated by a letter of appreciation John Myers, the intern at the Center who would go on to a successful career as Bishop of Peoria, wrote to a woman at the USCC: "Thanks, lovely ladies, for all the experience and all your help."[10]

The Center took its intellectual inspiration from liberation theology and two of its leading thinkers, Uruguay's Juan Luis Segundo SJ and Peru's Gustavo Gutierrez. Ryan had known the Uruguayan Jesuit since his student days at Louvain and later learned about the brittle realities of life in southern slums while touring the barrios of Montevideo on the back of Segundo's motor scooter during his first trip to Latin America in 1969. A few months later he had met the Peruvian (whose work would eventually make him a target for Vatican inquisitors) when the two became friends at a SODEPAX meeting in Geneva and spent an extra day at the conference centre getting to know each other better. Ryan recognized Segundo and Gutierrez as founders of liberation theology and was aware that their ideas had made them pariahs in certain circles. He later recalled Segundo being "alone and isolated" among his Jesuit brothers in 1969, and when he started the Center of Concern he eagerly welcomed the two Latin Americans to the converted living room in northeast Washington for long sessions with its staff. The North Americans were receptive to the need for what Gutierrez called a "liberating praxis" of specific action in solidarity with the poor as well as his criticism that the spirituality with which they had grown up was overly individualistic, elitist and romantic. Gutierrez, who would frequently be accused of reducing theology and spirituality to politics, also wrote: "An awareness of the need for self-liberation is essential to a correct understanding of the liberation process. It is not a matter of 'struggling for others,' which suggests paternalistic and reformist objectives, but rather of becoming aware of oneself as not completely fulfilled and as living in an alienated society."[11]

Bill Ryan took this message seriously. Just as the Center was getting started, he used his Jesuit contacts to help arrange the first English publication of Gutierrez's work in the Jesuit scholarly journal *Theological Studies*. The new Center's rejection of the opulent trappings of official Catholicism and Bill Callahan's commitment to simple living and antipoverty work buttressed its credibility as an authentic anti-poverty organization. Pete Henriot preached and celebrated Mass each Sunday in a poor black parish. And the Center's first publication was a document whose radicalism was one more "sign of the times."

The Quest for Justice was a twenty-page tabloid, its columns filled with a closely argued case for witnessing to justice. Peppered with quotes from the documents of the recently completed synod, it was a call to live out the values of social justice in action and decision making. American society had to change and the Church had to change with it. Charity was fine, as far as it went, but structural social injustice was "sin." It was one thing for the Church to make grand pronouncements, but what about equal pay for equal work by men and women employed in Catholic schools? The lifestyles of bishops should be "sharply modified" and bishops chosen exclusively from lists of people nominated by local churches. Women should be ordained as priests, since no theological basis for their exclusion had ever been demonstrated. As a way of identifying with the poor, Church authorities and tax-exempt clerics might consider paying taxes, a move that would also sharpen their interest in tax reform because their own money would be involved. There was scarcely an issue the publication did not address. Disarmament, conspicuous consumption, environmental degradation, strategies for local organizing, prison reform, housing, the engagement of young Christians – *The Quest for Justice* was a virtual manifesto.

And a deftly presented manifesto it was, its radical proposals surrounding statements that leading American bishops had made at the 1971 synod. Aside from a few simple line drawings from a recent American Bible Society version of the New Testament, the only graphics consisted of large photographs of four prelates who had attended the synod, an archbishop and three cardinals – including Ryan's nemesis, Cardinal John Krol. It was as if the American hierarchy was calling for a thoroughgoing democratization of the country, the Church and the world. Ryan knew the Church, so the document carried a prudent front-page disclaimer indicating that its judgments were those of principal author Bill Callahan and not the Center of Concern. Still, the Center held the copyright to these "guidelines to a creative response by American Catholics" to the "Justice in the World" statement from the synod. The publication was successful in putting the Center of Concern on the map. Eighty thousand copies of *Quest* had been distributed within eleven months of its publication in 1972. With its circulation eventually topping 200,000, it would emerge as a forerunner to the American bishops' bicentennial campaign on the theme of "Liberty and Justice for All."

Nowhere was *Quest* better received than among women religious. Many orders asked for copies in bulk, distributing them to all sisters and to their schools. It called explicitly for redress of the "discriminatory and unjust treatment" women had received within the Church, urging them to speak out publicly for full participation. In case there was any mistake about the connection between social reform and institutional change, one statement that had been made by the bishops at their 1971 synod was repeated twice on the front page: "The examination of conscience which we have made together, regarding the Church's involvement in action for justice, will remain ineffective if it is not given flesh in the life of our local churches at all levels."[12]

Quest represented a pointed call for the Church to look inward as well as outward, to reflect critically on the sins of its past. It was perhaps the closest Bill Ryan would come to being directly associated with this sort of frontal public critique of internal Church practice, the way it was organized and the manner in which it excluded women. Rather than promoting justice in the Church, he preferred to concentrate on the Church's external role in promoting justice in the world. He was also by temperament more inclined to adroit institutional politicking, scheming behind the lines rather than mounting the barricades directly, using his influence and leadership to provide room to allow people who were more openly critical to manoeuvre. One of those was Bill Callahan. Always an admirer of Ryan's, Callahan was the most impatiently radical of the three Jesuits who first worked at the Center. Like both of his colleagues, Callahan was a shrewd observer of the politics around him; he saw Ryan as an accomplished institutional poker player who knew when to hold 'em and when to fold 'em.

"Bill was politically adroit, always able to duck his head when the volleys were coming, to know when he could speak out boldly, when it was time to keep his mouth shut," explained Callahan, who stayed with the Jesuits until he became so frustrated with the institutional Church of John Paul II that he was expelled from the order for publicizing internal correspondence. Callahan would not have disagreed with Ryan's blunt assessment of his exit: "He knew what he was doing." According to Callahan, Bill Ryan also knew the lay of the land: "He understood early something that somebody like Dan Berrigan understood. As long as you stay away from internal church reform, and stay with social justice and social teaching, you'll not come under fire of a certain kind from the Vatican.… The Center of Concern from its beginning has been part of the social justice movement of the Church, not the Church reform movement."

In 1972 there were ample opportunities for Ryan and the Center of Concern to help animate the movement for social justice. It was a movement that was becoming particularly engaged in the struggle against what was known at the time as "underdevelopment," an essentially economic notion that had become shorthand for the fact that the peoples of the Third World – most of whom had then only just emancipated themselves from the clutches of colonialism – were still mired in material poverty. The modernizing economists led by Walt Rostow hoped that the Third World (a term that was just beginning to gain currency when Bill Ryan was studying economics at Harvard, down the street from Rostow's MIT) would grow its way to the exalted "stage" that had been achieved in post-war North America.

This path to progress would, of course, fall under increasing critical scrutiny as its costs, both environmental and social, became evident. The suburbs of Phoenix and the slums of Calcutta were evidence of the limitations of this model, as was the startling realization that acid precipitation and ultraviolet radiation had made the rain and the sun, once simply life-giving blessings, into potential threats to planetary life. Some thinkers had already realized that it was possible to have growth without development, although it would still be some time before that elusive notion of development began to be modified by the adjectives *sustainable* and *human*. In June 1972, just as the first UN Environmental Conference got underway in Stockholm, the Center of Concern's *Quest* stated that the world's finite resources had to be redistributed fairly, their control shared between rich and poor. Only then would "future growth of the less developed nations be possible within the context of limited natural resources and the interrelated ecology of our planet."[13]

It was an exhilarating time to be a well-connected Jesuit based in Washington and travelling around the world in pursuit of social justice. The Center of Concern didn't organize anything itself, adopting instead a strategy of trying to influence gatherings organized by others and to follow the rhythms of United Nations conferences. In April 1972, shortly before the Stockholm meeting, another pivotal international gathering meeting took place in Chile. The United Nations Conference on Trade and Development (UNCTAD) convened its third meeting just as all the talk of a "New International Economic Order" was building. Bill Ryan was there.

The NEIO, as it was called, was a plan for the reform of the global economic system, an agenda developed in the early 1970s by the "Group of 77" non-aligned countries of the south. Third World commodity producers linked their continued poverty to a corrosive combination: they received low prices for the sisal, sugar, bauxite and a hundred other commodities they sold to the affluent north but had to pay high prices for the manufactured goods they bought from the rich countries in turn. The goal of the NEIO was an "Integrated Program on Commodities" that would have restricted the supply of primary exports from the south, thus avoiding market gluts and providing a stable income for producers. The NEIO was not really a radical agenda. It simply envisaged an end to neocolonial trading relations, along with a world order based on "equity, sovereign equality, independence, common interest and co-operation among all states." In the Chilean capital of Santiago, humble ministerial delegations from Gabon and Bolivia mixed with bejewelled sheikhs from oil-rich sultanates discussing "terms of trade." The Organization of Petroleum Exporting Countries would would soon give substance to the demands for a just trading system by raising the price of oil. Suburban motorists in North America suddenly faced gasoline shortages, gaining a tiny taste of life in the south, where shortages of clean water were commonplace but where, as Ivan Illich had put it, thirst was being transformed into the desire for a Coke. There were initial rumblings about the growing power of "multinational corporations" like the American soft-drink manufacturer.

The venue was nearly as important as the substance of the six weeks of UNCTAD meetings. If there was ever a hopeful place at a hopeful time, Chile in 1972 was it. Salvador Allende's attempt at a democratic revolution was in full flower. Official greetings were extended not just to the delegates to the official meetings – social justice advocates at the parallel gathering (every UN conference would have its activist counterconference) also met the country's socialist president. For partisans of the international left who attended, the atmosphere was electric. They joined their Chilean counterparts in a march down the Alameida, where John Foster of the United Church recalled holding aloft a portrait of Ho Chi Minh. Allende's agriculture minister announced the latest land-reform measure at a session of the counterconference.

For Bill Ryan, Santiago was also an upbeat scene because it was a hotbed of Jesuit social thinking. Renato Poblete and Mario Zanartu had been at Louvain. Gonzalo Arroyo, a well-known socialist, also had a doctorate in economics. Ryan also knew Patrick Cariolla, who had studied education at Harvard when he was there. As a result, he was able to indulge his zeal for international gatherings while strengthening his links to the network of international contacts that is available to Jesuits. Ryan was becoming accustomed to using this unique resource that was so helpful in keeping abreast of social and political events around the world. The Society of Jesus was filled with well-educated, well-connected men who shared his social concerns. The order was still a mixed bag, however. Ryan also met Roger Vekemans in Santiago. The Belgian intellectual who had also studied at Louvain had been dispatched by Pedro Arrupe's predecessor Jean-Baptiste Janssens to fight socialism in Chile years before. A right-wing zealot ("I'd take money from the devil himself if it were necessary to stop the communists"), he served as a conduit for CIA funds to Christian Democratic parties and trade unions. Vekemans, who later repaired to an opulent mansion in Colombia, had been intimately involved with American attempts to keep Allende from coming to office. He never tired of denouncing liberation theology as a mere plot for Marxist infiltration of the Church.[14]

Returning briefly to Canada, Ryan denounced the Canadian government's lack of sympathy with Third World demands and the NIEO. He and John Foster, the United Church staffer with whom he had passed several evenings in a smoky communist bar listening to Chilean flute music, participated in a successful press conference in Ottawa.

Canadians could take no pride in the role their government had played in Santiago, where its delegates kept looking back to see how the American delegation was voting. At a subsequent meeting at Toronto's St. Michael's College, the UNCTAD monitoring initiative gave rise to GATT-Fly, one of the most enduringly radical of Canada's emerging network of interchurch coalitions. The Toronto group began publishing in-depth research on Canadian and international economic issues, approximating the solid analysis that Ryan promoted at the Center of Concern. GATT, the General Agreement on Tariffs and Trade, has since evolved into the World Trade Organization, and GATT-Fly has been renamed the Ecumenical Coalition for Economic Justice, but almost three decades after its founding the organization is still carrying on the struggle against a world trading system controlled by rich countries and weighted against the poor. The left wing of the Canadian Catholic Church was central to GATT-Fly as it was to all the ecumenical coalitions. And Bill Ryan, during his years in Washington, made sure that he kept in close touch through his friend Everett MacNeil, general secretary of the Canadian Catholic Conference, with what his successors at the Conference were doing on the social justice front.

——◆◆◆◆——

The NIEO was proclaimed at the sixth special session of the United Nations in April 1974. The United States was steadfastly opposed, while Canada abstained. It was formally rejected by the rich countries in December of that year. It was the same year that Friedrich von Hayek won the Nobel Prize for economics. The gospel according to the free market, soon to be proclaimed with evangelical zeal, was beginning its return to favour. The International Monetary Fund and the World Bank, Washington-based and U.S.-controlled, would become its principal instruments of enforcement. A "Washington Consensus" gradually began to congeal.

The rejection of the NEIO by the rich countries did not dampen the enthusiasm of Bill Ryan and the Center of Concern for the social justice gospel. Though the Center was based in Washington, Ryan felt that the United Nations was the ideal forum for this work. Just after the Center gained formal consultative status at the UN, four staffers went to the 1974 UN conference on population in Bucharest, Romania – the first time that Ryan and his colleagues participated officially in a UN meeting. The UN orientation would provide a source of funds, with money also begining to flow from major American foundations like Ford and Rockefeller.

The delicate situation in which this strategy placed the Center of Concern was nowhere more evident than at the Bucharest population meetings, attended by official delegates from 136 countries and 1,100 participants in the "Tribune," a parallel meeting of non-governmental organizations. A new Center staffer, Jane Blewett, formerly a nun and medical missionary in Pakistan who accompanied Ryan to the population conference, put it succinctly: "We tried to walk a very narrow line."

The politics of the situation were complex. The United States was a key backer of the conference and had formulated the proposed "Action Plan." Although Richard Nixon had resigned in disgrace just days before the Bucharest meeting, the Republican administration's line reflected the thinking then still dominant in many policy circles. If only the world's poor would stop breeding so fast there would be more food to go around, so that the problem of poverty could be addressed. The American delegation, headed by Caspar Weinberger, was pushing specific population "targets." Weinberger, who would go on to be Ronald Reagan's Defense Secretary, didn't want to hear complicated arguments about how consumption patterns in affluent countries like his own might be relevant to the issue of world population. At Bucharest, the Americans dismissed what they termed the "so-called" NIEO as mere rhetoric.

The Vatican was clearly on record as opposing contraception and, by extension, programs that would allow women to exercise more control over family size, and Pope Paul VI and his curia made good copy for the thousand or so journalists attending the meetings. If there were too many people in the world and the pope had lectured the United Nations about how irrational it was to diminish the number of guests at the banquet of life, then headlines like "Vatican Dissents" and "Holy See disassociates itself from world plan of action" followed easily. Radical critics, particularly in the feminist movement, also denounced population control, but not because they agreed with the pope. They saw Western population-control programs as a means of controlling the lives of Third World women and another way of reinforcing the client status of poor people in poor countries without interfering with the structures of neo-colonialism.

Officials at the United Nations and the foundations that were simultaneously funding population-control programs and the Center of Concern tried to marry the need for birth control with the need for economic development. But if birth control was straightforward enough, "development" meant many things to many people. Was it economic growth? The expansion of world trade? Did it involve land-to-the-tiller efforts at wealth distribution inside Third World countries? Empowering women? Demographers (Bill Ryan had hired one and brought him along) argued that population always increased when peasants began to feel economically secure, child mortality declined and people gained more control over their own lives.

Integral to the Center of Concern's delicate balancing act was its position as a Catholic organization not controlled by the bishops or the Vatican. It could push the Church's social justice position without hewing specifically to the official line on birth control. This made it an effective conduit for the message of egalitarian development as a precondition to population control. Ryan, Blewett, Henriot and Mike Henry, the Australian demographer who was working with them, came to Bucharest with a trilingual (English, French, Spanish) pamphlet. It was free of jargon and outlined ten population-policy principles. The main message was that population policy could not be divorced from the social context, that population problems were social problems whose solution required an improvement in the status of women and the elimination of poverty and illiteracy. Feminists, to whom Ryan was starting to listen, could agree. Vatican orthodoxy could accept the statement that "the need for fertility reduction in the poor countries is...over-stressed." Third World reformers would agree that the goal of population policy should be to "change economic and political structures which maintain the unequal distribution of power, wealth and resources among and within nations."

For Bill Ryan and Pete Henriot, writing in the Jesuit magazine *America* after Bucharest, the "unexpected 'radical prophet' of Bucharest" was John D. Rockefeller III. The Rockefeller Foundation was a major Western funder of Third World population-control efforts, and as such a target for the radicals. For the Jesuits from the Center of Concern, however, Rockefeller was taking his distance from the State Department by arguing that each country had to solve its own problems in its own way, that "women must have greater freedom of choice in determining their roles in society" and that economic growth had to enhance "the well-being of people generally."[15] Unknown to most of the delegates, Rockefeller's speech had been drafted by the staff of the Center of Concern.

Ryan felt that the Center's participation at Bucharest was a success. Its behind-the-scenes diplomacy contributed to changes in the U.S.

administration's proposed Action Plan on fertility control. The final text was more holistic than the American scheme. For Ryan, Bucharest was "primarily a political meeting, not a technical meeting of experts." He and his staff had been able to gauge the political winds (or, once more, "the signs of the times") in advance and push their own position as far as they could, both in pre-conference preparatory meetings and in Bucharest itself. Jane Blewett recalled:

> From the point of view of the foundations and the UN, the pope and the Vatican were big stumbling blocks to this whole thing. So to the foundation people we said, "You cannot just talk about condoms and birth control if you do not understand the religious and cultural setting of the people. However your message is tailored it has to come out of that." To the Catholic Church we said, "As long as this is boudoir morality in your minds and is limited to what goes on in the bedroom between two people and you do not see it as an immense social question, you're out of the loop. You might as well stay home."

Ryan and Henriot felt that the Vatican had not emerged from Bucharest that badly. If only the official Church could better hone its communications strategy, realizing that "the medium is the message," it would be able "to take a more radical, unambiguous prophetic message on behalf of the poor and powerless." Despite the "admirable record" of the Holy See in Bucharest, its delegates had still not overcome the perception that its position on birth control was driving its agenda. The Jesuits wrote in *America* that the Vatican's delegates "did not succeed in convincing the world assembly, the observers or the press that its major preoccupation at Bucharest was genuinely with social justice for the poor and the powerless and not rather with protecting its own specific teachings on family life."[16]

This analysis blended two things: Ryan's visceral optimism and his keen sense of politics as the art of the possible. As a shrewd observer of Church politics, he was aware of the sensitivity of the "family life" (read, birth control) dogma and the likelihood that it could trump concerns for social justice. Although he had been able to skate around the issue at Bucharest, he and Henriot saw the episode as a small skirmish in a larger war. He took the longer view, believing that with time and with enough successful skirmishes, things would work out and the Church would be able to cope with its huge contradictions.

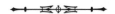

Another tension the Center of Concern was trying to manage in those years was between spirituality and the pursuit of social justice. In the 1960s and early 1970s, while the Jesuits were becoming increasingly committed to social justice work, they were also rethinking and renewing the Spiritual Exercises of St. Ignatius. The "preached retreat" Ryan had experienced as a novice in the mid-1940s and during his tertianship in the late 1950s, where periods of silent prayer were punctuated by homilies given by the retreat leader, was giving way to a new format, the "directed retreat." Taking their inspiration from the way Ignatius himself had given the Exercises, the reformers scrapped the homilies and replaced them with one-on-one meetings between the retreatant and a spiritual director who acted as a counsellor, monitoring the retreatant's spiritual progress and prescribing the forms and subjects of prayer that were most germane to his or her individual situation. Some of the early work on this change was done under Paul Kennedy SJ at St. Beuno's in Wales, where Ryan's Canadian contemporary John English studied in the 1950s. Back in Canada, English helped make Loyola Retreat House in Guelph a leading centre of the new method.

Father General Pedro Arrupe, the inspirational leader of the move towards a greater Jesuit commitment to social justice, was also a passionate believer in the Spiritual Exercises, which he saw as the underpinning for all Jesuit activities. But what was the connection between the two currents? Could Ignatian spiritual methods be used to lead people towards greater social awareness and involvement? In late 1973 the Center of Concern assembled a task force to explore these questions. Nine of the fourteen members were primarily spiritual directors and counsellors; the other five brought a primary interest in social thought. All were Jesuits except for Margaret Brennan, superior of the Sisters, Servants of the Immaculate Heart of Mary of Monroe, Michigan, who would later teach at Regis College in Toronto. Ryan, Henriot and Callahan were all on the task force, as was English, who had briefly lived with Ryan in Montreal ten years earlier but had not previously collaborated with him.

The task force met four times between December 1973 and May 1974, and by the end of the fourth meeting its members had written and revised papers based on their personal experience but also informed by the discussions of the group. After the fourth meeting, a team of editors headed by Callahan was assigned to edit the papers for publication. In the interests of speed and affordability, Callahan's team decided on a tabloid format similar to that of the Center of Concern's earlier *Quest for*

Justice. The new tabloid, *Soundings: A Task Force on Social Consciousness and Ignatian Spirituality*, appeared during a time of intense discussion and anticipation in the Jesuit world. Arrupe had called a general congregation, scheduled to convene in late 1974. Jesuit provinces all over the world were meeting to elect delegates to the Congregation and adopt resolutions, known as *postulata*, for the Congregation to consider. A set of Mexican *postulata* defining the pursuit of justice as a fundamental orientation of the Society was gaining momentum as other provinces endorsed it. Meeting at Easter, the Upper Canada province had unanimously passed the Mexican *postulata* and elected one of their chief supporters, Bill Ryan, a delegate to the Congregation.

Ryan's contribution to *Soundings* reflected these developments. He criticized the prevailing "mindset" in North American society, which he characterized as oriented towards results, efficiency, success, competition and consumerism. He quoted economist Gail Stewart: "We have built a whole society in the image of a factory…. We are marching forward under the terrible technological imperative of growth at any cost – more things, more things, more things."[17]

The previous year's International Symposium on Jesuit Spirituality in San Francisco, he noted, had focused on the question of mindset: "There the question posed was why persons highly attuned to the Spiritual Exercises of St. Ignatius often show little sensitivity to the acute demands of involvement in social justice issues. The answer suggested was that such persons simply do not perceive their own involvement in sinful structures and so do not relate it to their daily life and prayer."[18] Referring to the Upper Canada province's meeting in preparation for the general Congregation, still fresh in his mind, he wrote that the meeting's "basic insight" was that "all discernment must begin with the fundamental Christian option of casting one's lot with the poor and powerless." This insight, he concluded, "has immediate relevance for all of us in our spiritual exercises and discernment."[19]

Other contributors looked at how specific elements of the Spiritual Exercises – the "Eighteenth Annotation," the "Graces of the Third and Fourth Weeks," the "Rules for Thinking with the Church" – could be given more substantial social content.[20] John English suggested that "the methods…given by St. Ignatius in the Spiritual Exercises for obtaining a free, personal response to God's invitations may be useful for promoting a self-appropriation of the truth presented in the social teachings of the Church." He added that "recent developments in the personally directed retreat and the Exercises are closely linked with the insistence of Vatican II upon humanity's responsibility for building-up the kingdom of Christ on earth."[21]

Soundings was a valuable early attempt to bring together two groups of people – spiritual directors and social activists – who often appear to have little in common. The need to keep the concerns and outlooks of the two groups in balance would not go away. It would be an important element in the discussions of the 32nd General Congregation, which convened in Rome in December 1974, and in the debates that followed GC32. Bill Ryan would be faced with the task of maintaining that balance in a number of contexts in subsequent years, and he would not always be as successful as he was at the Center of Concern.

—————

There is a story about Bill Ryan and the 32nd General Congregation of 1974–75, when the Jesuits adopted their famous – and famously controversial – Decree 4 declaring the struggle for social justice "indispensable" to evangelization. When the Jesuits again gathered in Rome for their 33rd General Congregation nine years later to pick a new general to succeed Pedro Arrupe, Bill Ryan and Peter-Hans Kolvenbach were delegates, as they had been at GC32. Just as GC33 got underway Ryan approached Kolvenbach to learn something of the man who, word had it, might be chosen to take over from Arrupe.

As Terry Walsh SJ, English-Canadian provincial at the time of GC32, tells the story, Ryan said, "Well, Father, I didn't hear you speak at all in the big hall at our last Congregation." To which Kolvenbach replied, "No. But you spoke enough for all of us."

Walsh laughs heartily, recalling that he first heard the story from Ryan himself. Actually, Ryan has a somewhat different version of the story. In his recollection, Kolvenbach's reply was, "And how did you know from the beginning how the Congregation would end?" Either way, it is clear that Ryan's efforts at GC32 did not go unnoticed.

If the early years in Washington were the high point of Ryan's career, he experienced GC32 as wearying and frustrating, "one of the most difficult experiences of my life." He had found it depressing and spiritually debilitating, "even a shock to my faith," to see his fellow Jesuits and their esteemed father general "misunderstood and humiliated for weeks on end" by the Vatican and Pope Paul VI. But, he assured an American audience in the wake of the crucial gathering, it was also "the strongest confirmation I have ever had of what Jesuit identity and mission are today and for the future."[22]

The story of GC32 and the events that followed is also the story of Pedro Arrupe and the Jesuits' often-stormy relations with a Vatican that almost exactly two hundred years previously had abolished "for all eternity" – but not extinguished – the Society of Jesus. Though the popular imagination had it that the Jesuits were the papacy's loyal foot soldiers, relations had often been tense.

The Jesuit Matteo Ricci, known also as Li Mateou, became a citizen of Nanking and would come to understand China and gain the ears of its highest officials in the late sixteenth century. Born in an Adriatic enclave of the Papal States, Ricci arrived in Macao after a stint in India. A pioneer in what would become known as Sinology, this amazing Jesuit polymath was no missionary in any bringing-the-truth-to-unbelievers sense. Living and dressing as a Confucian scholar, Li Mateou won the respect of Chinese intellectuals. His years of exposure to Chinese life and culture and his embrace of Chinese ways led him down an intellectual path in search of spiritual roots common to the belief systems with which he was most familiar. Rome, however, subsequently condemned Jesuit links to Confucianism. Meanwhile, in South America the famous Jesuit reductions, model self-reliant communities of indigenous people under Jesuit control, collapsed in a welter of imperial intrigue, a prelude to the "eternal" suppression of the Society in 1773.

Between 1814, when they were officially restored by the pope (eternity being short-lived), and 1860, the Jesuits, always as close to controversy as they were to various popes, were banished, reinstated, redissolved and rerestored some seventy times in various European countries. The order played an essentially reactionary role in the nineteenth century, standing with the papacy in attempting to expunge the viruses of "progress, liberalism and modernization." Pietro Picirillo SJ, the editor of the Vatican newspaper *La Civiltà Cattolica* in the 1860s, was a close adviser to Pius IX who consulted almost daily with the pope during the First Vatican Council. That council would produce the declaration of papal infallibility that, along with the Syllabus of Errors and the doctrine of the Immaculate Conception, did as much damage to the Church as its refutation of liberalism, Darwinism and socialism. During this period, the Jesuit reputation was as foot soldiers and shock troops (the metaphors for the Company of Jesus were almost always military) in the papal crusade against various errors and ideologies. "In the whole wide world, apart from two muleheaded Belgians," declared one Canon Morel in 1876, "a liberal Jesuit is a phenomenon no longer to be encountered."[23]

Things had changed by the eve of the Second Vatican Council, when the thinking of Jesuit theologians like Karl Rahner, Henri de Lubac, John Courtney Murray and Jean Daniélou did so much to contribute to the reformist atmosphere. But although he had a Jesuit confessor in Father Paolo Dezza, Pope Paul VI had uneasy relations with the Society during his papacy. Things came to a head at GC32, only the fourth Jesuit Congregation in more than four centuries called for any reason other than to elect a new general.

The 31st General Congregation in the 1960s had not only opened the door to social justice work within the Jesuits. It had also opened the door, period, providing the same sort of spiritual renewal that Vatican II offered the Catholic Church as a whole. Jim Connor, who was Jesuit provincial for Maryland at the time, had entered the Order in 1946 as one of sixty under the direction of a single master of novices. Everything was very orderly, very static, with no big surprises. The path of a teaching career seemed straightforward, with little opportunity for initiative or creativity. Connor senses that Vatican II and GC31 were the products of a clash as the Enlightenment broke into Catholic consciousness. He recalls looking out his office window during a thunderstorm and watching as lightning struck a beautiful tree that he had always admired, smashing it to the ground: "It wasn't until then that you could see it was totally hollow and rotten inside. I said, 'There's the Maryland Province.' And it wasn't our fault. We had been indoctrinated in a lockstep, mechanical way. We had never been socialized in the proper sense into the sprirituality of the Ignatian charism. There had been no opportunity for that."

The opening up had mixed results. It would animate Jesuits like Ryan and Connor, who would participate together at GC32 when the order declared that working for social justice was integral to the mission of every Jesuit. But it would have a different effect on other Jesuits who decided that the priestly life was not for them. "[GC]31 really opened the door to modernity for the Jesuit order," said Connor, who went on to head up the Woodstock Theological Center at Georgetown University. "It broke out of the cloistered monasticism and all the external trappings.... So many Jesuits were being held together by the external trappings without an interior life. As soon as you opened those doors they just flew right out. They had no anchor to hold them."

This may have been among the anxieties of Catholic conservatives, including some Jesuits, who opposed modernity and all of its malaises. Complaints about the direction in which Arrupe was taking the Society began very early in his term, especially among some Jesuits in Spain who called themselves *jesuitas de la fidelidad* or "Faithful Jesuits."[24] The voices of these dissident Jesuits reached the Vatican and formed part of the backdrop for the tensions between the Society and Pope Paul VI that would emerge at GC32.

The dissidents, however, were a minority. Immediately after GC31, Arrupe sent a questionnaire to every Jesuit asking for a "deep, objective, wide-open scrutiny" of the world and the Church.[25] Arrupe's advisers, notably Jean-Yves Calvez from France and Vincent O'Keefe from the United States, scanned the questionnaire and sensed a demand for social justice. Ryan took to the spirit of reform with a zeal that would lead him to play an active and influential role in GC32, particularly in bringing about its declaration that "since evangelization is proclamation of that faith which is made operative in love of others, the promotion of justice is indispensable to it."[26] For him, the road to that conclusion went through Louvain, Vatican II, GC31, Medellín and Montreal and, most importantly in his experience, the 1971 Justice in the World synod, at which the bishops had used the word *constitutive* instead of *indispensable*.

When the 236 Jesuits convened on December 1, 1974, they were for the most part strangers to one another. The *aula*, or hall, was nearly two storeys high, a gallery running along both sides and the back, where the translators' booths were located. A raised desk at the front had places for the general, the secretary and a moderator. It was all quite stately and old-fashioned, with delegates seated in alphabetical order so that Ryan was placed between a Sicilian and a Filipino. The only modern wrinkle was an imposing electronic affair that resembled the scoreboard at a basketball game except that it registered with coloured lights the results of the votes: aye, nay or abstention. Ryan, with a penchant for efficiency and smooth-running meetings, found unclear procedures and inexperienced chairpersons so frustrating that he felt some delegates were never sure what was going on. Terry Walsh recalled that all the preliminary work, the pre-convention planning, that would have been done by the bureaucracy in most organizations had to be shouldered by small groups of delegates once the meeting got going. Another participant described "the donkey-work" of digesting and integrating *postulata*, amendments and proposals into readable texts as laborious and time-consuming. Ryan even employed the phraseology of the day, blurting out that the Congregation was itself a "sinful structure." Whether sinful or merely disorganized, the Congregation appeared ill-equipped to introduce some order into the mountains of *postulata*, nearly a thousand, that had been submitted by Jesuits around the world.

The delegates' task was complicated by the nervousness of the Vatican about what the assembled Jesuits would do. As the Congregation got underway, Pope Paul arrived with some words of warning for the order of priests that had over the centuries done so much to help and to aggravate the papacy they were pledged by their unique Fourth Vow to obey. He advised the Jesuits to examine where they came from, where they were and, most important, where they were going. He reminded them that "you are united with the pope by a special vow." The speech was couched in strong, precise language, warning of "spiritual decadence" and declaring His Holiness' awareness of "a strong state of uncertainty, indeed a certain fundamental questioning" about their very identity among the men arranged alphabetically in the *aula*: "Readiness to serve can degenerate into relativism, into conversion to the world and its immanentist mentality, into assimilation with the world that one wanted to save, into secularism and into fusion with the profane. We exhort you not to be seized by the *spiritus vertiginis*."[27]

The Jesuits were uncertain about what the man from up the street meant by this last reference. But a sizable number among them were convinced that, even though Pope Paul had issued the socially progressive encyclicals *Populorum Progressio* and *Octogesima Adveniens*, he would be averse to the spirit that animated various *postulata* before them.[28] Ryan, whose goal at the Congregation was to ensure that the essence of the "Mexican *postulata*" on the centrality of social justice worked its way into the final documents, later speculated that it was perhaps an overemphasis on socio-economic analysis that caused "some of our misunderstanding with Pope Paul VI," adding that GC32 took pains to strengthen the spiritual and theological underpinnings of what would become Decree 4.

In fact, the pope's uneasiness had more to do with the feeling among many Jesuits that the spirit of egalitarianism animating their social justice work should also enliven the internal workings of the order. Why not move to greater equality between priests and brothers? And why shouldn't all Jesuits, brothers as well as priests, be allowed to pronounce the same vows, including the special Fourth Vow of obedience to the pope? Ironically, it was precisely this vow of obedience that made the pope and his curial advisers edgy. So edgy that on December 3, the same day the pope gave his opening speech to the Congregation, Vatican Secretary of State Cardinal Villot sent Arrupe a letter indicating that any change in the Fourth Vow would present "grave difficulties" that could well stall approval by the Holy See.[29]

Jesuit–Vatican tensions were one problem. But at least as pressing a concern for Ryan and his allies who hoped to see a strong statement on social justice come out of GC32 was the sheer weight of inertia that could overcome a gathering as long and complex as a Jesuit Congregation, particularly since the meeting lacked the basic preliminary organizing necessary to enable the diverse group to digest the controversial agenda. Ryan later recalled being shocked to realize that many Jesuits were suspicious of the expression "social justice," with delegates from eastern Europe regarding its proponents as trapped by communist ideology, or at least liberation theology. Many of the canon lawyers, theologians and moral philosophers present, Ryan found, were not used to working with "social scientists or process people."[30]

On December 12 the Congregation considered forty-eight suggested priority areas and approved six of them by majority vote: "the criteria of our apostolate today"; "mission and apostolic obedience"; "poverty"; "the promotion of justice (as a criterion of our life and apostolate)"; "the fourth vow"; and "formed members." A commission would be set up for each of these areas. Although social justice was one of the priority areas, Ryan and his allies were still worried. Would this structure produce a clear statement that social justice was fundamental to Jesuit identity and mission, or would the potential unifying effect of the Mexican *postulata* get lost in the commissions? They convinced the Congregation as a whole to spend a few days discussing a "priority of priorities" before the work of the commissions began. This tactic served its purpose, Ryan felt: "It helped clarify the notion of 'fundamental option' and of 'justice' for many delegates, and it brought into very sharp focus our need to clarify the relationship between the promotion of justice and evangelization."[31]

The document that came out of this discussion was entitled "Jesuit Mission and Justice in the World," but it was still up to the separate commissions to decide how to interpret and incorporate the priority of priorities. Not surprisingly, this task was taken up most enthusiastically by Commission IV, the commission on justice, of which Ryan was a member. Delegates worked hard to relate the promotion of justice to previous understandings of Jesuit mission, from "reconciling the estranged" as it had been formulated in the sixteenth century to the emphasis on fighting atheism that GC31 had adopted at the behest of Pope Paul. In a speech to the delegates on December 20, Arrupe gave strong support to the option for justice, calling it "a priority in the sense that it is to be treated first in the Congregation and ought to influence our entire life." He warned the delegates that they would pay a price if they accepted this option. Lifestyles would change. Friends and benefactors would disappear along with prestige and social standing. "Have you got only an academic interest in the promotion of justice?" Arrupe asked. "If not, then let us be prepared to preach the justice of the Gospel through the cross and from the cross."[32]

Still, many delegates wondered why the commissions were continuing to work separately, potentially undercutting the priority of priorities. Finally, at the end of January, Commission IV was merged with Commissions I and II, which dealt with issues relating to Jesuit mission. Now the task for Ryan and his colleagues became to ensure that Commission IV's understanding of justice would be the basis for the document that would emerge from this larger group. Commission IV had the advantage of having developed the clearest formulation, but its work went through several drafts and thousands of amendments, most of them directed towards clarifying the relationship between the promotion of justice and the service of faith.

In the midst of this toil the Jesuits got another shock from the Vatican in the form of a letter from the pope dated February 15. He again warned against any watering down of the priestly character of the order and forbade any further discussion of the Fourth Vow. The pope also mentioned "certain orientations and dispositions which are emerging from the work of the General Congregation. Is the Church able to have faith in you here and now, the kind of faith it has always had?"[33]

Putting aside the historical record of four centuries of sometimes-harmonious, sometimes-fractious relations between the Vatican and the Jesuits, the pope was, according to two Canadian Church historians, warning the Jesuits that "there would be no creeping egalitarianism under the banner of *aggiornamento*." And as the Congregation ended three weeks later, the pope sent another missive underlining his right to intervene in the proceedings and telling the Jesuits, "Be loyal!"[34]

Some Jesuits became physically ill with doubt after the several papal interventions. Others, like Ryan, just wanted to get on with the task. This group took its inspiration from Pedro Arrupe, whom one delegate described as a spiritual optimist who genuinely believed that if you sincerely wanted to do the Lord's will, no matter what the opposition or difficulties, all would be well. Confronted with the repudiation from on high, the gentle Basque summoned a dramatic, unscheduled general session where he simply read out the letter as an expression of the Holy Father's will and gave thanks for God's clear guidance. The Vatican's efforts to influence the course of the Congregation also had the unintended effect of intensifying the sense of solidarity among the delegates. Suspicions and misunderstandings dissipated as the delegates struggled towards a common goal under outside pressure. "At the end of December," Ryan later recalled, "there were at least fifty delegates with whom I disagreed fundamentally and emotionally and felt like giving a swift kick. By the end of February my 'enemies list' was reduced to two, and later to one!"[35]

After another round of amendments in which delegates tried to come up with wording that would not push any papal buttons, the Congregation approved the final text of Decree 4 in a near-unanimous vote on March 4. The next day, an exhausted Bill Ryan boarded a plane for Washington, worried that something essential might have been lost in these last-minute changes. But as he read the text the delegates had approved and realized that the core ideas had not been diluted, his spirits lifted. Despite the difficulties with the Vatican, the pope would approve the GC32 documents unchanged within two months. Reflecting on his experience of the Congregation for a Catholic audience a few years later, Ryan read out what was for him the "richest paragraph" to emerge from GC32. He told of how it had at first been "censored" and then "unanimously restored":

> It is in this light that we are asked to renew our dedication to the properly apostolic dimension of our religious life. Our consecration to God is really a prophetic rejection of those idols which the world is always tempted to adore, wealth, pleasure, presitige, power. Hence our poverty, chastity and obedience ought visibly to bear witness to this. Despite the inadequacy of any attempt to anticipate the Kingdom which is to come, our vows ought to show how by God's grace there can be, as the Gospel proclaims, a community among human beings which is based on sharing rather than on greed; on willing openness to all persons, rather than on seeking after the privileges of caste or class or race; on service rather than on domination and exploitation. The men and women of our time need a hope which is eschatological, but they also need to have some signs that its realization has already begun.[36]

Of course, he acknowledged, the Congregation had not extended the Fourth Vow to all. But, he continued in a cheery manner, "We surely lived it deeply! Attempts to censor our draft documents and to wall-paper over our own rhetoric with papal or pious rhetoric were angrily refused, even by more conservative delegates."[37]

Arrupe's inspirational leadership was undoubtedly one factor in creating a consensus in favour of the social justice imperative. Among the delegates, Latin Americans played a major part – after all, Decree 4 had its origins in the social justice proposals from Mexico, the so-called Mexican *postulata*. However, Jean-Yves Calvez, a general assistant to Arrupe and a delegate to GC32, also maintained that there would have been no Decree 4 without the theological reflection that came from Europe and North America. More precisely, added Calvez, the "most active editors of the Decree came from North America and Canada."[38] Maryland provincial Jim Connor, who had known Ryan since his arrival in Washington, said that "Bill Ryan played a big role. He left saying 'I got most of what I wanted.'... When Bill got to Rome he really wanted the pursuit of justice to become a constitutive dimension of the Society of Jesus."

The decree's supporters knew that they would have a hard sell once they got home, for they were not all returning to be surrounded by the activists that Bill Ryan worked with at the Center of Concern. Few critics were as acerbic as one right-wing former Jesuit who pilloried Decree 4 as "a pitiable model of false doctrine...stitched together with the trill-notes of spiritual-sounding mush,"[39] but many Jesuits remained unconvinced that faith and justice were as integrally related as the General Congregation maintained. "It wasn't an easy marriage at all," said Terry Walsh. "The justice people were saying, 'Well these people want to reduce everything to faith and spirituality and not deal with the real problems.' And the others were saying, 'If these people are not Marxists they tend towards Marxism or some form of materialism.'"

Jim Connor had to tell academics that Decree 4 did not mean they had to drop their briefcases and start work in soup kitchens. He even had to try to convince a Jesuit political scientist that the decree was relevant to his work. And as Connor noted, these misunderstandings lingered for a long time:

> Here are the faith people saying, "What we really need to do is to develop a more intense prayer life. Secularization is moving into our world. We're losing our fundamental root, the central-ity of Christ, the love of Christ, the self-sacrifice of Christ. Jus-tice is okay but this is really what the Church and Jesuit life are about." These are not bad people. And justice people would come

back with, "We've got to be serving the poor. We've got to be liberating the world from the shackles of economic and political oppression." And to this day that divide in many places has not been healed.

⟶►•◄⟵

The sweaty swampland that the American republicans chose for their capital has never been a successful city. Dickens would describe spacious avenues "that begin in nothing and lead nowhere" and "public buildings that need only a public to complete." By the 1970s, Washington had become a place where monumental, even imperial public ornaments and buildings attracted tourists and shielded the largely black slums just beyond. Presumably the market would take care of those grim neighbourhoods.

Ryan, never a big-city type, liked to relax by taking long walks. Initially seeking refuge from Washington's heat and the pressure of a busy schedule by strolling through Rock Creek Park, he soon realized that it was too dangerous for solo wanderings. But the Blue Ridge Mountains, the Shenandoahs and the great Appalachian Range with its Long Trail stretching north towards Canada offer residents of Washington an escape. Ryan often spent his Saturdays on his favourite one-day spiritual retreats, hiking in the rich temperate woodlands. He also made his way back to the boreal forest outside Ottawa every Christmas and Easter, celebrating and preaching Mass at St. Francis Xavier in Renfrew, visiting family and taking to the woods when possible. Jesuit spirituality finds God in all things, and nowhere did Ryan find soulful solace more than in forest and mountain. He was now travelling so much that he became something of a connoisseur of challenging alpine trails, climbing and skiing in the Rockies when doing workshops with the priests of the Denver archdiocese, exploring the Matterhorn and Mount Zinal when attending UN meetings in Geneva.

Ryan was by this time a leader among the Jesuits. He would sometimes take Pete Henriot climbing in the Alps or in the western United States. Henriot came from the Pacific northwest and his brother was a noted mountain climber, but the American Jesuit got dizzy at heights. Still, the two continued to hike, with Ryan urging Henriot on to try a more challenging trail. Henriot, whose mother was initially convinced that Ryan was a communist who was leading her son astray, would succeed Ryan as the Center of Concern's director and go on to live in Zambia, campaigning against Third World debt.

Another colleague from Ryan's Washington days who, like Henriot, kept in contact with him over the years was Joe Holland. A former priest, Holland was a leftist who had lived in Chile before the destruction of the Allende government's attempt at democratic socialism. After Ryan left the Center, Henriot and Holland wrote a successful book, *Social Analysis: Linking Faith and Justice*, that sold some 50,000 copies in its first edition. The book explains better than their mentor's somewhat circuitous writing the connections between spirituality and radical politics. Holland's preface to the second (1983) edition points to the failure of the traditional left to acknowledge the spiritual roots of creative energy and the unwillingness of the classical religious right (by this time fundamentalist Protestant zealots of the New Right were on the rise in the United States) to be open to the creative transformation of our civilization. The book presents a practical, how-to guide to pastoral work on social justice, underpinned by a theoretical analysis that made it a useful text for theologians.

Holland's preface also indicated that he had often heard Bill Ryan talk about discerning the signs of the times, assessing the prevailing energy flow. Appreciating culture is important to radical political action and the deepest source of cultural energy is "participation in divine creativity…. But in the crisis of our present civilization these energies of creativity are being converted on a massive scale into energies of destruction."[40] Henriot and Holland dedicated the book to Bill Ryan, crediting his leadership and friendship in helping them link faith to justice.

During his time at the Center of Concern, Ryan lived at a large Jesuit house that Holland, the self-described socialist at the Center, called "the elite Jesuit house downtown." He would live at 1729 New Hampshire Avenue near fashionable Dupont Circle for longer than any place he had stayed since he had left his parents' house at the corner of Quarry and Lynn twenty-seven years previously. The Jesuits, always mindful of a good real estate deal, got what one of its residents called "the little mansion" on the cheap in the 1960s after it had fallen into disrepair during its years as a student boarding house. The corner building with the neo-classical design had huge windows and enough space by the front door that its original owner, an affluent Washington lawyer, could have his guests pull their carriages and cars off the street. Renamed Leonard Neale House after an early Jesuit archbishop of Baltimore, during Ryan's years there it was home to some fifteen Jesuits, mostly men who worked in national Jesuit offices. Spacious and centrally located, Neale House had ample room for Ryan to arrange day-long meetings.

As the Center of Concern grew – its staff reached ten soon after Ryan returned from GC32 – its quarters became inadequate for anything but small gatherings. And as its publications and activities multiplied, the house up on 13th Street got increasingly cramped.

One new member of the staff, and new resident of Neale House, was Phil Land, who arrived from Rome in 1975 after twenty years at the Gregorian University and seven on the Pontifical Commission for Justice and Peace. Ryan's long-time friend had pushed things too far on birth control during the lead-up to the Bucharest conference. "At that time," said Land, "I discovered that the Vatican worked with a certain syllogism on population: If there is a population problem, people will practise birth control. But birth control is evil. Therefore there is no population problem."

Ever since the proclamation of *Humanae Vitae*, Land, a distinguished economist and theologian who always had a twinkle in his eye, had been quietly embarrassed by his Church's stance when attending ecumenical gatherings where population was discussed. Grateful to Protestant colleagues who recognized his difficult position and didn't press things, he was appointed to the Vatican delegation to Bucharest by a former student, by then a bishop who realized that his lively old professor would bring a wealth of insight and international experience to the UN population discussions. Land proceeded to prepare a paper on population that ran contrary to a document written by the head of the delegation. The American, long used to the baroque intrigues of Vatican politics, was still surprised by the reaction.

It was as if he had just stepped up to the plate. Strike one came when a representative of the secretary of state, one of the most powerful Vatican officials, arrived to read a statement to the delegation that would be going to Bucharest. Not only did they have to support *Humanae Vitae*, they had to push it: *"Il faut le pousser."* The secretary of state, Cardinal Villot, was French, an anomaly in a bureaucracy dominated by Italians. Strike two came in the form of a letter from the Cardinal the next day. "Father Land must, in front of witnesses, affirm that he has *'loyauté totale'* – total loyalty – to the encyclical," was Land's recollection of the content of the letter. "So I said, 'Tell Cardinal Villot that I have complete loyalty to the encyclical.' And then I added, 'according to the norms of Vatican II.' The next day I learned that was not enough loyalty."

Land recalled the incident not with any bitterness but with characteristic humour. The next day his Jesuit superior told him that Cardinal Villot himself had just called. Strike three was a hard slider that caught the inside corner. The cardinal was demanding that Land attest before witnesses that he had no questions about *Humanae Vitae* and that, furthermore, he could not question the word from on high either externally or internally. This attempt at thought control surprised even Land, a man of conscience and deep faith who thought he had heard it all: "I told my superior, 'Tell the good Cardinal that I can't take that oath. I will stay home and pray for the delegation.'"

Land had struck out. He related the incident in confidence to a fellow professor at the Gregorian, a moralist who rebuked him gently for not simply taking a "mental reservation" that would have involved accepting the demand with the caveat that the person making the demand cannot do so. Such psychological gymnastics were apparently not uncommon in the Vatican. But they had become too much for the sixty-four-year-old Jesuit. Obedience was one thing; this was quite another. "You can't so invade my conscience," he reflected later on. "I've thought about that, but that's the trouble with the Vatican. Everybody there uses mental reservations. That's corrosive. Sometimes plain talk is required."

Land was put on the shelf, his travel funds cut off with no explanation. He stewed silently for months, reading and writing letters but not really doing anything. Father Arrupe at the Jesuit curia on Borgo Santo Spirito was supportive but could do little. Publications seemed out of the question: "I said to myself, 'Land, you've talked a lot about justice, but you've never suffered for it. Now you've got to suffer for it.'" After a few months of inactivity he came to the conclusion that the Vatican commission for justice and peace had been reduced to a study group, that it was no longer witnessing for justice. He made the painful decision to tell his colleagues this. He did not want to return to a full course load at the Gregorian, where he had still been teaching a seminar during his years at the commission.

In June 1975 he received a letter from the man whom he had tried to recruit to Rome a few years earlier. Ryan, whom he described as "a very powerful figure," asked him to join the Center of Concern. He welcomed Land back to the United States, not with any instructions but by asking him what he wanted to do and encouraging him to do it. Land began by doing three things. He joined the board of Georgetown University. He sat on a key social justice committee (not just a study group) of the U.S. bishops just as the USCC was edging towards more social engagement. And his interest in the links between spirituality and the social and political order led him to the Jesuit Seminar on Spirituality.[41]

Ryan brought Land to the Center of Concern because he knew that Land's deep faith and personal warmth would be helpful in firming up the spiritual grounding of an organization that, of necessity, concerned itself on a daily basis with the secular world of UN conferences, foundation fundraising and policy research. Ryan's sensitive political antennae may also have sensed that Land's presence would enhance the Center's credibility in certain circles. Land recalls driving to a meeting with Ryan and Msgr. Jack Egan and Egan commenting to Ryan, "Well, Bill, let's acknowledge it. You brought Phil Land here because you needed to have a more conservative image."

Land wasn't particularly flattered by this observation. But he jumped right into work at the 13th Street house, where life had become rather different than he was used to in Rome or, for that matter, in the Jesuit order. Priestly life had been a cloistered affair and, even if Vatican II had attempted to open up the Church, many clerics had continued to exist in splendid isolation from the day-to-day realities of the world. Land arrived at the Center of Concern with an immaculate set of files, his documents neatly arranged. But they had been arranged by someone else. He had no social-security number and was puzzled by the prospect of opening his own bank account. He was used to a very structured environment. The Vatican bureaucracy was so stultified that one official could not talk to his opposite number down the hall without getting clearance from that official's superior. Now Land found himself at a place Eileen Olsen described as a "free-for-all."

"When he came to the Center he had never polished his shoes," recalled Jane Blewett, who knew about Jesuit life. Her brother was a member of the order and she married a former Jesuit. "Someone had bought his clothes for him. He didn't know how to open a can. He was cared for in Rome." Then there were the feminist signs of the times that the priests at the Center of Concern were being called on to recognize and adapt to. The collaborative style of the Center meant that Land had to get used to getting his draft papers back from Blewett, full of red marks indicating each time he had used *he, man* or *mankind*. Land would arrive at the office full of the joy of the morning and say "Good morning, girls!" and Eileen Olsen would say, half-jokingly, "We're not girls!"

Of the Center's staff of ten, six were women. Though the men all had formal religious affiliations and were called "staff associates," the women were "staff assistants" with the exception of Sister Elizabeth Carroll.[42] Still, as a Catholic organization, the place was moving to address issues of women in both the Church and society. While at the

Center, Betty Carroll worked on an issue of *Theological Studies* devoted to women in the Church that was later published in book form. Jane Blewett represented the Center at the UN's World Food Conference in Rome in late 1974 and Mary Burke was its delegate to the first World Conference for Women in Mexico City in 1975, sponsored by the United Nations to mark International Women's Year.

The feminist movement was having its impact on the international-development enterprise and the UN conference circuit that was a main focus of the Center of Concern. Danish economist Ester Boserup's pioneering 1970 book *Women's Role in Economic Development* had shaken up development agencies by pointing out that conventional growth-as-development was actually resulting in the deterioration of women's lives in the Third World. In the succeeding years, informal networks of feminist development workers, project managers, academics and activists emerged and the Center tapped into them, extending its critique of conventional development.

In the wake of the International Women's Year events the Center organized an interfaith gathering on the role of religion in what was coming to be called "women and development." Bringing together twenty-three Buddhist, Hindu, Jewish, Muslim and Christian women (including future United Church of Canada Moderator Lois Wilson) and men for three days outside Washington, the meeting was a departure for a group that usually stuck to participation in events organized by others. The Center published a summary report on the meeting. It concluded that, for the men who attended (including Bill Ryan), the discussions represented a new way of hearing the "universality of frustration" existing among women. "Human development" involved "mutuality" between the sexes and freeing the human spirit, and religion could do much to bring about this new stage of development. But for this to happen, "Religion itself must be purified of its corrupting and oppressive tendencies. Women must begin to define their own religious reality."[43]

Talk of ecclesiastical corruption and oppression was certainly not Ryan's style. Yet his willingness to put the Center's name on the report of the interfaith conference was an example of an emerging pattern with Ryan: his eagerness to use his position to provide space for those whose approach might be more confrontational, their views out of step with – or at least out in front of – conventional thinking.

Ryan's interfaith work would continue. Joe Gremillion, now back in the United States as a fellow at the University of Notre Dame, played a leading role in mounting a conference at Bellagio, Italy, in 1975 on the food-energy crisis and world faiths. Attended by Muslim, Jewish, Buddhist, Hindu and Christian leaders, the Bellagio conference led to a book, edited by Gremillion,[44] and to an organization called the Interreligious Peace Colloquium (IRPC). In 1976, at Gremillion's request, the Center of Concern agreed to house the IRPC's secretariat, with Ryan as executive secretary and Blewett as administrative assistant. In that capacity, they organized a second conference, on global economic and social issues, at a small hotel near Lisbon, Portugal, in 1977. Though billed as "a Muslim-Jewish-Christian search," the conference also included Buddhist participants and academics such as Richard Falk from Princeton and Robert Bellah from the University of California.[45] Ryan's work with the IRPC whetted his appetite for interfaith conversation on world issues, and bringing together a variety of religious voices to address those issues would be a major outlet for his considerable energy after he left his last institutional position in 1990.

———⇒»·0·«⇐———

By the mid-1970s, the Center of Concern had become a nationally and internationally known U.S. social justice organization. Despite Ryan's hopes for an international organization based in Washington, the staff was, except for the director, all American. They still did workshops and retreats, particularly with women religious whose orders also continued to give the Center additional gifts of cash. Commissioned writings by staff generated extra income. Although the Center did not yet have a full-time fundraiser, the three women who worked as support staff also handled tax-deductible contributions from individuals. The $140,000 budget for 1976 was augmented by the foundation grants that had become a staple, assisting the Center in its participation in international conferences.

Using its official status, the Center tried to influence the agenda and content of UN meetings, participating in the so-called "prep-coms," the preparatory commissions that do much to influence outcomes. In the seven months after the end of GC32, Mary Burke attended the UN World Conference for Women in Mexico City, Joe Holland joined the International Labour Organization for a World Employment Conference in Geneva, and Ryan accompanied Jane Blewett and Pete Henriot to a special session of the UN that adopted the Charter of Economic Rights. In following and trying to influence the UN schedule, Ryan's Center did acquire an international presence, part of the rapidly emerging world of non-governmental organizations (or NGOs) that were becoming an important part of the architecture of international relations. As the era of what would soon be called "globalization" dawned, the NGOs would assume greater prominence as something called "civil society."

In 1975–76 the Center of Concern played a role at three Church meetings in Detroit. Ten years on, Vatican II was still very much in the air, the generation of priests, nuns, bishops and lay people that had been galvanized by the Council having achieved more influential positions in the Church.

"Theology in the Americas" was the name given to a liberation theology gathering organized by an exiled Chilean priest named Sergio Torres working out of Maryknoll. Joe Holland, who had known Torres in Chile, co-ordinated the pre-conference research on behalf of the Center of Concern. The meeting itself was an ecumenical gathering that brought together some 200 theologians from all parts of the hemisphere, giving the Latin Americans generally associated with liberation theology a chance to meet and solidify networks with black, feminist and Native American thinkers.

Three months later, in November 1975, the first Women's Ordination Conference took place in Detroit, with the Center of Concern represented by Betty Carroll. The issue of equality was by this time bubbling over in Catholic circles and the Center, with its base among women religious and a staff that included Catholic feminists, was part of the ferment. Since women are fully gifted, human and graced, any structure that called that into doubt was unjust. Of course, the issue of ordaining women was a hot potato, and the Center's strategy would avoid confronting it directly. As Bill Callahan, who had by this time left the Center to start his own Quixote Center in Washington, put it, Ryan's Center tended to be "more scholarly, more politically savvy, taking a longer view of Jesuit-episcopal collaboration to move the social justice teaching of the Church from the textbooks into the consciousness of the Church leaders." Callahan's approach was more direct. He placed an article on the opposite editorial page of the New York *Times* apologizing on behalf of the Vatican for lack of action on women's ordination: "We apologized for the sexism of our church. You wouldn't do that at the Center of Concern."

Just before their 1976 seminar on women, religion and development, Jane Blewett, Betty Carroll, Phil Land and Bill Ryan went to the "Call to Action" meeting in Detroit. The Center of Concern saw the gathering as important: aside from the Bucharest population conference, it was the largest delegation that the Center had dispatched to a meeting. Blewett looked back on it as "a major achievement on the part of the national Church."

The Call to Action meeting was animated by what the lay Catholics, priests and nuns who attended saw as the spirit of Vatican II, a vision of a more collaborative Church in which lay people could be more involved in decision making. Their hopes had been further bolstered by *Octogesima Adveniens*, Pope Paul VI's 1971 "Call to Action" urging Christian communities "to analyze with objectivity the situation which is proper to their own country, to shed on it the light of the gospel's unalterable words and to draw principles of reflection, norms of judgement and directives for action from the social teaching of the Church."[46]

The direct call to local communities to shape their own culture and social order seemed a propitious sign of the times, coming as it did from the pope himself. What's more, the U.S. Call to Action initiative was backed by some extremely influential members of the hierarchy, including Cardinal John Dearden of Detroit, a former president of the U.S. bishops' conference. The atmosphere among the 1,400 people who gathered at Detroit's Cobo Hall was almost euphoric. Going in, those more experienced in the ways of the Church worried that the bishops would steamroll the conference and, in the words of the Center of Concern, "pack the assembly with the tried-and-true, conservatives [and] curialists."[47]

As it turned out, the conference was a definite high point for liberal-minded Catholics. For the Center of Concern, looking back in the immediate aftermath of the "Call to Action," it was a mini-Medellín that made Catholic history, in good measure because a meeting under the chairmanship of a cardinal had voted not only for an agenda of social action but for an agenda that also included "justice in the Church itself." The hierarchy had placed its trust in the people in the pews, and "in priest, sister and brother." The Center reported that the Detroit meeting understood that the Church was a loving, trusting community of believers, a "servant" church ministering to the needs of all but most particularly to the poor and the powerless. A majority voted for women's ordination and married clergy. According to the Center's analysis, these prickly issues were not matters of dogma, merely Church practice. As such they could be changed.[48]

Looking back from the vantage point of 1988, Ryan described the "historic" gathering as "a major Church-related experience in the Center's early history," presaging a new openness that would give rise to the massive consultation processes launched by the U.S. bishops as they prepared their left-leaning pastoral letters on peace and on the economy in the 1980s.[49] Twelve years later, Jane Blewett had a different assessment, describing a spirit that had "energized people to the core" as having been "squashed," in part by the U.S. bishops and in part by Rome. "The Vatican went on red alert," said Joe Holland. "Historically the Vatican accepted democracy for civil society only at the end of the [nineteenth] century and even then only reluctantly. It was terrified it would permeate the Catholic Church. It always felt that if there was a danger to democratizing the Catholic Church it would come through North America, particularly the U.S. They really had to keep that U.S. Church in line."

———◆———

By the time the Call to Action meeting had wrapped up, Bill Ryan had already been in touch with the Jesuit curia to explore the possibility of moving on. The response from Francisco Ivern, a close adviser to Pedro Arrupe, was cautious. He and Ryan had been discussing Ryan's departure for some months and although headquarters had been surprised by all that the Center of Concern had achieved and the prestige it had gained, Ivern felt that the apostolate was still in its initial stage and that Ryan's presence was "very much required." Apparently there was uncertainty with respect to support for the Center from some North American Jesuit provinces and the Jesuit curia was about to pressure them to change their tune.[50]

When Ryan was appointed provincial of Upper Canada in early 1978, the matter was still unresolved. "I see the Center as one of the most important social apostolates sponsored by the Society in North America, even though it is strictly not fully under Jesuit control," said Pedro Arrupe in a letter to Jim Connor, by then president of the U.S. Jesuit Conference. Arrupe asked the North American Jesuits for one or two well-qualified Jesuits to be assigned as full-time staffers at the Center.[51]

Evidently, Ryan had been correct in putting the Center on an independent footing. Two decades after his departure, it had doubled in staff size to twenty people, of whom only one was a Jesuit. And although three of its dozen board members were Jesuits, funding from the

Society was negligible, with only the Maryland province giving more than $5,000. The Chicago, Detroit and New Orleans provinces each gave between $1,000 and $5,000. This was out of a total budget of just over a million dollars.[52]

The people who worked at the Center of Concern in the 1970s describe a place that was convivial and co-operative, a place where they managed to accomplish important things. It was partly the right chemistry, partly the right times. For Ryan, the exhilaration of working with a team of "strong people" made his years at the Center – and especially the initial period when they had few resources and the future was cloudy – particularly invigorating.

Like Ryan, Jane Blewett feels that working at the Center was a high point for her – "one of the most graced times of my life." As for Pete Henriot, he finds that, after thirteen years in Africa, one of his principal tasks involves something he learned from Ryan: mentoring younger people in the work of justice and peace. "Bill taught me a lot, by explicit example and by hands-on lessons of reviewing drafts of my papers, encouraging me in public presentations," says Henriot. "I try to do that here, with both younger African Jesuits working on our team and the young lay women and men who work on the team."

Ryan realized that effective leadership combined an intimate knowledge of organizational (read, Church) structure; an aptitude for working with people, gauging their capabilities, pushing them on; a sense of going somewhere and a willingness to take calculated risks to get there; and the capacity to work hard at analyzing shifting political winds. He could do all of this. He could also, according to Pete Henriot, miss what others might be saying because he had his own agenda. Ryan was not always clear in explaining to others what that agenda was. Henriot, who worked with him for longer than anyone else, says that it was difficult to get Ryan to listen to someone else's point of view: "Sometimes I had to stop him in the middle of something he was excited about in order to tell him what I was excited about." Ryan talks a lot about himself – his own feelings, opinions and accomplishments. He is an interesting person who usually has something interesting to say, but his quick intelligence, his singlemindedness and his pride can interfere with an understanding of the agendas of friends or colleagues.

Joe Holland recalls Ryan's intuitive ability to read situations and people: "Bill was uncanny. He had a sixth sense of how to move when. Some leaders just have that gift. It's a spiritual gift almost like witchcraft that he was given, that he was born with – not necessarily Christian."

Such shrewdness had its downside, according to Holland: "I always felt he was very much alone, the poor guy. He always had everyone else figured out. He was always on the move. I think his life was kind of lonely in the way he had to work."

Bill Callahan, more comfortable with simply living his beliefs than with playing the institutional game, nevertheless respected Ryan's tactical mastery. "His approach is not to have a demonstration," says Callahan, "but to dig a hole in the barrier and come up the other side and see what he can find over there. 'I'll go talk to so-and-so who I know....'" Eileen Olsen agrees. Olsen, the first person hired by Ryan, left at the same time as her boss. Though she had been raised as a Catholic, she learned something new about the Church in her eight years with Ryan: "I *never* thought the Church was so political. I was still naive. The priest didn't get up in the pulpit on Sunday and say, 'By the way, I had the bishop approve this before I came up here.'"

Olsen was as savvy as the program staff who, she felt, knew how far they could go: "I don't think they were interested in tearing down the walls, just pushing them back." The institutional savvy that Ryan had honed in his years at the Center of Concern would serve him well in his next posting. Though the Upper Canada province of the Society of Jesus was not a place where he felt the need for tearing down walls, there were still possibilities for designing entire new structures. And Bill Ryan was always an enthusiastic architect.

---

[1]   George Bernard Cardinal Flahiff, "Christian Formation for Justice," presentation to the International Synod of Bishops, Rome, October 20, 1971, in Edward F. Sheridan SJ, ed., *Do Justice! The Social Teaching of the Canadian Catholic Bishops* (Sherbrooke, QC: Éditions Paulines, 1987), 218–19; Bishop Alexander Carter, "Super States and Multi-National Corporations in a Developing World Community," presentation to the International Synod of Bishops, Rome, October 20, 1971, in Sheridan, ed., *Do Justice!*, 223–24.

[2]   Alexander Carter, "Facing the Challenge of Injustice," *Compass*, summer 1987, 18.

[3]   Quoted in Edward F. Sheridan SJ, "Introduction," in Sheridan, ed., *Do Justice!* 28

[4]   *Oral History of Phil Land: Interviews Conducted, Transcribed and Edited by Judy Mladineo,* mimeo (Washington, DC, 1992), 40; see also Philip S. Land, *Catholic Social Teaching: As I Have Lived, Loathed and Loved It* (Chicago: Loyola University Press, 1994), 33.

[5]   Center of Concern, untitled document (Washington, D.C., 1971).

[6]   Center of Concern, "Social concern of U.S. Religions to take new step," press release, May 4, 1971.

[7] William F. Ryan SJ and Fr. Joseph Kononchak, "The Liberation of Men and Nations: The Role of the Church in the Americas," *Catholic Mind*, September 1971.

[8] Center of Concern, *The Quest for Justice: The First Year's Chronicle* (Washington, DC: Center of Concern, 1973), 1.

[9] Barbara Ward, *The Lopsided World* (New York: W.W. Norton, 1968), 87, 99.

[10] Letter from John Myers to Catherine Schaeffer, September 15, 1971, in University of Notre Dame Archives, CCOC, box 1, reading file September 1971.

[11] Gustavo Gutierrez, *A Theology of Liberation*, quoted in James Bacik, *Contemporary Theologians* (Chicago: Thomas More Press, 1989), 167.

[12] Center of Concern, *The Quest for Justice* (Washington, D.C.: Center of Concern, 1972).

[13] Center of Concern, "The Quest for Justice," 3–4

[14] Penny Lernoux, *Cry of the People: The Struggle for Human Rights in Latin America – The Catholic Church in Conflict with U.S. Policy* (New York: Penguin, 1991), 25–28, 305–9.

[15] Willian F. Ryan SJ and Peter Henriot, "Message from Bucharest for Washington and Rome," *America*, November 2, 1974.

[16] Ibid.

[17] Gail Stewart, *One Woman's Thoughts – Challenging Society's Assumptions* (Queen's University, May 31, 1973), 12–13, quoted in William F. Ryan SJ, "Mindsets and New Horizons for Discernment," in *Soundings: A Task Force on Social Consciousness and Ignatian Spirituality* (Washington, DC: Center of Concern, 1974), 5.

[18] Ryan, "Mindsets and New Horizons for Discernment," 5.

[19] Ibid., 6.

[20] Bernard J. Bush SJ, "The Eighteenth Annotation of the Spiritual Exercises of St. Ignatius and Social Sinfulness," in *Soundings*, 20–22; Dominic Maruca SJ, "The Graces of the Third and Fourth Weeks," in *Soundings*, 25–27; Daniel Lewis SJ, "Rules for Thinking with the Church: A Contemporary Approach," in *Soundings*, 31–32.

[21] John English SJ, "The Ignatian Method and Social Theology," in *Soundings*, 35–36.

[22] William F. Ryan SJ, "Our Mission Today: A Personal Experience of its Genesis in the 32nd General Congregation," Baltimore, June 15, 1980, 16–17, 26.

[23] Quoted in Jean Lacouture, *Jesuits: A Multibiography*, tr. J. Leggatt (Washington, DC: Counterpoint, 1995), 377.

[24] Ignacio Echániz SJ, *Passion and Glory: A Flesh-and-Blood History of the Society of Jesus*, vol. 4, *Second Spring: 1814–1965–1999* (Anand, Gujarat, India: Gujarat Sahitya Prakash, 2000), 338–39.

[25] Quoted in Lacouture, *Jesuits*, 463.

[26] Society of Jesus, 32nd General Congregation, Decree 4, "Our Mission Today: The Service of Faith and the Promotion of Justice," quoted in Jean-Yves Calvez, *Faith and Justice: The Social Dimension of Evangelization* (St. Louis, MO: Institute of Jesuit Sources, 1991), 174.

27   Quoted in Calvez, *Faith and Justice*, 41–42.

28   Ryan, "Our Mission Today," 7.

29   Calvez, *Faith and Justice*, 43.

30   Ryan, "Our Mission Today," 17–18.

31   Ibid., 12.

32   Quoted in George Bishop, *Pedro Arrupe SJ: Twenty-eighth General of the Society of Jesus* (Anand, Gujarat, India: Gujarat Sahitya Prakash, 2000), 259.

33   Quoted in Douglas Letson and Michael Higgins, *The Jesuit Mystique* (Toronto: Macmillan, 1995), 67.

34   Ibid., 67–68.

35   Ryan, "Our Mission Today," 22.

36   Society of Jesus, 32nd General Congregation, Decree 4, quoted in Ryan, "Our Mission Today," 20–21.

37   Ryan, "Our Mission Today," 20.

38   Calvez, *Faith and Justice*, 36.

39   Malachi Martin, *The Jesuits: The Society of Jesus and the Betrayal of the Roman Catholic Church* (New York: Touchstone Books, 1988), quoted in Letson and Higgins, *The Jesuit Mystique*, 131.

40   Joe Holland and Peter Henriot, *Social Analysis: Linking Faith and Justice*, 2nd ed., (Maryknoll, NY: Orbis Books, 1983), xiii–xv.

41   *Oral History of Phil Land*, 58–59.

42   Center of Concern, *Purpose, Progress, Plans: Five-Year Report of the Center of Concern* (Washington, DC: Center of Concern, 1976).

43   Center of Concern, *New Woman/New Family/New God: Report of a Consultation on the Impact of World Religions on Women and Development* (Washington: Center of Concern, 1976), 21–22.

44   Joseph Gremillion, ed., *Food/Energy and the Major Faiths* (Maryknoll, NY: Orbis Books, 1978).

45   Proceedings of the conference were published as Joseph Gremillion and William F. Ryan SJ, eds., *World Faiths and the New World Order* (Washington, DC: Interreligious Peace Colloquium, 1978).

46   Quoted in Land, *Catholic Social Teaching*, 50.

47   Center of Concern, "Detroit: Catholic Milestone," *Center Focus*, 18 (January 1977), 2.

48   Ibid., 1–3.

49   William F. Ryan SJ, "The Center of Concern: Past and Future Challenges" (mimeo, 1988). Ryan prepared this document as his contribution to a Festschrift for his long-time friend and colleague Peter Henriot.

50   Francis Ivern to William F. Ryan SJ, May 4, 1976, Ryan files.

51   Pedro Arrupe to James Connor, February 9, 1978, Ryan files.

52   Center of Concern, *Annual Report*, 1999–2000.

Chapter 5

His Way of Proceeding

Looking back over the last half dozen or so provincials of the Upper Canada province of the Society of Jesus, one Jesuit divides them into "innovators" and "sustainers." Another Jesuit has a different classification system: "low-key" and "fireworks." But whatever the terminology, Bill Ryan is universally regarded as an activist provincial, and his term of office – 1978 to 1984 – as a time of significant change for the province. "It was an exciting time to be a young Jesuit," remembers Doug McCarthy, who was in his thirties at the time.

In many ways, Ryan was not an obvious choice to take over the leadership of the Upper Canada province in 1978. Most provincials come to the job with some experience of leadership in the province's own institutions – the parishes, colleges and high schools. Ryan had virtually no such experience. Except for his year teaching high school in Winnipeg while in formation and another year at Loyola College in the early 1960s, all his work and study had been outside the context of the province since his departure for St. Louis in 1951.

And yet the idea of recommending Ryan as his successor was germinating in the mind of Terry Walsh, who had become provincial in 1972 when Ed Sheridan was called to Rome to be an adviser to Father Arrupe. Having been a delegate to GC32, Walsh was sensitive to the need for a stronger social justice thrust in the Upper Canada province. A new generation of Jesuits were completing their formation – strong social justice advocates who were products of the Arrupe era and were fired by GC32's vision. One of these, Jim Webb, was living and working with poor people in the inner-city Toronto neighbourhood of south Riverdale. The next provincial would need to direct this new energy and mediate between it and the more traditional concerns of the province. From that point of view, Bill Ryan's credentials – his doctorate in economics, his leadership of the Center of Concern, his prominence at GC32 – looked pretty good.

The initial reaction to the idea was not one of unbridled enthusiasm. When Walsh mentioned it to Arrupe, the general first expressed surprise, then skepticism. Was not Ryan too outspoken for a job in which *cura personalis* – the Jesuit term for the care and management of individuals – played a large role? Ryan, after all, had been one of the most forthright critics of the antiquated organization of the general congregation. Walsh consulted some Canadian Jesuits who knew Ryan well, and they expressed similar reservations. One cited a "weakness in sympathetic appreciation for the perspective of others"; another suggested that he "is not temperamentally sympathetic to weakness." His "feel for power" was cited as both an asset and a liability; his tendency to be "personal-success-oriented" was something else he would have to watch. How Ryan would fare, one Jesuit said, "depends on the kind of provincial needed. If the need is for strong challenging leadership rather than *cura personalis*, for vision under driving leadership, for a high image of the provincial in the life of the Church, then Bill Ryan would be a fine provincial."

Arrupe came to see things that way too, and agreed to Ryan's appointment early in 1978. In April, Ryan went to Rome and had a long rambling conversation with the general, in which the subject of Ryan's new job came up only at the very end. "You'll have lots of problems," Arrupe said. "When you have a problem you can't solve, get on a plane and come over here, and we'll solve it in ten minutes."

The problems of running the Upper Canada province would be exacerbated by new winds that were beginning to blow through the Church in 1978. Although the effects of the climatic changes would not be visible for some years, developments in 1978 provided the first warnings of the storms to come. On August 6, less than a week after Ryan formally took office as provincial, Pope Paul VI died, and when his successor, John Paul I, died a month after taking office, the cardinals elevated Karol Wojtyla, a strong-minded Polish archbishop with a reputation as an intellectual. Ryan heard about Wojtyla's election when he was about to get on a plane to India, and the name meant little to him. But the new Pope John Paul II would have very firm ideas about papal authority, and by the end of Ryan's term as provincial the Jesuits would feel the full force of those ideas.

Also in 1978, a new archbishop was appointed to the see of Toronto, which would be Ryan's home as provincial. Ryan was well-acquainted with Emmett Carter. He had worked with him at the Canadian Catholic Conference in the 1960s and had appreciated his support at the Center of Concern. With his own skill at manoeuvring within the institutional Church, Ryan respected the same quality in Carter. He also understood that the newly appointed archbishop, who was quickly made a cardinal by the new pope, was far from being an ideological conservative. At the same time, however, Carter was deeply concerned with resolutely upholding the authority of the Church hierarchy, and had little tolerance for dissent.[1] While he would have had some sympathy for the goals of the Center of Concern, the freewheeling atmosphere that prevailed there would not have been to his taste. Furthermore, Carter cultivated people in power. Again, this trait was similar to Ryan's own inclinations, but while Ryan's Top People were likely to be United Nations officials or World Bank economists, Carter numbered business tycoons, prime ministers and premiers among his friends. Implementing Pedro Arrupe's vision in Pope John Paul II's Church, in Emmett Carter's Toronto – this would be Ryan's challenge over the next six years.

Neither Arrupe nor Walsh ever told Ryan that his mission would be to put GC32's Decree 4 on social justice into practice in English-speaking Canada; it was simply understood. But this mission was far from representing the full extent of his job. The Upper Canada province was not the Center of Concern, where management by improvisation was both his privilege and a necessity. Ryan was inheriting the weight of a half-century of institutional history and responsibility for more than 300 Jesuits, every one of whom he was required to visit in each year of his term. In theory, a provincial is a near-absolute ruler; like a bishop in his diocese, he is the superior to a group of people bound to him by an oath of holy obedience. However, unlike a bishop, who generally serves until retirement age, a provincial holds office for a fixed term, and will himself be in holy obedience to a new provincial in a few years. In practice, a good provincial operates less as an absolute ruler than as a consensus manager.

In addition to the institutional traditions of the province, Ryan also inherited Terry Walsh's socius, Bill Addley, whose finely tuned people skills would prove invaluable in ensuring that the changes Ryan would introduce did not come at the expense of the *cura personalis* side of the provincial's job. Feeling that it was important to bring a member of the younger generation of Jesuits into the province curia, Walsh had named Addley socius in 1975, when he was only thirty-one. Addley served as socius throughout Ryan's term, frequently travelling with Ryan on his visits to Jesuits throughout Canada, and eventually succeeded Ryan as provincial in 1984. Two Jesuits in their early forties were also key members of Ryan's team: J.P. Horrigan, the province treasurer, a genial presence presiding over a period of expansion and financial good times for the Canadian Jesuits, and Brother Art White, executive secretary and unfailing source of insight and advice. Ryan also came to depend on the advice and support of Jean-Marc Laporte, an expert in systematic theology with a practical bent not always typical of theologians, and John English, who by now had an international reputation for his work on the Spiritual Exercises and would be the guardian of the spiritual element in the changes Ryan would introduce.

Some changes had already taken place. In the early 1960s, not long before Arrupe became general, the province had bought a lavish house on Hawthorn Gardens in Toronto's exclusive Rosedale neighbourhood, where Jesuits attached to the province curia both lived and worked. The quiet of the tree-lined street was occasionally broken when tour buses pulled up in front of the home of Lord Thomson, two doors from the Jesuit house. Arrupe first saw the house during a visit to Toronto in the early 1970s, when he was scheduled to meet Archbishop Pocock there. Approaching the house, Arrupe assumed that it must be the archbishop's palace, and was astonished when Terry Walsh took out his keys and opened the door. It quickly became clear that a mansion in Rosedale was not quite a suitable place to locate the headquarters of an order that was supposed to be in solidarity with the poor. A few years later, Walsh moved the province curia from the mansion to new and less ostentatious quarters in the High Park area of west-end Toronto. Another significant move took place around the same time. Regis College, which in the early 1960s had left the old building by the railway tracks where Bill Ryan had studied philosophy in favour of a self-contained campus in suburban Willowdale, moved back downtown to a location on the edge of the University of Toronto campus. Developing this new location became the responsibility of Ryan as provincial and Jean-Marc Laporte as college president. Regis, one of the province's central institutions, became much more integrated into the life of the city, as groups of Jesuits took up residence in co-op-style houses in the downtown area. The college also became less exclusively focused on training Jesuits and began serving a wider range of students, not all of them Catholic.

In his effort to focus and direct the new reform spirit that had already begun to animate the province, Ryan undertook preparations for what he called a "retreat/insitute" at Ignatius College in Guelph in June 1979. The idea was to bring together the leadership cadre of the province: the community superiors and directors of apostolates (as the Jesuits call their programs and projects). They would use methods of Ignatian discernment to help set priorities for the province, and yet it would be like no Ignatian retreat any of the invited Jesuits had ever experienced. The ten-day duration planned for the event was itself unusual: retreats were generally eight days long, or thirty in the case of the full Spiritual Exercises.

Early on, Ryan called in the expert in Ignatian spirituality, John English, and asked him what the best way would be to teach discernment. English said that if it was to be a true exercise in discernment, there had to be money attached – a concrete outcome that would give some reality to the decision-making process. Ryan agreed to allocate $100,000 to whatever project the Jesuits assembled in Guelph decided was the "priority apostolate" for the province in line with the goals of GC32. Jesuits involved in various apostolates would make presentations indicating what they would do with the money, and then the group would determine which was the most deserving.

Assisted by former provincial Gordon George, English played a major role at the retreat/institute, leading the Jesuits in reviewing and praying over the "blessed history" and "sin history" of the province. This process, based on the conviction that our personal and collective stories reflect God's presence, would help them better understand the province's situation and reach the state of consolation that Ignatian spirituality prescribes for making major decisions.[2] Another resource person was Jim Connor, Ryan's friend and former housemate from Washington and the president of the U.S. Jesuit conference. Connor, Ryan and Pat Malone, all of whom had been at GC32, answered questions about the implications of the congregation's decree on social justice. The next day, Ryan addressed the Jesuits, noting that his reading of the signs of the times had left him apprehensive: "It looked as though we were losing any possibility of shaping our own history, that circumstances more and more were making decisions for us." This was why it was important to set priorities, he said, as he announced the $100,000 prize.

There were a number of strong contenders. Education of youth, carried out through the Upper Canada province's four high schools, struck a deep chord among Jesuits. Social communications had a contemporary feel and had been identified as a priority by Father Arrupe; it was also an area where the province was strong, with several Jesuits teaching communications at Concordia University in Montreal, which incorporated the old Loyola College. The social apostolate, dear to Bill Ryan's heart and newly invigorated by the work being done in the east end of Toronto, clearly had an important claim on the province's resources. But in the end, it was a presentation on behalf of the Native apostolate in northern Ontario by Father Mike Murray, a soft-spoken but persuasive Jesuit in his early forties, that carried the day.

On one level, no apostolate had deeper roots among Canadian Jesuits than missionary work among Native people. It was, of course, what brought the Jesuits to this part of the world in the first place, in the seventeenth century, and a large part of what brought them back when the restored order returned to Canada in the 1840s. At the time, they established a mission on Manitoulin Island, where Indians from various parts of northern Ontario were being settled at the government's direction, and where the Jesuits retain a strong presence today. Like other missionaries, the Jesuits saw their task not only as bringing Christianity to the people but also as erasing the Natives' own spiritual and cultural traditions.[3]

By the 1970s, while the missions remained, the conception underlying them was changing, and Mike Murray was on the cusp of this change. At West Bay Indian Reserve on Manitoulin Island, where Murray was pastor in the early 1970s, the church was destroyed by an explosion and fire. The new church, built under Murray's guidance, opened in 1972: its round shape evokes a Native tepee, and from the totems of the Anishinabe people on the inside of the front doors to the Thunderbird over the altar, the work of Native artists working in their traditional idiom sets the tone. The Stations of the Cross, by local Native artist Leland Bell, use Native imagery to depict Jesus' final journey.[4]

New ideas about the relationship between Christianity and culture were beginning to emerge all over the world, and Jesuits working in the Native apostolate in Canada were hearing about what was going on in Latin America, Africa and the Philippines. The development of a Native church became their goal. The celibacy requirement was a serious obstacle to the ordination of Native priests, but the training of Native deacons seemed a realistic objective, and the Church was in fact doing this in Alaska and South Dakota. Murray and his colleagues wanted to train Native deacons in northern Ontario, and their proposal to the Jesuits assembled at Guelph was the establishment of a spiritual centre where the main focus would be a diaconate program. Their enthusiasm was infectious, the concrete nature of their proposal was appealing, the long Jesuit association with Native people created a deep sense of obligation, and all of a sudden Murray and his colleagues had access to $100,000 to carry their plan forward.

A few months before the Guelph retreat/institute, Pedro Arrupe gave a talk on the subject of "Our Way of Proceeding" at the Centrum Ignatianum Spiritualitatis in Rome.[5] The title evokes a phrase that appears frequently in the writings of St. Ignatius, who used it to refer to "all those specific and differentiating qualities in the Society that distinguish it from other religious Orders."[6] The Society's way of proceeding relates to its essence, and yet it evolves over time: "I am not judging the past but looking for the perennial – and today's – version of the Jesuit way of proceeding, as our Founder would do if he were alive, so that, while preserving the permanent elements that transcend any given era, I can find the image best suited to this post-conciliar world of ours. In other words, I would like to contemplate Christ again in terms of the modern world, as Ignatius himself would do."[7] In the rapid change of this "post-conciliar world," Arrupe identified some, from the "full-time protester" through the "irresponsible Jesuit" to the "fanatically traditionalist type of Jesuit," who had lost a true sense of the Society's way of proceeding.[8] But he embraced change as necessary for the Society: "The Society, like the Church, has to live in terms of today. And this is not always easy: sometimes the changes have to be made amid shifting points of reference and competing values that must all be respected. In our search for new forms, we can commit errors. But sometimes it is worse not to try to change."[9]

Reading the text of Arrupe's talk in Toronto, Bill Ryan saw it as a potential framework for his project of setting new priorities for the Upper Canada province, a project that would ultimately lead to a document entitled *Our Way of Proceeding in the '80s*. His friend Julien Harvey, the French-Canadian provincial, had already drawn up a similar document for his province, but Ryan felt that it was less effective than it should be because it reflected Harvey's priorities rather than those of the province as a whole. Ryan used the Guelph retreat/institute as the launching pad for a two-year exercise in consultation, which – economist that he is – he later estimated involved "almost 12,000 man-hours of prayer and reflection."[10] He left much of the routine administration of the province to Bill Addley as he threw himself into the exercise, working through a "Committee of 15" that brought together the directors of major apostolates and the province consultors. The committee organized one-day regional meetings and meetings on the various apostolates. Mike Murray remembers that, while the Native apostolate had previously "had its little life," through the Committee of 15 it began to see itself as part of the work of the province as a whole.

But even for a provincial as committed to collaborative work as Bill Ryan, consultation only goes so far. When it came time, in the spring of 1981, to distil the masses of material into a workable document, Ryan went off by himself to the village of Belfountain northwest of Toronto where he had recently arranged the purchase of a house for the provincial (or other Jesuits) to use as a getaway cabin. After five days in these quiet surroundings, he had produced a draft to present to the Committee of 15. The committee recommended only minor adjustments, and Ryan sent the document to Rome where it received Arrupe's stamp of approval: "I must leave execution to you and your successor, but I wish it known in the Province that 'our Way of Proceeding in the '80's' is the Province orientation and direction, and not to be changed in any notable respect, without serious consultation and my own or my successor's full approval."[11]

Not surprisingly for a Bill Ryan document, *Our Way of Proceeding in the '80s* began with a detailed reading of the signs of the times – in the world, the Church, Canada, the Jesuit order and the Upper Canada province. These signs of the times included declining church attendance, materialism, alienation and shrinking numbers in religious orders, including the Jesuits:

> The most immediate and troubling yet instructive sign of the times for us Canadian Jesuits is the fact that we no longer have the manpower to carry on all our apostolates in their present forms.... Right now we are so short of experienced and skilled middle-age Jesuits (age 38–56) that it is extremely difficult to find a sufficient number of superiors and directors of apostolates. Moreover, many if not most of those who now carry these responsibilities are so overworked and overburdened that they often risk harming their personal health and spiritual well-

being, and have little opportunity to grow as contemplatives in action.[12]

When Ryan updated *Our Way of Proceeding* a couple of years later, he buttressed this warning with some stark figures. In comparison with 1943, just before Ryan had entered the Society, the Upper Canada province was a smaller and older community. Numbers were down from 327 to 307. More dramatically, whereas 60 per cent of the 1943 Jesuits were under thirty-five, now only 19 per cent were in that younger cohort. By contrast, 34 per cent of English-Canadian Jesuits were now over sixty-five, as compared with only 9 per cent in 1943.[13] When a journalist asked him about the fact that there were only seven novices in the Upper Canada province, Ryan said that the number was "about as low as we get." Still, he remained optimistic. "We're not afraid to see people leave," he told the curious writer. One of Ryan's colleagues employed a typical Jesuit device with the journalist: "Why do you ask why people leave? Why don't you ask what makes them stay?"[14] The question of numbers, which would grow only more acute as time went on, underlay many of the specific changes that Ryan recommended in the 1981 document. Some Jesuit commitments were to be scaled down or phased out: St. Paul's College in Winnipeg, Brebeuf High School in Toronto, parishes in Montreal and Vancouver.

Nevertheless, with his inveterate optimism, Ryan insisted that the manpower shortage should be seen not as "a source of discouragement" but rather as "a special grace, a sign of the times that requires careful and prayerful discernment."[15] And so other Jesuit programs were to be expanded, revitalized or redirected. For the Native apostolate, "our goal here is a Native Church." Regis College "will be given the highest priority to become not only a centre of excellent formation for our Jesuits but also a truly national Catholic intellectual centre at the service of the Canadian Church and society…. It will be expected to be ecumenical in the widest sense." The Jesuit Centre for Social Faith and Justice, founded "on a priority basis" to work in the social field, "should strive for intellectual excellence and ecumenical outreach in its attempts to develop integrated social, spiritual, and theological approaches to the urgent problems and needs of the day." The Farm Community in Guelph, also initiated "on a priority basis to attempt to bear witness to our preferential option for the poor and marginalized people," was to "pioneer a model to be imitated elsewhere in Canada." The Guelph Centre of Spirituality "should become a training centre for Jesuits in spiritual and communal discernment." In the area of communications, "the feasibility of launching a popular publication, perhaps called 'The Canadian Jesuit,' should be explored," as should "the feasibility of establishing a small pastoral communications centre in association with [Concordia University's] Communications Department."[16]

So it went, apostolate by apostolate, city by city. And along with the specific recommendations came some general guidelines: Jesuits should embrace GC32's call for a preferential option for the poor in the service of faith and the promotion of justice; they should learn to collaborate with non-Jesuits in all their apostolates; they should be critically aware of communications and learn to use the mass media; they should grow in Jesuit community and identity and foster creative cooperation among apostolates; and they should take opportunities to pray, reflect, study, renew themselves and update their skills.

—————⟫•0•⟪—————

The story goes that when Pedro Arrupe received Ryan's *Our Way of Proceeding* document, he gestured towards his office furniture and said, "We have filing cabinets full of great plans" – most of which, of course, had come to nothing. But Bill Ryan's time as provincial produced not only plans but also a remarkable constellation of new apostolates that, taken together, redefined the Jesuit presence in English Canada. The Jesuit Centre for Social Faith and Justice became an important actor on issues relating to Central America, refugees, public health and social justice in general. The Farm Community deeply affected the lives of many people who lived there over the years. In 1980, the Jesuits purchased property on Anderson Lake near Espanola, Ontario, where they built the Anishinabe Spiritual Centre and began training Native deacons. The Jesuit magazine, *Compass*, reached several thousand readers. The Jesuit Communication Project (established in Toronto instead of in conjunction with Concordia University in Montreal as originally envisioned) and a volunteer program for youth called the Jesuit Companions were also products of initiatives taken in Bill Ryan's time.

Several factors were favourable to the development of new Jesuit initiatives in the late 1970s and early 1980s: the presence of eager young Jesuits in their twenties and thirties (perhaps the last such generation in the Upper Canada province), the momentum created by GC32, relative prosperity resulting from good real estate deals and lucrative investments, and the presence of a provincial whose attitude was that if the province had money, the right thing to do was to spend it on new initiatives, especially ones related to social justice. While before Ryan's time there had been no institutionalized financing of apostolates by the province – each apostolate was expected to be financially self-supporting – Ryan established an apostolic fund that provided a steady flow of province money to the Jesuits' various projects. These grants were supposed to be temporary, designed to allow the apostolates to become self-sufficient. At least that was the theory.

A decade later, when the province had aged further, investments had turned sour, a sexual abuse case had drained province funds, and Jesuits compared the reality of the apostolates unfavourably with their initial promise, this theory would get the province into financial trouble. But through the 1980s, for the most part, the apostolates flourished. None had a higher profile, or proved to be more expensive, than the Jesuit Centre for Social Faith and Justice.

Building on the work that Jim Webb was already doing in south Riverdale, the Jesuit Centre opened its offices in the gritty working-class neighbourhood in 1979, the year the Sandinista revolutionaries toppled the Somoza dictatorship in Nicaragua and a year before Archbishop Oscar Romero was assassinated in neighbouring El Salvador. The Centre was located in a Presbyterian church not far from a Canada Metals plant, the focus of a bitter lead-pollution dispute that pitted the company against a community worried about its health. But local struggles never became its main area of interest. Rather, it concentrated on the wars in Central America (particularly Canadian foreign and refugee policies) as well as health care and a growing number of Canadian social justice issues. The Centre was very successful, supporting interchurch coalitions and human-rights advocacy work and reaching out to as many different communities as it could.

In the beginning, the Centre was staffed by several up-and-coming Jesuits in their thirties, notably Webb and Michael Czerny, who had joined the Society after graduating from Loyola High School in Montreal and now had a Ph.D. in social philosophy from the University of Chicago. In addition, Gordon George and Ed Sheridan, two Jesuits older than Bill Ryan who had played important roles in bringing social justice and the spirit of Vatican II into the order, were given office space at the Centre. But as the Centre grew, it was increasingly staffed by non-Jesuits. Dr. Rosalie Bertell, Grey Nun and public health activist, was brought in from the United States in 1980 to be the Centre's public health specialist. Another early recruit was Central America specialist Tim Draimin, a Jew who developed a fruitful collaboration with the Jesuits. Draimin

and Czerny formed a powerful team, an important part of Canada's growing Central America solidarity movement.

Another early Jesuit Centre project was a book on "social analysis." The Center of Concern had published Joe Holland and Peter
Henriot's very successful book on the subject in 1980, so it seemed natural
that the Canadian Jesuits would also aim a volume at a Church-based
social justice constituency. The Toronto Centre hired Jamie Swift (co-
author of the present volume) to work with Czerny and, in collaboration with a broader team, they produced *Getting Started on Social Analysis
in Canada*, published in 1984. The Canadian book was different from the
American volume in that its principal text was a secular analysis rather
than an analysis explicitly informed by a spiritual tradition. The Christian element of *Getting Started* consisted of quotations from the social
teachings of the Canadian churches in sidebars sprinkled throughout
the text. But although the Jesuit Centre's social analysis differed from
that of the Center of Concern, it was no less successful, going through
three editions and selling some 45,000 copies in fifteen years. Its main
market turned out to be university and college instructors who found it
a useful teaching tool.

At the beginning, Bill Ryan's relationship to the Jesuit Centre
was the source of some apprehension. People working at the Centre
feared that he would try to dominate it and turn it into a Canadian
version of the Center of Concern; others less sympathetic to social justice issues feared that he would use it as a base to turn the whole province into a Center of Concern writ large. Neither happened. One person who worked at the Jesuit Centre during that period describes him as
"remarkably hands-off." It was certainly important to Ryan that the Centre
existed and did its work, but he had no need to run it. He also continued
to emphasize the connection between social justice and the Spiritual
Exercises, encouraging Czerny and John English to direct retreats together focusing on justice. They conducted the retreat three times with
different groups of Canadian Jesuits.

While the Center of Concern had based its early expansion on
money from private foundations, the Jesuit Centre soon began getting
public funds from the Canadian International Development Agency. It
also started to raise money from individual donors, quickly moving from
an informal network of personal contacts to a sophisticated direct-mail
operation run by professional fundraisers. The province was committed
to matching the money raised from direct-mail appeals, a flow that grew
to flood proportions in the wake of the publicity surrounding the mur-

der of six Jesuits, their housekeeper and her daughter in El Salvador in 1989. The staff complement expanded in lockstep with the income, so that by the early 1990s some fifteen activists were working out of an office that threatened to overflow a space where the Presbyterian ladies' auxiliary had once hosted afternoon teas and bake sales.

While the Jesuit Centre dealt with national and international issues, the Ignatius Farm Community tried to create justice and love within one small group of people. Like the Jesuit Centre, it built on work that had been started before Bill Ryan became provincial. In 1976 Doug McCarthy SJ and some lay associates set up a haven for people who had been in prison or psychiatric hospital. It was located in a tumbledown red house across the road from Ignatius College on the outskirts of Guelph. Their initiative was part of a strain in the Christian tradition that responds to Jesus' call to live among the poor and not to turn anyone away, and was strongly influenced by the L'Arche communities for mentally handicapped people founded by Jean Vanier in 1964. McCarthy had had a life-changing experience when he spent four months in a L'Arche community during his theology studies. However, the Red House, as it was known, differed from L'Arche in its target population and also in its more radical breaking down of barriers – L'Arche still maintained clear distinctions between "residents" and "assistants."

The people who came to live in the Red House were supposed to get jobs in local industries, but this turned out to be more difficult than originally anticipated, and McCarthy had to struggle to find a new economic basis for the community. In 1979 he approached Bill Ryan with a proposal: the Red House would take over the farm that surrounded Ignatius College (where Ryan had "kept sane" by shovelling manure as a novice thirty-five years earlier), and the farm would provide work for the people in the community. Ryan accepted the proposal; the Jesuits purchased an adjoining property; a second house, the Farm House, was opened; and the Ignatius Farm Community was born. Two more Jesuits, Dan Phelan and Bill Clarke, joined the community, which became a chaotic but vibrant mix of Jesuits, volunteers (most of them young), and the troubled, disturbed and rejected. Speaking about the project in its early years, McCarthy observed, "The community that lives with marginal people, people who have seen kind of the rough side of life, people who have suffered rejection, is always going to be a very fragile community, and because of its fragility, you are forced to live almost constantly on a kind of a knife edge and it's there where you experience healing and growth."[17]

When McCarthy was appointed master of novices at Ignatius College in 1983, he pleaded with Ryan to be allowed to stay at the Farm Community. Jesuits were not supposed to become too attached to any one apostolate, but McCarthy regarded the Farm Community as his life's work. Ryan agreed to let him stay, and McCarthy remained with the community for another ten years, although in 1986 he turned the directorship over to Clarke, whose life had also been marked by a L'Arche experience. Except for a two-year period when a layperson named Don Gingerich served as director, Clarke remained as director of the community until it closed in 2001. The Farm Community was an apostolate that had to be experienced to be appreciated, and one of the disappointments expressed by its pioneers is that it never caught the imagination of the province as a whole. "From the outside it seems stupid and a waste of time," Clarke acknowledged, and yet many of the people who lived there continued to feel a deep attachment to this radical experiment in Gospel values long after they left.

McCarthy and Clarke, along with Ryan and Michael Czerny, were also involved in the creation of another new program, the Jesuit Companions, which began in 1981. Several American provinces had Jesuit Volunteer programs, where lay people helped in Jesuit works; the Jesuit Companions program was to be similar but less hierarchical. The Jesuits would not only teach and direct the young people who would join the program but learn from them as well – especially about how to live in community. Bill Clarke became the first director of the program, and the Farm Community became the training ground and most consistent placement for Jesuit Companions.

Meanwhile, using his influence with northern Ontario bishops, especially Alex Carter of Sault Sainte-Marie, Ryan leveraged the province's $100,000 commitment to the new Native retreat centre into broader Church support. In October 1982 the Anishinabe Spiritual Centre on the shores of Anderson Lake, just north of Manitoulin Island where Jesuit priests serve a number of Native parishes, was inaugurated in a ceremony in which Bishop Carter gave it his blessing. As with the church at West Bay, the log construction of the centre and its round chapel reflect an effort to incorporate Native idioms. The diaconate program got off the ground and Regis College faculty members who had experience working with Native people, notably an American Jesuit named Carl Starkloff, came to Anderson Lake to teach classes. Several Native deacons graduated from the program and began assisting with services in the Jesuit parishes on Manitoulin Island and in surrounding

Early Years (Ottawa Valley)

Joe, Jim (later Father Jim) and Frank (later Father Frank/Father Bill SJ) at Masham, Quebec, summer 1930. Their father's year-round work in the logging industry meant that the nine Ryan children saw much of him only in the summer.

Bill, Jim and Joe Ryan, altar boys at St. Francis Xavier in Renfrew, ca. 1939. The Ryan children trooped off to mass before school every morning and two of the four Ryan boys became priests, with Jim joining the Oblates.

As a member of the Renfrew Collegiate cadet corps, 1942. The young Bill Ryan considered an Air Force career, but as the Allies were gaining a foothold in Normandy he received a mysterious inner call to join the Jesuits: "I've never had that happen before or since."

Bill Ryan spent teenage summers working with his father, a lumber camp foreman. The heavy work was often hazardous, but it appealed to a serious lad who worked hard while developing a love for the outdoors.

With his parents after taking first vows as a Jesuit,
Guelph, 1946. Ryan "stayed sane" through his
studies by working on the farm on which the
novitiate was located.

Renfrew, 1959. According to Helen, the youngest of the Ryan clan, "My mum really
wanted perfection. It was no good to come second." Back: "Frank," Bill Sr., Lena, Jim.
Middle: Bernie, Helen, Kay, Eileen. Front: Bob, Theresa, Joe.

Early Training

The novitiate in Guelph, Ontario, where Ryan entered the Jesuit order in 1944. The novitiate closed in the early 1990s, and the last Jesuits in the building moved out in 2001. The handful of Canadians now entering the novitiate are trained in Wisconsin.

Phil Land SJ taught Ryan at Saint Louis University in the 1950s before going on to the Gregorian University in Rome. Adviser to the Pontifical Commission for Justice and Peace, the impish American liked to insert the word "liberation" into Vatican pronounce-ments. In 1975 Ryan brought Land to the Center of Concern, where he kept arguing that the Church had to get its own house in order if it wanted to have credibility when it proclaimed the need for equality elsewhere.

At Louvain, Belgium, 1956. The atmosphere at the Catholic university took Ryan outside the rigid certainties of the standard Jesuit formation of the time. Ideas that would blossom in the next decade with Vatican II and the emergence of liberation theology circulated relatively freely at Louvain despite Vatican disapproval.

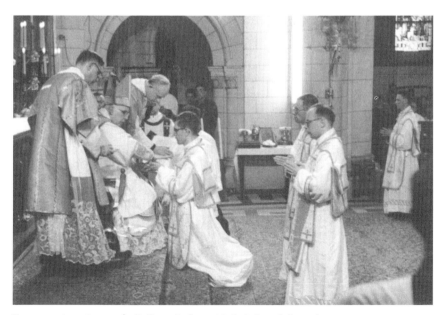

Ryan is ordained a priest, Collège de Saint-Michel chapel, Brussels, 1957. Ordination was the occasion for a rare visit from three of his sisters.

Center of Concern

The opening of the Center of Concern was formally announced at the United Nations on May 4, 1971, although secure financial arrangements were not yet in place. From left to right: Father Tipton; Father Tucci; Center of Concern intern Father John Myers; Msgr. Marvin Bordelon, international affairs staffer at the U.S. Catholic Conference; Father Francisco Ivern, social justice adviser to Jesuit general Pedro Arrupe; Father Arrupe; UN Secretary General U Thant; U.S. Catholic Conference general secretary Father Joseph Bernardin; Ryan; Father Small; Father Mitchell; Father John O'Connor, head of the U.S. Jesuits' Conference of Major Superiors; Father Jim Connor, Maryland Jesuit provincial; Father Guindon.

During the heady days of the early seventies, the Center of Concern struggled to address issues of women in Church and society. According to Bill Callahan, one of the Center's first staffers, "The women religious were the backbone of the early days of the Center of Concern. The backbone of the funding, the backbone of the commitment to the ideas of social justice that we were proclaiming." Left to right: Joe Holland, Mary Burke, Jane Blewett, Peter Henriot, Bill Ryan and Betty Carroll stand outside the northeast Washington house that served as the Center's office, 1976.

Bridging the Solitudes

Mgr Bernard Hubert, bishop of Saint-Jean–Longueuil and Ryan's "soul buddy" during his stint as general secretary of the Canadian Conference of Catholic Bishops in the 1980s.

Julien Harvey SJ, a close friend of Ryan's from the 1960s on and French Canadian provincial during Ryan's term as provincial in Upper Canada. The two appeared together at a "freewheeling" press conference in Montreal in 1981 where they expressed their incomprehension at the pope's decision to appoint his own delegate to run the Jesuit order.

When in Rome...

Lower right, the back of the Jesuit Curia in Rome. The Jesuit headquarters is close to the Vatican, but over the years relations with the Holy See have often been strained. In 1773 the Vatican had abolished "for all eternity" – but not extinguished – the Society of Jesus.

Some of the 236 Jesuits who assembled in the *aula* at their Curia for their 32nd General Congregation in 1974. Bill Ryan is seated in the back row, third from the right. Ryan, who liked efficiency and smooth-running meetings, found GC32's procedures so unclear that he felt some delegates were never sure what was going on.

Delegates to the 32nd General Congregation (including Ryan's friend Julien Harvey of the French Canadian province, centre front) head back to the Jesuit Curia after an audience with Pope Paul VI. A proposal to extend the special Fourth Vow of obedience to the pope to Jesuit brothers led to tension between the Jesuits and the Vatican throughout GC32.

Pope John Paul II's appointment of his own delegate to head the Jesuit order in 1981 caused a crisis in the order and put Ryan and the other provincials in a difficult position. In February 1982 the provincials gathered at Cavalletti outside Rome and reaffirmed their commitment to the pursuit of social justice. At the conclusion of their gathering they met in Rome with the pope, who told them that their concern for justice had to be exercised in conformity with their vocation as priests.

With Pope John Paul II at the 1987 Synod on the Laity. Ryan had by this time become an old hand at international gatherings, some of them momentous. But this meeting, like the 1985 extraordinary synod to celebrate Vatican II, achieved no breakthroughs. Phil Land felt that the Synod on the Laity "failed miserably."

World Traveller

Visiting the Jesuit school at Kathmandu, Nepal, as Upper Canadian provincial, 1978 (the other people in the picture are identified as Brother Quinn, L, and Ludwig St. Iler, R). Canadian Jesuits have long maintained a presence in Nepal.

With Sri Lankan Buddhist scholar Lankaputra Hewage and Center of Concern staff member Jane Blewett at an interfaith conference on world issues near Lisbon, 1977. Ryan was executive secretary of the Interreligious Peace Colloquium, which organized the conference, and became increasingly involved in interfaith work over the years.

Addressing a meeting in preparation for the 1974 United Nations population conference. Ryan's Center of Concern did a delicate balancing act between Vatican opposition to contraception and the feminist critique of population control as "development." As the Center's Jane Blewett put it, "We tried to walk a very narrow line."

Jesuit Relations

"Injustice is atheism in action": Pedro Arrupe SJ. Elected as Vatican II ended in 1965, the Jesuit Father-General with the sunny disposition presided over the order's embrace of social justice as an essential part of its mission. Arrupe's openness to change did not endear him to conservative Jesuits or the Vatican curia.

With Dutch Jesuit Peter-Hans Kolvenbach (centre) and Bernard Hubert, 1980. Three years later Kolvenbach was elected Jesuit general at a general congregation at which Ryan played a prominent role.

With Juan Luis Segundo SJ at his installation as chancellor of Regis College, Toronto, 1983. Ryan first met the Uruguayan Jesuit during his student days. He was deeply impressed when Segundo, a prominent exponent of liberation theology, took him on a tour of Montevideo's slums in 1968.

Ryan chats with (left to right on couch) Cardinal Emmett Carter, Eric Maclean (Upper Canadian provincial from 1990 to 1996) and Angus Macdougall (provincial from 1963 to 1969) at a Jesuit synod in 1990. Ryan was diligent about keeping his working relationship with Carter in good repair, and the relationship served both of them well over the years.

The Ottawa Jesuit Community, with visitors, 1995. Bill Ryan, Benoît Malvaux, Norman Dodge, Michael Czerny, Peter Knox, Eric Maclean, Mike Doiron. By the 1990s English Canada's Jesuits were confronted with an aging membership and a dwindling number of recruits.

Canadian Conference of Catholic Bishops

A meeting of the Social Affairs Commission shortly after the publication of *Ethical Reflections on the Economic Crisis* in 1983. Bishop Remi De Roo (far right) is presiding; Tony Clarke is to his left.

When Tony Clarke joined the bishops' conference staff in the 1970s, he continued the social justice thrust that Ryan had helped start. But when Ryan returned to the conference a decade later, the two had a falling out.

As general secretary of the Canadian Conference of Catholic Bishops in the 1980s, Ryan hired a management consulting firm to help restructure the organization. Seated, from left, are Touche, Ross consultants Mike McFarland, Ross Roxburgh and Bob Brouillard. Alex Taché, French general secretary of the CCCB, and CCCB staff member Bernard Daly are also seated. Ryan is standing.

Everett MacNeil, Ryan and Dennis Murphy held the position of English general secretary of the Canadian Conference of Catholic Bishops in succession from 1968 to 1990. The three priests, savvy institutional players, developed a close friendship, sharing golf and ski holidays.

Bill Ryan at work in 2002

areas. Native women – not eligible to be deacons – were trained to do pastoral work in a separate program. The Anishinabe Spiritual Centre also hosted other programs such as Alcoholics Anonymous and marriage-preparation courses. As Jesuits came and went, two Sisters of St. Joseph, Dorothy Regan and Patricia Hassett, became its mainstays.

In the development of the Jesuit Centre, the Farm Community and the Anishinabe Spiritual Centre, Ryan used his position as provincial to support the work of others. To a much greater extent, *Compass: A Jesuit Journal* was the result of his own initiative. His idea of a Jesuit magazine was a typical Ryan project in that it was vaguely defined and left lots of room for interpretation, but he obtained the support of the province consultors and then hired his old friend Grant Maxwell, with whom he had worked at the bishops' conference in the 1960s, to be its editor. Maxwell, whose extensive experience as a journalist and as an interpreter of Catholic teaching did not include magazine editing, moved to Toronto in 1981 to begin planning the magazine, whose offices were set up adjacent to the provincial's office in the west end of the city.

Our Way of Proceeding had described the purpose of such a venture as being "to make Jesuits and Jesuit undertakings and opinions known more widely in Canada in order to inform and encourage our friends, promote vocations and reach a growing public."[18] This implied that the magazine would be at least partly promotional, and much of the early *Compass*, which began publication in 1983, was devoted to "telling the Jesuit story." It was also one of the magazine's problems. The editors did not show much discrimination in terms of which Jesuit stories to tell, and Jesuits themselves, especially younger ones, felt that *Compass* was not putting the province's best face forward. With time, the magazine improved. A 1985 redesign made it more visually accessible, and more thoughtful, well-written articles began to appear, such as a piece on agriculture by Louisa Blair, a young Jesuit Companion living at the Farm Community, or an account of a visit to Toronto by Jesuit General Peter-Hans Kolvenbach (who had succeeded Arrupe in 1983) by Ryan's friend Janet Somerville,[19] but *Compass* as a whole continued to lack focus and edge.

Maxwell was sixty when he took on the editorship of *Compass*, and he had not foreseen a long tenure. By 1986 he was ready to retire, and a publishing policy committee made up of four Jesuits – David Eley of the Jesuit Communication Project (a team of Jesuits and others in Toronto working primarily on media education and media literacy issues), Michael Czerny of the Jesuit Centre, Ryan's close associate Jean-Marc Laporte and former provincial Angus Macdougall – was concentrating on finding a new concept and a new editor for the magazine. Their search eventually led them to one of the authors of this book, Bob Chodos, a practising Jew who was more than a little surprised to receive a phone call from a Father Michael Czerny inviting him to consider becoming the editor of a Jesuit magazine. Czerny described *Compass'* rough start and the continuing sense among many Jesuits that it was still not the kind of magazine they wanted. As discussions with Czerny and other Jesuits proceeded, it became apparent that Jews and Jesuits who shared an interest in publishing a "religious affairs" magazine that interpreted its mandate broadly could in fact easily work together. By the fall of 1986, planning was underway and the first issue of the revamped magazine appeared in the spring of the following year.

A personal recollection by Bob Chodos is in order here:

It is difficult to write with any sense of detachment about a project that occupied me intensely for ten years, so I will confine myself to a few observations. First, perhaps more than I realized at the time, the leap of faith involved in hiring a Jewish editor reflected a remarkable spirit of openness and possibility that pervaded the Jesuits of English Canada in the late 1970s and 1980s. Second, looking through back issues and old correspondence, I realize how naive and ignorant I was regarding the Catholic world in those years. In my naïveté and ignorance, I did not know that the Catholic activists of Bill Ryan's generation were the obligatory spokespeople on social justice questions or that we were crossing a boundary when we ran a cover cartoon of a bishop holding back a horde of laypeople. Some of these trespasses no doubt contributed to the freshness of the magazine, but I am also grateful for the wise guidance and support I received from the Jesuits and lay Catholics who in time constituted a very strong editorial board. Third, reading for the first time Bill Ryan's five criteria for all Jesuit apostolates – preferential option for the poor, collaboration with non-Jesuits, use of mass media, creative co-operation among apostolates, and opportunities to pray, reflect and study – I am struck by the extent to which *Compass* made good on all of those criteria. When the Catholic Press Association named *Compass* the best general-interest Catholic magazine in North America in 1990, earning us a warm letter of congratulation from Bill Ryan, the judges had this to say: "*Compass: A Jesuit Journal* is a publication that tackles difficult Church issues but in a style that encourages the engagement in these debates by a wide selection of readers. In other words, it is informative, clear, and provocative."[20]

⟫⟩-◦-⟨⟪

While he was presiding over all the changes in the Upper Canada province, Bill Ryan was also continuing to lead the life of Bill Ryan. He had no sooner returned to Canada in 1978 than he was back in the United States, making a presentation on transnational corporations to the U.S. conference of religious superiors in Cleveland. A journey across Canada included a side trip to Anchorage, Alaska, where he gave a workshop on social justice and spirituality to the local Jesuits. In October he was off to visit the Canadian missions in Zambia and then India and Bhutan, where he took a two-day trip across the foothills of the Himalayas in a Jeep. After Christmas he revisited the Center of Concern, meeting with Pete Henriot and Irving Friedman. He later went to Ireland and England where Jesuits were interested in setting up an organization along the lines of the Center of Concern, to Chile for the Fourth Interamerican Meeting of Religious, and to India and Bhutan for a return visit. The travel never ended.

Ryan made his most significant and extensive foreign trip in the summer of 1979, soon after the retreat/institute in Guelph, when he went to China for three weeks as part of a Western delegation to discuss "Values and Ideologies in Science, Medicine, Technology, and Law" with the Chinese Academy of the Social Sciences. The delegation, under the auspices of the Kennedy Institute of Ethics at Georgetown University in Washington, included such Top People as Kennedy family member and former U.S. vice-presidential candidate Sargent Shriver and theologians Richard McCormick SJ and Hans Küng. The United States had just established full diplomatic relations with China and western contacts with the Chinese were by no means routine, especially for religious leaders. Ryan spent much of his time in China meeting with Chinese Jesuits, including three who were confined to labour camps, and other Chinese Catholics, from both the government-approved "Patriotic Church" and the semi-underground "Roman" Church. Toronto *Globe and Mail* correspondent John Fraser helped facilitate many of these meetings, which had to be organized outside official channels. Reconciliation between "Patriotic" and "Roman" Catholics, Ryan acknowledged, "will require heroic virtue and trust," but he was still able to find a bright spot in that "the Jesuits I met from the labor camps were neither bitter nor judgmental concerning these 'patriotic' priests."[21] On the same trip he stopped in Japan, where he made the acquaintance of the rector of Sophia University, the Italian Jesuit Giuseppe Pittau.

His position as Jesuit provincial combined with his personal stature also gave him a high profile in the Catholic world within Canada in those years. In 1978 he organized a three-day workshop on social justice for the Ontario bishops, bringing in Pete Henriot and Joe Holland from the Center of Concern as well as Canadian facilitators Janet Somerville, Marcel Gervais (later archbishop of Ottawa) and Tony Clarke. On the basis of the experience of the Guelph retreat/institute, he and John English organized a workshop for Canadian major superiors of religious communities on "Praying over Our Graced and Sin History in View of Choosing Apostolic Priorities." Ryan repeated this workshop at the meeting of religious superiors in Chile, and English wrote a workbook based on it. Later, Ryan organized a seminar on "Religious as Contemplatives in Action" for Ontario religious superiors.[22] This time he brought in John Kavanaugh SJ, philosophy professor at Saint Louis University, as well as John English. One person who did not fail to notice the prominence Ryan acquired was the archbishop of Toronto, Cardinal Emmett Carter, who made use of Ryan's position to get himself out of a political jam in 1983. But before that happened, there was something that Carter was able to do for Ryan.

In 1980 Ryan received a confidential request from Pedro Arrupe for his endorsement of the general's decision to resign. This apparently straightforward appeal for support, which Arrupe sent to all the Jesuit provincials, reflected some complex and delicate Church politics. The ensuing controversy had its roots in GC31, the general congregation that elected Arrupe in 1965, which opened the possibility of a general's resignation for reasons of old age or incapacity.

A Jesuit provincial serves a six-year term. A bishop is relieved of his diocesan responsibilities at age seventy-five or when his state of health makes further service inappropriate. Even in other religious orders, there are provisions for the superior to leave office. But traditionally a Jesuit general was like a pope: the only way he could end his term was by dying. It could be argued – in both cases – that the interests of stability would be better served by a fixed term or a retirement age. That is not the way the Vatican perceived things, however. So it viewed Arrupe's wish to resign with some alarm – especially since the resignation of a

Jesuit general might be regarded as a precedent that could apply to the pope.

Though still in good health in his early seventies, Arrupe had not had an easy time as general. The dissension that had begun early in his term and had contributed to the tense relationship between the Jesuits and Pope Paul VI during GC32 continued after the general congregation. The Vatican received a steady stream of reports from dissident Jesuits, local bishops and other sources that the order was becoming too political and too secular. These reports reached the ears of the new pope, John Paul II, who called in Arrupe and Jesuit leaders from fourteen countries and told them that their conduct had caused "confusion in the Christian people and concern to the Church."[23]

At the same time, the martyrdoms that Arrupe had predicted would be a result of the Jesuits' preferential option for the poor began to occur. On March 12, 1977, Father Rutilio Grande, a Jesuit doing pastoral work among peasants in a rural area of El Salvador, was ambushed as he drove from his home to a neighbouring town to celebrate Mass.[24] Grande's death helped radicalize the newly appointed archbishop of San Salvador, Oscar Romero, who began to speak out strongly against repression and abuse of human rights by the Salvadoran military. According to Vincent O'Keefe SJ, Arrupe's American assistant, the papal nuncio sent back reports to Rome that Romero was being "manipulated by Jesuits and Marxists."[25]

Senior Vatican officials were conspiring to have Romero removed from his position, but before they could act, on March 24, 1980, Romero was gunned down while celebrating Mass. In Rome, Pedro Arrupe said Mass for the slain archbishop, but Pope John Paul and his subordinates at the Vatican did not. Even for Jonathan Kwitny, the pope's highly sympathetic American biographer who entitled his book *Man of the Century*, "John Paul's treatment of Archbishop Romero, and his continued treatment of Romero's memory, are an injustice like no other he has done anyone."[26]

These were the circumstances under which Arrupe decided to press forward with his plans to resign. Ryan was one among a large majority of provincials who agreed that he had sufficient reasons to resign if he wished to.[27] Arrupe had already received the approval of his general assistants, and so his next step would be to call a general congregation to accept his resignation and appoint a new general. But before he did that Arrupe decided to inform the pope of his intentions. John Paul asked Arrupe not to resign "for the good of your society and the Church," although he did promise to begin a "dialogue" with Arrupe with a view towards a general congregation. But the dialogue proceeded at glacial speed, and the tug-of-war between Arrupe and the Vatican was still in progress when the Jesuit general left Rome on July 25, 1981, for a twelve-day visit to the Philippines to celebrate the four hundredth anniversary of the Jesuit presence there. Taking precautions in case anything should happen to him, he appointed Vincent O'Keefe, his chief assistant, vicar until the end of August.

After a stopover in Bangkok, Arrupe boarded a plane for Rome on August 6, 1981, the thirty-sixth anniversary of the bomb attack on Hiroshima. When the plane landed the next morning, Arrupe suffered a severe stroke and was taken immediately to Salvator Mundi hospital. As his condition worsened and it became clear that he would never be able to resume his responsibilities as general, provisions had to be made for the future. In the Jesuit constitutions, article 787 allowed for the appointment of a vicar when the general was temporarily incapacitated. During the extended final illness of Father Janssens in the early 1960s, John Swain, the Jesuit from the Ottawa Valley who had accepted Bill Ryan into the Society in 1944, had served as vicar under this article. Now Arrupe, still able to express his wishes, used it to extend O'Keefe's mandate beyond the end of August. O'Keefe appeared to be Arrupe's chosen heir – but as a liberal and an American, he was not trusted in the Vatican. In early September, Arrupe was transferred from the hospital to the infirmary at Jesuit headquarters.

On October 6, the Vatican secretary of state, Cardinal Agostino Casaroli, came to visit Arrupe carrying a letter from the pope, who was himself just back at work after recovering from the gunshot wounds he had endured in May. The letter, addressed to "my dear Son Pedro Arrupe, Superior General of the Society of Jesus," was warm in tone, but its intent was clear:

> I asked you last year to defer offering your resignation since, as I indicated to you in our conversations in the early months of this year, I saw the need for a more thorough preparation of the Society for the General Congregation and I hoped to set this in motion with you. Unfortunately this has not been possible due to my long stay in hospital and now to your present state of health. Therefore, after long reflection and prayer, I have decided to entrust this task to a Delegate, who will represent me more closely in the Society, look after the preparation of the General Congregation, to be called in due time, and also, in my

name and by my appointment, superintend the government of the Society until the election of a new Superior General.[28]

The delegate John Paul chose was Paolo Dezza, who had managed to maintain insider status both at the Jesuit curia and at the Vatican. A former rector and long-time professor of metaphysics at the Gregorian University, Dezza had been one of four general assistants elected by GC31, along with O'Keefe, Swain and the Hungarian Andrew Varga. He had also been confessor to three popes: John XXIII, Paul VI and John Paul I. By October 1981, Dezza was close to eighty years old and nearly blind, and so the pope also named a deputy, the Japanese provincial Giuseppe Pittau, a Jesuit of Ryan's generation whom Ryan had met on his Asian trip two years earlier.

Casaroli met with Arrupe alone, then called for O'Keefe: he couldn't understand what Arrupe, whose speech had been impaired by the stroke, was saying. O'Keefe spoke with Arrupe, then told Casaroli that the general wanted him to meet with Father Dezza – a request that O'Keefe, who had not yet seen the pope's letter, found mysterious. While Casaroli met with Dezza, O'Keefe picked up the letter and read it to Arrupe. Arrupe was in tears; O'Keefe, whose authority was being swept out from under him, later described himself as being "kind of stunned." So, too, as the news filtered out, was the whole Jesuit order.

In much the same way that memories of the Holocaust will affect the Jewish psyche for generations, or that francophone Quebecers remain haunted by the memory of the defeat on the Plains of Abraham in 1759, the suppression of the Society by Pope Clement XIV in 1773 looms large in the collective Jesuit memory. The suppression, which had more to do with European court intrigue than with religious doctrine, lasted forty years, and its memory helped produce the conservative, conformist nineteenth-century "restored order" of which significant vestiges lingered at the time of Bill Ryan's formation. Even now, no Jesuit can completely forget that a pope could, and under some circumstances would, end the Society's existence with the stroke of a pen. So John Paul's appointment of a personal delegate to run the Society elicited fears of a "new suppression." Even if it didn't mean the end of the Society, would it mean the end of the social justice thrust of GC32? Or would Jesuits simply have to pay more attention to their relations with the Vatican and with local bishops? Would Jesuits around the world accept the pope's decision, or would there be open revolt? No one knew for sure.

A key role in controlling the flow of information, mediating the response of local Jesuits and dealing with local bishops would inevitably fall to the provincials. In Rome, the secretary of the Society, Louis Laurendeau, informed the provincials of Dezza's appointment a week after Casaroli's ominous visit to Arrupe. But he instructed them to keep the information under embargo until the appointment became official on October 31. Anti-Arrupe Jesuits in Spain leaked the story to the press, however, and on Friday, October 23, the Jesuit press office in Rome confirmed Dezza's appointment.[29]

Bill Ryan, in Montreal for a visitation to the Loyola Jesuit community, felt that he had to act. He addressed a letter to the superiors of Jesuit communities across the country, enclosing the pope's letter to Arrupe and other documents from Rome, still with the embargo date of October 31. He urged each superior to be the only official spokesperson for the Jesuits in his local area, and to "stay with the documentation and avoid speculation" in public comments:

> The fact that the Pope's letter is warm and affectionate is significant – as well as the fact that he sees us with the help of his delegate moving to a General Congregation to elect a new Superior General. The only unusual thing in his letter is his initiative in naming a personal delegate, which is not provided for in our Constitutions. Nevertheless, it is clear that he intends that Father Dezza prepare a General Congregation according to our Constitutions. Father Dezza is a very respected older Jesuit, while Father Pittau is an energetic modern Jesuit responsible for the present vitality of Sophia University in Tokyo. I mention these facts only because they may help you deal with one or other troubled Jesuit. You can be sure that I will myself be seeking all the clarification and advice I can get and will share it with you.

He asked each superior to "be in touch with the local Bishop on October 31 so that he too as a friend of the Jesuits may have accurate information," noting that in Toronto he would assume this responsibility himself by contacting Cardinal Carter. He acted on this promise much more quickly than the letter indicated.

At about five o'clock that afternoon, Ryan felt the need to talk to someone about what was happening. Knowing Carter's habits, he realized that the cardinal was probably having his late-afternoon gin, and so he called Carter in Toronto and filled him in on the situation, establishing a bond of trust or at least mutual non-aggression that strengthened Ryan's delicate position in dealing with the new regime.

He followed up with a letter, enclosing the documentation from Rome. The reply from Carter – who had also suffered a stroke, although not as debilitating a one as Arrupe's – served Ryan's purposes perfectly:

> It is not my place nor my privilege to make any comment on what has transpired recently between the Holy Father and the Society.... As one who has gone through, all too recently, something of the same crisis as Father Arrupe, I can well understand his frustration at his illness and the need for interim government. The Pope has chosen to take certain actions which, in his wisdom, he has deemed appropriate. I repeat that I am not called upon to offer any judgment but I can judge and appreciate the obedience and the calm prudence of the Society in the face of this crisis. Your own letter is a model of religious dedication and obedience and not only do I thank you for being kept informed, but also for the kind of insight and balance which your contribution brings to all of us under these painful and difficult circumstances.
>
> I hope that I don't have to tell you that my co-operation and my support at this time, as at all times, is assured.

One of the causes of the difficulties in which the Jesuits found themselves was their failure to pay close enough attention to keeping their relations with local bishops in good repair. It was clear that Bill Ryan was not going to make *that* mistake.

At the suggestion of his friend Julien Harvey, Ryan joined three Quebec Jesuits – Harvey, Bernard Carrière, who had just succeeded him as French-Canadian provincial, and Irénée Desrochers – at a press conference on Monday, October 26. The press conference, which Ryan later described as "freewheeling,"[30] was a response to the unusual level of media interest in the Jesuits occasioned by the news of Dezza's appointment. The main message that the four Jesuits conveyed to the press was that they "did not understand" the pope's unprecedented action. Ryan ventured a possible explanation: the pope, accustomed to living under a totalitarian regime, did not have the same view of the world as people living in capitalist countries. Just as he feared that trade unions would become political parties and too closely tied to the state, so he feared the same outcome for the Jesuits. Harvey, meanwhile, noted that while the overall tendency was for popes to become more democratic in exercising their authority, they also sometimes returned towards centralization: "Every time they've done it, it has been a mistake. Some day they'll realize it!"[31]

A few days later, in an interview with the Toronto *Star*, Ryan said that if the pope's appointment of Dezza was "innocent" – if he just wanted an interim leader whom he could trust – then the next general congregation should take place in about two years: "If the preparation drags on longer than that then our people will begin to get very uneasy."[32] In a letter addressed that same week to all Upper Canada province Jesuits, in which he enclosed the pope's letter to Arrupe and the letter from secretary Laurendeau to the provincials, Ryan took a different tone:

> This unusual initiative taken by Pope John Paul will, I am sure, come to many of you as a surprise – even to some as a serious test of faith. As your Provincial, I ask all of you as true Jesuits "to receive this decision in a spirit of full and filial obedience" as Father Arrupe has asked us to do. The Pope has spoken: let us give clear evidence to the world that we Jesuits will obey. Indeed, such spontaneous obedience has been an essential quality of our own Jesuit way of proceeding since our very beginning.

But as this letter urging obedience went out to the Jesuits, word of the Montreal press conference was getting back to Rome. In some of the reports, the four Jesuits' statement that they "did not understand" came out as "we do not accept" the pope's action, and Ryan had to explain himself. He sent a package to Rome in which he included his own notes from the press conference, his letter to the Jesuits of his province and, perhaps most significant, Cardinal Carter's letter to him. The matter soon blew over.

It also gradually became clear that some of the worst fears about the impact of the papal intervention would not be borne out. Dezza and Pittau proved to be skilful diplomats rather than heavy-handed authoritarians. In his initial homily on October 31, Dezza said that the pope "does not want his intervention to upset our internal order but rather that, with the exception of the person of the Delegate instead of the Vicar, everything will remain unchanged and in conformity with the norms of our Institute which remain in full vigor and should be religiously observed." That this statement would have at least some substance became clear at a meeting of Jesuit provincials in February 1982 at Cavalletti, a Jesuit villa outside Rome where barbed wire served as a reminder of its former incarnation as German headquarters during the Second World War. Preoccupied with managing the situation in his own province, Ryan had little idea of what to expect of the other provincials, and looked forward to the meeting as an opportunity to sense the "energy" in the Society. He very quickly realized that the energy among the provincials at Cavalletti was pro-Arrupe and pro-GC32. After Dezza and Pittau gave their opening remarks, provincial after provincial stepped up to the floor microphones to praise the stricken general. Ryan concluded that the Jesuits were not about to abandon their commitment to social justice as an integral element of their religious work, although greater efforts would be made to maintain good relations with the Vatican and local bishops, which he could fully appreciate. A hug Dezza gave Ryan before they left Cavalletti encapsulated the spirit of the meeting.

Even when the pope spoke to the provincials in Rome after their meeting, his message to the Society was fairly muted. To be sure, his remarks on the relationship between faith and justice were very different in tone from the ringing declarations of the 1971 synod and GC32: "It must not be forgotten that the necessary concern for justice must be exercised in conformity with your vocation as religious and as priests." The pope went on to quote a speech he had given the previous year: "The priest's service is not that of a doctor, of a social worker, of a politician or of a trade unionist. A priest might give such services in certain cases, but only in a supplementary way." Equally significantly, however, the pope expressed his confidence "that it will be possible, within the year, to convoke a general congregation" and thus to resume the Jesuits' normal mode of governing themselves. In fact, the general congregation was announced that fall for September 1983 – almost exactly the two-year time frame Ryan had envisioned.

On his way to Rome for the 33rd General Congregation, Ryan met his friend Pete Henriot from the Center of Concern, who was attending the congregation as a delegate from the Oregon province, and the two went climbing in the Alps while they plotted strategy. Their goal was to carry forward the spirit of Cavalletti: to maintain the social justice thrust of the Jesuits while keeping relations with the Vatican in good repair.

On the first day of the congregation, Pope John Paul paid a rare visit to the Jesuit curia to celebrate Mass. He once again told the delegates that they needed to carry out their work for justice only as it conformed with their role as priests, and once again he couched his warning in sufficiently general terms that Ryan could find a way to agree with it: "The only caution he put on us, and the caution we've always had in our documents, is that our role has to be as priests and religious men. It isn't our job to supplant the laity."[33]

The congregation went on to the formal acceptance of Arrupe's resignation and then, after hearing from Dezza, to the election of a new general. This was a choice that had to be exercised with care. O'Keefe and others closely identified with Arrupe were out of the running since the choice of someone from that circle would be a direct slap at the Vatican. Nor could the delegates choose Pittau, who under other circumstances might have been a candidate, because that would be too enthusiastic an endorsement of the pope's extraordinary action. They needed a dark horse, and they found one in Peter-Hans Kolvenbach, a fifty-five-year-old Dutch Jesuit who had spent the better part of twenty years in Lebanon before coming to Rome in 1981 as rector of the Pontifical Oriental Institute. Kolvenbach, elected on the first ballot, was more attuned to Vatican diplomacy than Arrupe while still being deeply committed to social justice.

Ryan was named chair of the commission that would produce a document on the Jesuits' mission in today's world, and he recruited Henriot to help draft the document. Not surprisingly, "Sent into Today's World," as the document was called, reaffirmed the Jesuit mission that GC32 had defined nine years earlier. It clearly indicated that social justice work would remain a central part of that mission, and made some suggestions and set some criteria for how that work would be carried out. For the social justice mission to be credible, the document said, Jesuits needed to collaborate with the laity, be in solidarity with the poor, and practise justice in their own lives and in the communities and institutions of the Society.[34] The congregation accepted the document unanimously.

A continued commitment to social justice, combined with a generally more positive relationship with bishops and the Vatican, would indeed characterize the Kolvenbach era in the Society. Meanwhile, in the same year that GC33 took place, a notable instance of Jesuit-episcopal co-operation was unfolding in Toronto, one that would involve Bill Ryan once again in the affairs of the Canadian Conference of Catholic Bishops (CCCB).

<hr />

While working in the social action office of the Canadian Catholic Conference (as it was known until 1977) in the late 1960s, Ryan had promoted the idea of a grand "Coalition for Development." The coalition never got off the ground, but the momentum developed in the 1960s did carry through into the 1970s, especially after the bishops' social justice work was given added impetus by the 1971 Justice in the World synod, at which the Canadian bishops were prominent players. The bishops' role as social critics was expressed primarily in two arenas: their participation in ecumenical coalitions, and their social statements which took on a more consistently radical tone during the 1970s and into the 1980s.

The coalitions that emerged in the 1970s reflected the new ecumenical spirit that was animating the country's Christian churches, and one participant observer called these organizations "the new experiments in Canadian ecumenism." The coalitions were staffed by energetic researchers and organizers, and funded by the Anglican, United, Presbyterian and Lutheran churches as well as the Catholic bishops, the newly formed Canadian Catholic Organization for Development and Peace, and various Catholic orders including the Jesuits. It was the heyday of Christian social justice work. United Church people had been deeply involved in laying the groundwork for social democracy in Canada, but never had the churches become so directly engaged in public issues on a co-operative, well-organized and ongoing basis.

Nuns and Presbyterian ministers stood up together at the annual meetings of Gulf Oil and Noranda Mines to call the corporations to account for their investments in southern Africa and Chile. Young activists, the children of missionaries in Korea and Bangladesh, sent home telex reports from United Nations conferences in Nairobi and Rome where they were making contacts with a growing international network of NGO activists. The flourishing community of Canadian Church activists that was on the receiving end of such dispatches was carrying out research, lobbying and education work, with the latter centring on the annual Ten Days for World Development. "Ten Days," as it became known in social justice circles, changed its name to Ten Days for Global Justice when the notion of "development" fell from favour. This busy period gave rise to such groups as the already mentioned GATT-Fly (international economic issues), Project Ploughshares (peace and disarmament), the Interchurch Committee on Human Rights in Latin America (Latin American solidarity work), Project North (support for Native people), the Task Force on the Churches and Corporate Responsibility, PLURA (anti-poverty work in Canada) and other efforts focusing on, among other things, Asia, Chile, Africa, and population growth. The list is long.

The Catholic Church was important on this front, providing money, organized networks and staff time. The Canadian Church itself sprouted numerous initiatives and by the end of the decade about a third of all dioceses had active social justice centres and offices. About half of these were located in Quebec, and although there was a lot of activity in the west and the east, Ontario was underrepresented. These efforts involved not just ecumenical work but also collaboration with secular activists involved in trade unions, the women's movement, the environmental movement and the peace movement.

During the 1970s, Tony Clarke of the CCCB's social affairs office emerged as an important figure in these networks. Clarke came to the bishops' conference in 1972 with a Ph.D. in social ethics from the University of Chicago and an Alinskyite view of confrontation politics. He represented a new generation and a new style in Catholic social justice work. While the activists of the 1960s, such as Ryan and Grant Maxwell, were unambiguously members of what Janet Somerville calls the Catholic "tribe," Clarke was an Anglican by background, one of the first of many non-Catholics (including the authors of this book) to become aligned with the Church as it expanded its field of activity. Energetic, bright, a good speaker, Clarke was a spark plug for social justice at the CCCB. He was also fortunate to enjoy the support of a generation of activist bishops such as Remi De Roo and Bernard Hubert.

Clarke's energy and the leftward turn of the bishops after the 1971 synod were reflected in a number of the social statements that emerged from the bishops' conference in the 1970s. In 1975 the bishops criticized the energy megaprojects then being planned for Canada's North, which they feared would bring about "forms of exploitation which we often assume happen only in Third World countries: a serious abuse of both the Native Peoples and the energy resources of the North." They called for "better ways of developing the Canadian North," which would have to involve "a just land settlement with the Native Peoples... effective participation by the Native Peoples in shaping the kind of regional development" and "adequate measures to protect the terrain, vegetation, wildlife and waters of northern areas."[35] By 1977, the bishops were saying openly that Canadian society was "a society to be transformed." In pursuing strategies for change, "no option is valid that does not unite people in efforts for the creation of a society based on justice."[36] The bishops refused to endorse Marxism as an alternative, but they were not hesitant about pointing out the serious flaws in capitalism.

In the first few years of the 1980s, those flaws were on full display. The economic difficulties of the 1970s, the decade of oil shocks and "stagflation," reached their peak in 1981–82. Fixated on inflation, which continued at above 10 per cent into the 1980s, Paul Volcker's U.S. Federal Reserve Board, followed in lockstep by Gerald Bouey's Bank of Canada, ratcheted up interest rates to unprecedented heights. The ensuing recession was so severe, with unemployment in Canada at levels not seen since the Great Depression of the 1930s, that talk of an "economic crisis" became routine. At the same time, the political will to deal with the crisis through government intervention ebbed, as the election of Margaret Thatcher in Britain in 1979 and Ronald Reagan in the United States in 1980 ushered in the era of neo-conservatism.

In Canada, the Trudeau Liberals were still determined to leave their interventionist mark after being unexpectedly returned to power in 1980, but business hostility and the intractable economic crisis had deflected their thrust by 1982. Their National Energy Program was undermined by ferocious opposition from the oil industry in Calgary and the Reagan administration in Washington and by a new stability in energy prices. Meanwhile, in his 1981 budget, Finance Minister Allan MacEachen (a Cape Breton Catholic in the tradition of the Antigonish Movement who in the 1960s had had Bill Ryan and his colleagues at the Canadian Catholic Conference write speeches for him) tried to close tax loopholes that benefited the rich. Under a barrage of business opposition, the Liberals withdrew the key measures in the budget, and MacEachen was shuffled out of the finance portfolio in the fall of 1982. In October of that year, Trudeau signalled the government's new economic direction in a series of televised speeches to the country: "Our challenge is to restore Canada's fitness to survive economically in a world where the survival of the fittest nations has become the rule of life…[in] a harder, leaner world, hungrier for customers, for investment, and for advantage."[37] Among those who were galvanized by the country's economic malaise and the government's neo-Darwinist response were Tony Clarke and his allies at the CCCB.

Clarke drafted a strongly worded statement, "Ethical Reflections on the Economic Crisis," whose central point was that the main focus of the government's concern should be unemployment, not inflation: "The fact that some 1.5 million people are jobless constitutes a serious moral as well as economic crisis in this country." It based its argument on two Gospel principles, "the preferential option for the poor, the afflicted and the oppressed" and "the special value and dignity of human work in God's plan for creation." Here the statement was following the lines of the most recent papal teaching: Pope John Paul's 1981 social encyclical, following the tradition of marking each decade anniversary of *Rerum Novarum*, dealt with work (*Laborem Exercens*) and emphasized the dignity and priority of labour. "Ethical Reflections" was also highly critical of the government's "survival of the fittest" thinking, which it said "has often been used to rationalize the increasing concentration of wealth and power in the hands of a few."[38] The document spoke favourably of labour-intensive industries, regional industrial strategies, self-reliance, and worker and community participation.

Clarke's power base among the bishops was the Social Affairs Commission, a group of eight bishops chaired by Remi De Roo. This commission initially hoped to present the statement to the bishops' plenary assembly, held soon after Trudeau's October television speeches, but was stopped by CCCB President Henri Légaré, archbishop of Grouard-McLennan in northwestern Alberta, who did not want such a potentially controversial statement to reach the floor. The next plan was to issue it as a statement of the Social Affairs Commission, for which the commission needed Légaré's approval. Under pressure from De Roo, the CCCB president finally agreed, and the statement went out to the bishops on December 22. On December 30, in the news trough between Christmas and New Year's, CBC television reported its existence, and the next day the full text appeared in the Toronto *Star*. From there, media coverage mushroomed, and in the flood of reports, comments and analyses, the nuance that this was a statement of the Social Affairs Commission and not of the bishops' conference as a whole tended to get lost. The general perception was that Canada's bishops – and the Catholic Church – were attacking the government's economic policies. In the world of Canadian public discourse, Clarke and the Social Affairs Commission had scored a major coup, but in the smaller world of intra-episcopal politics, there was a problem. Some of the bishops who had not seen the statement in advance and heard about it for the first time in the media were not pleased – Cardinal Emmett Carter least of all.

Carter's displeasure focused on both the content of the statement and the manner of its release. He immediately called a press conference, pointing out that "Ethical Reflections" was a statement of the Social Affairs Commission and that "there was no consultation with the collectivity of the Bishops." He also expressed "serious reservations concerning some of the material and attitudes contained therein while not contesting the right of the [Social Affairs] office to express its opinion." Carter's dissent quickly became part of the media story. Soon afterwards, Carter wrote to Archbishop Légaré, maintaining that "the thrust of the

[December 30 CBC] newscast was clearly to implicate all Canadian Bishops. We were in full flood of attribution without consultation, responsibility without participation, conclusion without dialogue."[39] An extended correspondence between the two followed, in which they disagreed over whether proper CCCB procedures had been observed (most subsequent observers have concluded that there was no violation of the letter of CCCB procedures[40]) and whether the arguments in "Ethical Reflections" represented something novel with respect to previous episcopal statements.

"Ethical Reflections" was a popular success, gaining endorsements from Protestant churches, newspaper editorialists and the New Democratic Party and crystallizing public dissatisfaction with the government's economic approach. By contrast, Carter came off poorly, appearing to stand with the corporate elite and its friends in government against his fellow bishops. Carter needed to reposition himself in relation to the document, and to do that he turned to his friend Bill Ryan.

In the flurry of comment that followed the release of "Ethical Reflections," Ryan had weighed in with a speech to a business audience on February 15, 1983, in which he took a sober and generally sympathetic look at the statement. He parsed what the bishops had said, put it in the context of previous episcopal and papal teaching, and analyzed the reaction to it. He defended the bishops' right to speak on economic matters: "Contrary to the wishes of government and business leaders that the bishops would stay with general principles if not pious generalities...whenever the image of God is defaced in people, in even one person, the Church must speak out to the concrete situation." Drawing on the work of two Quebec economists, Diane Bellemare and Lise Poulin-Simon, he proclaimed his faith in the essential soundness of the bishops' analysis: "Massive unemployment is too costly in both economic and human terms to our society and full employment is achievable if we work together as a community for it." At the same time, in keeping with the measured tone of his remarks, Ryan identified "some of the weaknesses I see in this very good statement." He regretted the absence of "a strong Spirit-filled, compassionate faith vision and call," and presaging the coming debates about globalization, he questioned whether the bishops' "neo-Keynesian" analysis was still valid in the light of the growing international mobility of capital: "Keynesianism in all its forms, including monetarism and Reaganomics, now seems largely dated and inadequate – given the emerging new world economy, which needs world controls to protect the poor but still has no controller."[41]

The *Catholic Register* headlined its report of Ryan's speech, "Jesuit superior defends bishops' statement." The Toronto *Star*, however, chose to focus on Ryan's critical points and ran its report under the headline, "Bishops' report on economy dated, inadequate, Jesuit says." (The headline prompted a letter from an irritated Ryan.) In March, the Toronto *Globe and Mail* ran excerpts from the speech.[42] The press coverage, along with the speech itself and his position as superior of a major religious order, helped cast Ryan as an independent and disinterested commentator on the bishops' statement. And he was, after all, a Harvard-trained economist. Who better to help Cardinal Carter climb down gracefully from his oppositional stance?

Carter invited Ryan to a meeting with him and his advisers, and they agreed on the strategy of putting together a high-profile panel to hear testimony on the issues raised by "Ethical Reflections," under the sponsorship of the archdiocese of Toronto. The archdiocese could then publish the panel's report, and Carter would have made a positive contribution to the substance of the debate instead of just criticizing from the sidelines. Ryan was helpful in recruiting panellists, including the distinguished Canadian diplomat George Ignatieff who served as chair. Ryan himself took the position of vice-chair, serving as the panel's expert on Catholic social teaching and Carter's unofficial representative. Rounding out the panel were Judge Lucien Beaulieu of the Provincial Court (Family Division); psychologist, educator and corporate director Reva Gerstein; and journalist John Fraser, the *Globe and Mail*'s national editor and its former Beijing correspondent who had served as Ryan's guide on his China trip four years earlier.

The archdiocese solicited submissions by letter and through ads in the Toronto dailies and in Catholic newspapers. From among the hundred-plus individuals and organizations that made submissions, the panel selected a smaller number to appear at the hearings, held over a weekend in mid-June at the Ramada Renaissance Hotel in suburban Toronto. These included politicians (Employment Minister Lloyd Axworthy, Ontario NDP leader Bob Rae), Church groups (Bishop John O'Mara of Thunder Bay for the Social Affairs Commission, the Reverend Roy Shepherd for the Anglican Church of Canada), business organizations (Canadian Bankers' Association), trade unions (Ontario Federation of Labour), NGOs (GATT-Fly), and representatives of the unemployed (Union of Unemployed Workers).

The venue was criticized as not being conducive to participation by the poor: prominent Catholic commentator Mary Jo Leddy of the Sisters of Sion referred to "the plush Ramada Renaissance Hotel miles from the city core, which you could only get to by car." The panel itself had wanted a more central, more modest venue (archdiocese staff maintained that this was the only location they could find for a three-day meeting) and in its report acknowledged "the inappropriate setting at a posh suburban hotel."[43]

Nevertheless, the hearing panel accomplished its mission. The bulk of the testimony was sympathetic to the thrust of the bishops' statement, and the title of the published report, *Canada's Unemployed: The Crisis of Our Times*, echoed the emphasis of the bishops' statement. The report began with a forceful summary of the testimony entitled "What the Panel Heard," which reflected Ryan's views: "There was a clear and broad consensus that unemployment was the major problem facing the nation. On this there was little, if any, equivocation. Few people thought it was merely a temporary aberration. If it wasn't clear to anyone before, it was certainly made manifest by the end of our proceedings that unemployment is not just a certain number of people without work: it is a scourge that destroys people and threatens to unravel the fabric of the nation."[44]

At the same time, Carter could endorse the report, which expressed a position so similar to that of "Ethical Reflections," as the outcome of a process of civilized discussion: "This series of Hearings was as exempt from partisan posturing as is possible in human affairs. We had no demonstrations. We had no placards. We had no publicity tricks.... We have had an experience of listening to one another, of listening with respect and of sharing in the views freely expressed in a free country. That experience is not without its value."[45]

Carter also appeared at the press conference at which the report was released and had favourable words for it, while Ryan served as chief spokesperson for the panel and emphasized its conclusion that dealing with unemployment had to be the main priority.

For Ryan, especially now that the difficulties with Cardinal Carter had been smoothed over, the impact of "Ethical Reflections" showed the possibilities of the kind of socially aware bishops' conference that he had helped set in motion back in the 1960s. He could see it as a positive sign of the times as he prepared to move on from the provincial's office in 1984, his sixtieth birthday not far away. There were other such signs as well. Major steps had been taken towards implementing the vision for the Upper Canada province that Ryan had outlined in *Our Way of Proceeding*, and his friend and successor, Bill Addley, was committed to continuing in the same direction. In Rome, Peter-Hans Kolvenbach would maintain the priority on the promotion of justice that had been Pedro Arrupe's hallmark, and with a new emphasis on diplomacy, some of the collisions that had punctuated the Arrupe era might be avoided. Ryan hoped that the tide that had carried him and other socially progressive elements in the Church since Vatican II would continue to swell. He and his allies had weathered the early storms occasioned by an authoritarian pope and a combative archbishop. The new storms on the horizon – more diffuse, more complex, more difficult to overcome – could not yet be discerned.

[1] See Michael W. Higgins and Douglas R. Letson, *My Father's Business: A Biography of His Eminence G. Emmett Cardinal Carter* (Toronto: Macmillan, 1990), 149–67.

[2] Donald G. Clifford SJ, "Canadian province plans center for Native people," *National Jesuit News*, October 1979, 11.

[3] Mary Lou Fox, at the time director of the Ojibwe Cultural Foundation at West Bay, Manitoulin Island, vividly described this approach in "Mukeekuniek, Medicine People, and Me," *Compass*, July/August 1991, 22–23.

[4] See "Kichitwa Maanii Namegamig, M'chigiing – Immaculate Conception Church, West Bay," pamphlet (West Bay, ON, n.d.).

[5] Pedro Arrupe SJ, "Our Way of Proceeding," SJ Press and Information Office Documentation no. 42 (Rome, June 1979).

[6] Ibid., n. 5.

[7] Ibid., n. 32.

[8] Ibid., n. 42.

[9] Ibid., n. 33.

[10] William F. Ryan SJ, *Our Way of Proceeding in the '80s* (Toronto: Society of Jesus, Upper Canada Province, 1981), n. 49.

[11] Arrupe to Ryan, May 5, 1981, included in Ryan, *Our Way of Proceeding in the '80s*.

[12] Ryan, *Our Way of Proceeding in the '80s*, n. 5.

[13] William F. Ryan SJ, *Update: Our Way of Proceeding in the '80s* (Toronto: Society of Jesus, Upper Canada Province, 1983), n. 15.

[14] John Lownsbrough, "God's Shock Troops," *Quest*, November 1982, 46.

[15] Ryan, *Our Way of Proceeding in the '80s*, n. 7.

[16] Ibid., nn. 93, 127, 113, 112, 114, 82, 90, 136, 137, 143, 156, 154.

[17] Doug McCarthy SJ, "The Risk of Building a Healing Community," address to the Risking Community Seminar, Humbervale United Church, Toronto, November 14, 1981.

[18] Ryan, *Our Way of Proceeding in the '80s*, n. 156.

[19] Louisa Blair, "Values at Stake in the Farm Crisis!", *Compass*, summer 1986, 20–22; Janet Somerville, "A Day in the Light of Peter-Hans Kolvenbach," *Compass*, fall 1986, 6–11.

20 "Critiques of Magazine Awards," *Catholic Journalist*, May 1990, 14.

21 William F. Ryan SJ, "The Catholic Church in China," *Kennedy Institute Quarterly Report*, vol. 5, no. 2 (fall 1979), 21.

22 Published as *Religious as Contemplatives in Action in the 80's*, "Donum Dei" series no. 29 (Ottawa: Canadian Religious Conference, 1984).

23 Jonathan Kwitny, *Man of the Century: The Life and Times of Pope John Paul II* (New York: Henry Holt, 1997), 403.

24 Ignacio Echániz SJ, *Passion and Glory: A Flesh-and-Blood History of the Society of Jesus*, vol. 4, *Second Spring: 1814–1965–1999* (Anand, Gujarat, India: Gujarat Sahitya Prakash, 2000), 350–55.

25 Quoted in Kwitny, *Man of the Century*, 321–22.

26 Kwitny, *Man of the Century*, 354.

27 It was a secret consultation and so accounts differ. According to Ignacio Echániz, fifty-eight out of sixty-two said yes (*Passion and Glory*, vol. 4, 344); according to Arrupe's biographer, George Bishop, it was fifty-two out of sixty-two (*Pedro Arrupe SJ: Twenty-eighth General of the Society of Jesus* [Anand, Gujarat, India: Gujarat Sahitya Prakash, 2000], 295).

28 Ioannes Paulus PP. II to Pedro Arrupe, October 5, 1981.

29 "Jean-Paul II nomme un « délégué personnel » à la tête de la Compagnie de Jésus," *Le Monde*, 25–26, October 1981, 11; "Après la nomination du Père Paolo Dezza: Le foi des jésuites français « mise à l'épreuve,»"*Le Monde*, October 29, 1981, 29.

30 William F. Ryan SJ, "My Life Between the Two Solitudes," *Compass*, January/February 1997, 13.

31 Denise Robillard, "L'intervention du pape: Les Jésuites ne comprennent pas," *Le Devoir*, October 27, 1981, 7.

32 Tom Harpur, "Pope's intrusion into leadership puts Jesuit order in an uproar," Toronto *Star*, November 7, 1981, H10.

33 Stanley Oziewicz, "Pursuit of justice not renounced: Sober message to Jesuits," Toronto *Globe and Mail*, November 12, 1983, 19.

34 John W. Padberg SJ, "The General Congregations of the Twentieth Century," in *Jesuits: Yearbook of the Society of Jesus 2000* (Rome: General Curia of the Society of Jesus, 1999), 20.

35 Canadian Catholic Conference, Administrative Board, "Labour Day Message – 1975: Northern Development: At What Cost?", in Edward F. Sheridan SJ, ed., *Do Justice!: The Social Teaching of the Canadian Catholic Bishops* (Sherbrooke, QC: Éditions Paulines/Toronto: Jesuit Centre for Social Faith and Justice, 1987), document 40, 277, 282.

36 Canadian Conference of Catholic Bishops, "A Society to Be Transformed," in Sheridan, ed., *Do Justice!*, document 46, 332.

37 Quoted in Christina McCall and Stephen Clarkson, *Trudeau and Our Times*, vol. 2, *The Heroic Delusion* (Toronto: McClelland & Stewart, 1994), 272.

38 Episcopal Commission for Social Affairs, "Ethical Reflections on the Economic Crisis," in Sheridan, ed., *Do Justice!*, document 55, 401, 399, 400, 403.

39 Quoted in Higgins and Letson, *My Father's Business*, 215–16.

40 Bishop John Sherlock of London, Ontario, who succeded Légaré as CCCB president, expressed that view in an interview in 2000. So did Bill Ryan, who became CCCB general secretary two years after "Ethical Reflections."

41 "Ethical Reflections on the Economic Crisis – A Commentary: Notes for an Address by William F. Ryan SJ, National Superior of English-speaking Jesuits in Canada, Dinner Meeting Sponsored by the King-Bay Chaplaincy, in the Board of Trade Quarters, First Canadian Place, Toronto, Tuesday, February 15, 1983," 6–8.

42 *Catholic Register*, February 26, 1983, 3; Toronto *Star*, February 16, 1983; Toronto *Globe and Mail*, March 10, 1983.

43 Leddy, quoted in Higgins and Letson, *My Father's Business*, 219; *Canada's Unemployed: The Crisis of Our Times: Report of the Hearing Panel on "Ethical Reflections on the Economic Crisis"* (Toronto: Archdiocese of Toronto, 1983), 1.

44 *Canada's Unemployed*, 2–3.

45 Ibid., ix–x.

Chapter 6

The Wind Shifts

It was a public happening the like of which had never been seen in Flatrock, Newfoundland, or even in Toronto. Hundreds of thousands of Canadians, the devout and the merely curious, flocked to see Pope John Paul II during his September 1984 Canadian tour. Millions more watched on television, the organizers at the Canadian Conference of Catholic Bishops having received some seven thousand applications for media accreditation. The usually cynical journalists covering the tour struggled breathlessly to find superlatives to describe the size and enthusiasm of the crowds in the eight provinces the pope visited in the course of ten days.

Most Canadians, of course, did not see the pope in person. They garnered their information and understandings in the same way they had been learning of the civil war in El Salvador or the repatriation of the constitution – through television. Unlike his predecessors, who rarely left Rome, the first global pontiff spent 10 per cent of his time on the road, spreading the Gospel to the world largely via television. But if the first-ever papal visit to Canada was a major media event, for Canadian Catholics it was also something more. It occupied their attention in ways that most such spectacles do not; many of them not only observed it but also lived it. For a brief moment it brought the Canadian Catholic "tribe" together, its emotional impact temporarily superseding the divisions that were already well-defined in 1984 – the mainstream, the social justice advocates, the feminists, the ultraconservatives. Questions about what the pope said or criticism of the sea of male faces surrounding the pope were saved for later. In retrospect, Doug McCarthy SJ described the papal visit as "a golden autumn for the church."[1]

The most commonly used comparison to describe Canadians' welcome for the pope was "like a rock star." The logistics, however, were more complex than accommodating Mick Jagger's tastes and security needs. Not only was this a man who grabbed attention wherever he went, but Karol Wojtyla had also been the victim of an assassination attempt that boosted the need for security and, in a grim way, added to his status. John Paul II was an intellectual who understood the power of symbol and gesture and believed that people could effectively express their aspirations through religious symbolism. This was a pope who knew how to play to the crowd in the manner of a seasoned populist politician.

The CCCB was determined to insulate the pope from partisan politics during a visit that coincided exactly with the arrival of a new federal government in Ottawa – having defeated Bill Ryan's former St. Pat's schoolmate John Turner earlier in September, Brian Mulroney was sworn in as prime minister two days before the pope departed. Conference General Secretary Dennis Murphy, aware that politicians who wanted a piece of the action would be keen to bask in the reflected glow of papal celebrity, had made it clear before the tour started: "No politician will appear on a public platform with the Pope during his visit."[2]

It was not that the pope was averse to sharing his platform with politicians. His subsequent visit to Chile featured an appearance on the balcony of the Moneda Palace with Augusto Pinochet after he celebrated the Eucharist with the dictator. Yet in Canada the enigmatic pope spoke in tones that pleased trade unionists implacably opposed to the Pinochets of the world who trampled worker rights. Within weeks of his departure, the Canadian Labour Congress published "A Vision for Humanity," a supplement to its magazine featuring a cover photo of a wheelchair-bound Aboriginal child being kissed by His Holiness. The congress chose its papal statements carefully: "The needs of the poor must take priority over the desires of the rich; the rights of workers over the maximization of profits; the preservation of the environment over uncontrolled industrial exploitation; production to meet social needs over production for military purposes."

In the end, the potent combination of religious spectacle, global celebrity and saturation media coverage combined to make the papal visit a huge success for the Canadian Church. Dennis Murphy, who had as much to do with the planning as anyone, saw it as "a great triumph" that Canadians, believers and non-believers, listened closely to a religious message for ten days. Murphy recalled being surprised that the lavish coverage was so uncritical of the pope and the Church: "Even the media willingly suspended their disbelief." The papal visit became an event of Olympian or World Cup magnitude and, like a major sporting event, required "colour commentary" for viewers at home. Bill Ryan provided it.

>➤-●-◄

In June 1984 Bill Ryan received two intriguing invitations. Bishop John Sherlock of London, Ontario, who was president of the CCCB at the time, called and asked if he would be interested in putting his name forward to succeed Dennis Murphy as general secretary. And CBC-TV called to see if he would appear daily as an expert commentator during the upcoming papal visit. He accepted both. But before agreeing to become the lead staff person for the Canadian bishops, Ryan made a few calls of his own, testing the waters. Dennis Murphy assured him that the job was his if he wanted it, even though there had to be at least one other candidate. Alex Carter was very keen. Emmett Carter muttered something about the general secretary running the place instead of the bishops, but finally urged Ryan to take the job. The Jesuits agreed as well. The other candidate was Father Bernard Prince, who had served as Murphy's assistant and could be seen as his natural successor. All that changed when it became clear that Ryan, with his impressive résumé, was available. With his academic background, his experience in running the Center of Concern and the Upper Canada province of the Jesuits and his wide range of international contacts, the bishops regarded Ryan as uniquely qualified to be general secretary. Prince, disappointed at being passed over, eventually went to Rome to work with the Congregation for the Evangelization of Peoples.

In the immediate term, Ryan felt up to the task of being a secular *peritus* for the CBC, interpreting for Canadians the remarks of a pope who had just firmly denounced homosexuals in England, indirectly reprimanded dictator Ferdinand Marcos in the Philippines and come out four square against priests in politics in the war zones of Central America. A person who speaks strongly about human rights while lecturing priests and nuns about the pitfalls of political action to obtain such rights is a person whose views are open to interpretation. In that task, however, Ryan had an advantage. Before the papal visit, Dennis Murphy had asked him to accompany Bishop Sherlock and CCCB vice-president Jean-Guy Hamelin to Rome to review the latest versions of the draft speeches that Canadian officials had forwarded to the Vatican for papal perusal. Having spent two weeks working on the pope's speeches, Ryan was well placed to interpret them for the television audience.

As for the Ottawa job, Ryan was intrigued by the challenge. His work at the Center of Concern and among Canada's English Jesuits had given him a taste for leadership. Having been chosen by all the bishops would enhance his influence: Ryan could always remind a bishop that he had supported his appointment as new general secretary. He was also confident that his skills in the game of organizational politics would serve him well in the Ottawa-based organization that had to perform a delicate dance – balancing the needs of Quebec bishops and those of prelates in the rest of Canada, respecting the orthodox *diktats* from Rome while recognizing that they no longer resonated with most Canadian Catholics. There were also enough Canadian bishops who shared his Vatican II views that he felt he could advance the social justice agenda. Besides, the Social Affairs Commission – both bishops and staff – had just scored a major success with "Ethical Reflections on the Economic Crisis."

Ryan persuaded Dennis Murphy to stay around the office until Christmas. This gave the new general secretary a chance to complete the work for the CBC and make a thirty-day retreat "to make sure that I would remain free throughout the ensuing six years." After the papal visit he went to Villa Manrèse in Quebec City, where he completed the Spiritual Exercises for the third time. Being free in Ignatian terms means being free of disordered attachments, of "everything that is not God."[3] But this unusual step of making a third thirty-day retreat indicated that Ryan he had doubts about how free he would be in his new job in a more conventional sense as well. For the first time since he had left what was then the Canadian Catholic Conference in 1970, Ryan would be working for someone else, in this case Canada's hundred-odd bishops. However strong his position might be, he would not have as free a hand as he had at the Center of Concern or in the provincial's office. And he may have sensed that the CCCB in the second half of the 1980s might not be as comfortable a venue for his brand of social justice work as either of his two previous workplaces.

Meanwhile, he and David Nazar, a recently ordained Jesuit, moved into a house near the University of Ottawa, where Nazar was doing his Ph.D. on faith and culture. There were eventually a half-dozen

Jesuits living at the house on Sweetland Avenue, where visiting Jesuits and others from out of town were welcome to stay. Like Neale House in Washington, the new Jesuit community in Ottawa became a stopping place for a fascinating group of travellers. The wars in Central America were raging, with Jesuits in El Salvador and Nicaragua in the thick of regional politics, promoting peace and opposing American intervention. A Central American solidarity activist from Saskatoon or the Nicaraguan ambassador might show up for dinner, although the idea of preparing it was new to Bill Ryan. "Bill wasn't accustomed to doing his own housekeeping or cooking," chuckled David Nazar. Ryan began gamely to do the dishes while Nazar, a priest of a younger generation more adapted to domestic labour, handled the cooking, at least in the early days.

The bishops' office was within a twenty-minute stroll, but though Ryan liked to walk in the woods, he preferred to drive to 90 Parent, where he began to relearn the ropes. The floors were just as highly polished, the old oils just as gloomy, the atmosphere just as institutional as it had been fifteen years before. Times, however, had changed. The Parti Québécois, a brand new formation when Ryan had left Ottawa, was completing its second term in office in Quebec. The new Mulroney government in Ottawa was a coalition of Quebec nationalists and traditional Tories, and with Quebec's signature still absent from the repatriated constitution, no one knew what the future held on the constitutional front. The CCCB was a sort of Canada-in-miniature, replicating the tensions between Ottawa and the regions, Quebec and the rest of Canada. It alternated between French and English presidents, had separate general secretaries for the English and French sides, and used both French and English at its Ottawa headquarters well before the federal government introduced official bilingualism. While Quebec's bishops were as convinced as ever that Quebecers constituted a people, their position had become more nuanced over the years as they tried the tricky manoeuvre of moving away from an ethnic definition of peoplehood. Like their English colleagues, the Quebec bishops had moved to the left during the 1970s. In the post-repatriation period, they were worrying publicly that Quebec nationalism was becoming unhinged from the movement for social justice.

The new English general secretary was well placed to relate to the Quebec bishops. He had worked with Quebecers as a boy, knew Quebec from his academic research and had good contacts there, particularly through his friendship with Julien Harvey, the former French-

Canadian Jesuit provincial. Though the two did not share the same position on the national question, they saw eye to eye on issues of social justice. The Quebec bishops had since at least 1980 been advocating the cause of immigrant women workers, particularly those employed in the unorganized service sector. Within a few months of Ryan's arrival at the CCCB, the Social Affairs Commission published a similar message.

The Canadian bishops had in the past issued their social statements on Labour Day. Indeed, Ryan's first effort on behalf of the bishops in the mid-1960s had been a Labour Day message on poverty in Canada. Until the mid-1970s, the tradition continued, with messages on northern development, social responsibility and inequality appearing on Labour Day. By 1985, the Social Affairs Commission under Bishop Remi De Roo and lead staffer Tony Clarke had moved things up to what the secular left knew as May Day and the Catholic Church celebrated as the Feast of St. Joseph the Worker. In 1984 De Roo and Bishop Adolphe Proulx of Hull had held a press conference and toured some factories on May 1, but resurrecting the feast as part of the liturgical life of the Canadian Church did not make much headway with the CCCB Liturgy Commission. Clarke concluded that it was not the first time that Social Affairs "was rebuffed in its efforts to reach out to the broader Catholic constituency in Canada through the programs of other pastoral commissions."[4]

Nonetheless, in 1985 the commission marked the Feast of St. Joseph the Worker and International Workers' Day with "Defending Workers' Rights: A New Frontier." The short statement pointed to the growing inequality in a society "deeply stratified" between regular full-time employees and a growing number of part-time and temporary workers who lacked benefits and job security. The commission noted that John Paul II's 1981 encyclical *Laborem Exercens* had defended the basic right of workers to organize unions. It pointed to a "new frontier" for workers' rights – the struggle of women in the expanding service sector, adding that Church social teaching maintained that attempts to deny the right of workers to organize or bargain collectively was an "attack on human dignity itself." This was all very straightforward and, in itself, not terribly controversial. What did stir things up was a bland-sounding mention of a labour dispute: "These concerns for justice are evident in the current dispute at Eaton's."[5]

Workers at Eaton's wanted to unionize and were in the midst of a high-profile strike in Toronto. Within a week of the statement, Emmett Carter had sent a letter to Remi De Roo denouncing the commission for taking sides in the Eaton's strike. Why the commission had not asked for the views of the Eatons (John Craig Eaton was a personal friend) was "incomprehensible" to Carter. In a backhanded slap at Catholics who supported the preferential option for the poor, Carter wrote that the Ottawa office had made a "preferential option for the unions." Bishops, added Carter, "are not trained to be economists." There was clearly no love lost between the imperious Carter and the combative De Roo, who shot back that "unbiased neutrality is impossible."[6]

United Church staffer John Foster was well aware of the internal politicking generated by an *engagé* Church. A social democrat who worked closely with Tony Clarke on the interchurch coalitions that emerged in the 1970s, Foster faced the same response to a United Church statement critical of Eaton's. He recalled that the reaction of the corporate elite to Church comments on the Eaton's strike was stronger than it was to the CCCB's "Ethical Reflections" document: "You were entering into the industrial struggle – with a Canadian icon to boot." For Bill Ryan, what became known as the "Eaton's Statement" was an early reminder of the controversies that invariably accompanied social justice work in the Church. Once you strayed from generalizations and approached the practical details of political conflict, repercussions were bound to follow.

Socialist theologian Gregory Baum, whose stint as a *peritus* at Vatican II was followed by an academic career following the ups and downs of social activism in the Canadian churches, wrote at the time that the social message of the Canadian bishops was more akin to Latin American liberation theology than it was to the more reformist social teachings of the American Church. For Baum, "The option for the poor here…expresses a more radical imperative, in some instances, to support a political struggle to change the inherited institutions."[7] For Cardinal Emmett Carter, on the other hand, politics consisted of influencing powerful men like Ontario Premier Bill Davis and the institutions they controlled. That way you could get things done, things like winning the extension of public funding to the final grades of Ontario's Catholic school system. Bill Ryan's position was ambiguous. While he shared Baum's analysis of the need to change institutions, he was sympathetic to Carter's savvy pragmatism, if not his pro-establishment politics.

Ryan recalled that he received the draft statement late on a Friday and approved it, uneasy about having to do so in a rush because the Social Affairs Commission wanted it finalized by the weekend. Concerned about what he felt was a lack of consultation with the bishops who might have to field questions about Eaton's in a message they had not read, Ryan said that he cited Catholic social justice teaching on subsidiarity (decentralizing decision making so as not to concentrate too many decisions at the centre of an organization or structure) in reminding Social Affairs about the need to communicate in advance with bishops affected by the actions of head office. The procedural problem foreshadowed things to come.

⟶►0◄⟵

Soon after Ryan moved to Ottawa, the Canadian bishops received a summons from the Vatican. In early 1985 the pope announced an extraordinary synod for the end of November, the stated intention being to celebrate, verify and promote Vatican II twenty years after the Council. Some felt that the pope would seek to turn back the clock, closing the famous windows opened by John XXIII. Others, less pessimistic, hoped for a reaffirmation of the Council's spirit, a recognition of the legitimacy of episcopal conferences and some sort of signal that the Vatican viewed synods as having a role in Church governance. Ryan recalled the issue at the extraordinary synod of 1985 as "What about Vatican II? Was it a mistake or not?"

Such doubts were prompted by more than the pope's orthodoxy on matters doctrinal. In the spring of 1985 Cardinal Joseph Ratzinger explained his views about the aftermath of Vatican II to an Italian journalist. John Paul had appointed the German theologian in 1981 to head the Congregation for the Doctrine of the Faith, and the so-called "Ratzinger Report" sketched a gloomy message about a Church infected by catastrophic and disastrous ideas. Women were ignoring their most important function as mothers. Lay people no longer believed in the devil. Ratzinger's message made big waves in clerical circles and beyond. Was Ratzinger speaking for the pope? Did John Paul agree that the post–Vatican II period had been a setback? Asked about the upcoming extraordinary synod, the pope was coy: "Oh, I leave that sort of thing to Cardinal Ratzinger."[8]

One thing was clear. Ratzinger was a close confidant of the pope, having been the Vatican official who was consistently appointed to the Council of the General Secretariat of the Synod of Bishops and who provided John Paul with regular advice. Catholic liberals were alarmed. They could smile wryly when Ratzinger's long-time enemy Hans Küng (the theologian had been banned from teaching Catholic theology) said things like "Cardinal Ratzinger is afraid. And just like Dostoyevsky's grand inquisitor, he fears nothing more than freedom." But they knew that the principle of subsidiarity was on shaky ground in a centralized Church whose priests and nuns could be told to stay silent until they corrected their "theological imprecisions."[9] As the controversy over the Ratzinger Report raged in the months preceding the extraordinary synod, the Vatican silenced the soft-spoken Franciscan Leonardo Boff. The Brazilian proponent of liberation theology, who argued that the Church of the poor had to be a more democratic Church, was told that he had promoted "revolutionary utopianism foreign to the church."[10]

The CCCB delegation to the 1985 synod included Bill Ryan, Ukrainian Catholic Archbishop Maxim Hermaniuk, and CCCB vice-president Archbishop James Hayes of Halifax. The lead delegate for Canada was Bishop Bernard Hubert of Saint-Jean–Longueuil, who had just been unexpectedly elected president of the bishops' conference. Long active in the Social Affairs Commission, Hubert was energetic and often outspoken.

The same plenary that elected Hubert had also, at the urging of Hermaniuk, instructed its delegates to the extraordinary synod to reaffirm the spirit of Vatican II's revolution of rising expectations. The Canadian hierarchy promoted the position that, instead of being merely consultative, synods should have more deliberative power within the Church. For Bill Ryan and the liberal-minded bishops he was now advising, the keywords for the synod were "collegiality" and "subsidiarity." James Hayes recalls that the Canadians were concerned that the synod would result in blowing the whistle on these things. The pessimists at the Vatican curia, on the other hand, intoned about "unity" and "excessive secularization."

Bernard Hubert made his presence felt even before the synod got underway. At a preliminary meeting between the presidents of episcopal conferences and a group of influential cardinals, Hubert challenged Jean-Marie Lustiger of Paris over subsidiarity and collegiality, arguing that it was problematic for the Church to hold up these principles and yet fail to apply them to its own interior life. Lustiger, an influential cardinal, was not impressed. Ryan, who was quickly coming to admire Hubert, was. He later applied a favourite accolade to the Quebecer, describing him as "fearless."

At this synod the proceedings were not exclusively in Latin, and Ryan, by this time adept at working the halls of international conferences, was in his element. Neither Hayes nor Hubert had ever been to a synod and Hayes recalled that the new general secretary was remarkably effective in such situations. In the end, there was no formal rollback of Vatican II. On the other hand, the bishops interested in grounding the spirit of the Council in the actual structure of the Church had no success. There would be no permanent synod of bishops elected by the General Synod that would decide, under the pope's authority, questions about the life of the Church. These remained the preserve of the Roman curia, so the extraordinary synod turned out to be quite ordinary. In fact, the matter didn't even make its way seriously into the deliberations. The message in Bernard Hubert's carefully worded summary was clear:

> Some major problems were not discussed…the interplay between the two ecclesiologies…which continue to color present debates in the Church. One, more communitarian, emphasizes the life of the Church as People of God and the co-responsibility of all baptized. The other, more clerical, insists on the hierarchical structure of the Church, Body of Christ, and on the role of ordained ministers…. Mention was made of the preferential option for the poor, the need for inculturation of the Gospel service of the world, but none of these topics was debated, voted or taken up with a clear vision of all the implications for Christian communities and the universal Church.

Hubert also noted that the status of episcopal conferences and the principle of subsidiarity in the life of the Church were referred to committee. Yet, in spite of these disappointments, Hubert's official report sounded an optimistic note, concluding that the Roman synod was "maturing." He felt that the pope hoped synods would be more collegial.[11] Hubert shared this perspective with Bill Ryan, in spite of mounting evidence that, by the mid-1980s, the spirit of Vatican II was no longer in fashion.

On the Church-reform front, doctrinaire men like Ratzinger occupied the most influential posts in a Church that showed no signs of becoming less hierarchical and still was prepared to crush those who spoke up too loudly. The pope himself might pronounce on worker rights and issue encyclicals that proponents of social justice could usefully cite in justifying their actions. But there was a gap between what John Paul II said and what he did – or what was done in his name. Faithful Catholics who dared to put social teaching into practice and speak out clearly for their beliefs, especially in Latin America, risked the wrath of the Vatican. During the 1980s there was a heated controversy over clergy and political involvement in Nicaragua, where the Cardenal brothers, both priests (one was a Jesuit) and ministers in the leftist Sandinista government, ran afoul of the pope's insistence that priests stay out of partisan politics. Fernando Cardenal left the Jesuits (he later rejoined), while his brother Ernesto was forced out of the priesthood. In 1985 the pope made Nicaragua's Archbishop Obando y Bravo, a right-wing supporter of the *contra* rebels in his country, a cardinal.

On the social justice front, the signs of the times pointed to growing social inequality. The Social Affairs Commission had been right when it pointed to a divided society. Bill Ryan himself was fond of using economist Vassily Leontieff's observation about people starving in paradise. The emergency food banks that has sprung up in the wake of the recession of the early 1980s did not close their doors; instead they were quickly becoming a fixture in Canadian cities even as the economy boomed later in the decade. The labour market was indeed the site of a growing divide between secure and contingent (often female) workers. The response of the new Conservative government was to embrace the 1985 recommendations of the Macdonald Commission – free trade, deregulation, privatization. It was the same "structural adjustment" recipe that was being applied in the 1980s by the International Monetary Fund and the World Bank to debt-burdened Third World countries. Canada's Church-based Ecumenical Coalition for Economic Justice (formerly GATT-Fly) was quoting Father Tom Burns, a Maryknoll missionary in Peru, who described a 30 per cent increase in the number of babies who die before they learn to walk.[12]

It was against this background that Bernard Hubert and Bill Ryan came up with the idea of a comprehensive review of the operations of the CCCB – how it operated, how it was funded, who was running the show.

———⊸•⊷———

Bill Ryan and Bernard Hubert hit it off when the bishop of Saint-Jean–Longueuil took over the presidency of the CCCB just months after Ryan settled into his job as general secretary in 1985. They had met at a Catholic social justice meeting when Ryan was still Jesuit provincial and the two priests quickly realized they were on the same wavelength. Both came from large families. Both their fathers had been involved in the lumber business. Ryan, who would always pinpoint the dangerous working conditions in the sawmills where he worked as a teenager as a wellspring for his concern for social justice, was surely moved when he heard that Hubert's father had been killed in a sawmill accident. Indeed, the two men had had similar boyhood experiences. "I hardly knew my father," recalled Hubert. "When I was a small child, he had to work in the lumber camps as a forest contractor because of the Depression."

Hubert's roots were in small-town Quebec, classical college and seminary. From his youth he gravitated towards the opposition elements in the Church and in society. The kinds of ideas with which he would be identified as a bishop were already present in the circles in which he travelled. Hubert was involved with the Jeunesse Étudiante Catholique, attracted to a movement that trained young lay people who could exercise leadership without, in Hubert's words, "being subject to the clergy."[13] The JÉC rejected the otherworldiness of traditional Quebec clerical nationalism, preferring engagement with concrete issues. For Hubert and his JÉC colleagues, religion should know the world, pinpointing and confronting its problems. The young Hubert read *Le Jour*, a paper founded by Jean-Charles Harvey whose novel *Les demi-civilisés* had been banned by the archbishop of Quebec, Cardinal Rodrigue Villeneuve, "under pain of mortal sin."

But if the Quebec Church was dominated by an ultra-conservative hierarchy, it was not the monolith of English-Canadian mythology, a point Ryan had pressed in his doctoral dissertation. In 1985 he found himself making common cause with a leading Quebec churchman who had from his youth rejected the traditional positions of the Quebec Church. By the 1980s, that Church was no longer the powerful social institution it had been in the days of Bill Ryan's youth, when a local curé like Father Filiatrault of Sainte-Cécile-de-Masham would warn the women of the parish that short sleeves and short skirts were the work of the devil and instruct his flock on how to vote. Priests like Bernard Hubert and Julien Harvey welcomed the challenge of accepting and, in Hubert's words, "loving" a new pluralistic, secular Quebec where economics was the "top priority" and the population was renewed through immigration and not the birth rate. And a challenge it was. The new Quebecers were humanists who subscribed to the "myths of progress and success":

Once secure and overly dependent on divine Providence, they are now filled with self-confidence and a positivistic kind of faith. Their vision of things has become devoid of the sense of sin. The future belongs to the human person, who depends on no one. Each person possesses all that it takes to provide his or her own happiness. The myth of progress has not only awakened the aspirations of Quebecers; it has also led to illusions, deceptive hopes, individualism, callousness, inequalities, marginalization of the poor, and reduction of human development to economics.[14]

Like Bill Ryan, Quebec's clerical intellectuals did not pine for the old days. Vatican II coincided with the Quiet Revolution, and Bernard Hubert was the product of both. If the birth rate declined among Catholic Quebecers, so be it, John Paul II and Cardinal Ratzinger notwithstanding. Quebec's bishops saw modernization in pragmatic, not dogmatic, terms. This clerical cohort was similar to the generation of English-Canadian priests seized so profoundly by the spirit of the Second Vatican Council. They wanted more room for the laity, less emphasis on triumphalism and authoritarianism, more work on social justice.

During the years when Bill Ryan was trying to put legs on these ideas at the Center of Concern, Hubert was chairing the CCCB's Social Affairs Commission and helping to move the Conference to the left. Tony Clarke, who guided the move to a more *engagé* conference from the staff side, credited Hubert's leadership as the organization became increasingly outspoken on issues from Aboriginal rights to global debt. During the furore over "Ethical Reflections," Hubert had backed the statement strongly in an interview with *La Presse*. Hubert was also a bishop who tried to maintain his community roots. As bishop of Saint-Jérôme in the 1970s, he had assisted workers trying to restart a closed textile mill as a workers' co-op and helped farmers fighting against federal government expropriation for the disastrous Mirabel airport. In this he was unlike the institutional operator Ryan, whose community was the Jesuit order.

As president and general secretary of the CCCB, Hubert and Ryan began to ponder the organization's future. They would often repair to Hubert's cottage overlooking the Richelieu River, spending a weekend talking and enjoying the meals that Hubert, a man with much *joie de vivre*, liked to prepare for his guests. The two became fast friends. "We were soul buddies," Ryan recalled in describing their relationship. Many Canadians and Quebecers, including those who lead institutions based in Ottawa, do not attempt to understand the other side of the Great Divide. Like Ryan's friend Julien Harvey, Bernard Hubert was a Quebec-firster. Yet the dapper bishop was also keenly interested in the world beyond Quebec and Ryan was particularly impressed with his willingness to visit dioceses in English Canada after he became president. This effort to cross over to the other solitude was important. Like the country as a whole, the Catholic bishops' conference must contend with national-regional, interregional and, of course, English–French/Canada–Quebec issues.

If the people in their dioceses, the People of God as Vatican II characterized them, opted for an independent Quebec (as many did in the 1980 referendum), then the bishops were certainly ready to walk with them down that path. As Hubert put it in 1990, "The desire for a French-speaking, autonomous Quebec is expressed almost everywhere."[15] And just as Quebec nationalism is always a factor in Canadian politics, the nationalism of the Quebec bishops affected the CCCB. In his job as general secretary, Bill Ryan had to take it into account. According to Dennis Murphy, who had worked closely with Hubert, the bishop of Saint-Jean–Longueuil "always had the inquiry light up as to how significant he would allow the national conference to be relative to the Quebec Assemblée des Évêques." The Quebec bishops, led by Hubert, wanted room to move, space in which they could reflect, autonomously from the Canadian Church, the distinctiveness of their own society. Bishop Remi De Roo, who had arrived at the Conference at the height of the Quiet Revolution, felt that when bishops like Hubert pushed Quebec's cause, they were expressing Catholic social justice theology: people should determine their own future. "Quebec bishops are very much bishops for their own people," observed De Roo. "So whether the people of Quebec went their own way or stayed within Confederation, the Quebec bishops made it very clear they would be with their people."

Ryan's relationship with Hubert, who by the 1980s was one of the principal leaders of the Canadian bishops as well as of the bishops of Quebec, was a big help in his job as general secretary. Although Ryan had the respect and admiration of all the bishops, he was becoming as close to Hubert as he was to anyone. Like Hubert, he had learned about what it was like on the other side of the Ottawa River and, though he did not share the nationalism of Quebec's bishops, he did attempt to understand it. Their new leadership role would lead them into conflict with the lay staff of an increasingly radical Social Affairs Commission.

Ryan became the principal staff person at a time when the CCCB was in a state of flux. Although it was a great public success, the papal visit had strained the resources of the Church. The event had been costly. Despite its often well-deserved reputation for being a highly centralized, hierarchical institution, the Vatican does not pay the bill when the pope visits a country. That is ultimately left to local dioceses and the bishops' conference that they support, while all Canadians paid for the pope's security. The CCCB hired accountants from Touche Ross who calculated net costs to host dioceses of $13.5 million, though the national body ended up with a half-million-dollar surplus.[16] The visit had also been a drain on the Conference's energies, with staff, volunteers and the bishops themselves spending huge amounts of extra time in meetings, on the phone and doing the thousand tasks that had come up. People were exhilarated but they were also exhausted. As Dennis Murphy recalls:

> There had never been a moment like that and it wasn't followed up on. There was no action taken by the national conference. I can say that with the same certainty at the diocesan level.... It was a sign of the fact that though the Conference was able to mount this significant national event, it couldn't come together both in terms of saying, "We're going to come up with strategies to follow up." And it couldn't say, "We're going to spend money on that." It really wasn't there.

For someone like Bill Ryan, adept at reading the signs of the times, it was clear that things had changed since his previous stint at 90 Parent Street in the optimistic 1960s. The Conference had been in expansionary mode well into the 1970s. By the mid-1980s, however, the Quebec bishops had long been feeling the squeeze of declining church attendance and those in the rest of Canada were starting to sense a shift as well. In 1965, 88 per cent of Quebec Catholics attended mass twice a month. Astonishingly, twenty years later, only 38 per cent participated regularly, with most nominal Catholics attending only the trinity of ceremonies – the wedding, the baptism, the funeral. In English Canada the numbers were less dramatic but still significant, with twice-monthly attendance dropping from 69 to 49 per cent of Catholics.[17]

The CCCB is supported by a per capita "tax" that each diocese pays to the national office, but that tax is based not on numbers of people in the pews but on Statistics Canada's data. The more people in a diocese who tell the census takers that they are Catholic, the more the local bishop pays to the Conference. This put particular pressure on bishops in Quebec, where most francophones were still identifying themselves as Catholic but not showing up at Mass – or putting money in the collection plate. The Quebec bishops continued to support the Canadian Conference, but the financial outlook underscored their feeling that whatever could be done at the provincial level should be done there. Subsidiarity made fiscal sense.

Quebec was not the only part of the country with its own bishops' conference. Ontario, always a dominant player in any pan-Canadian organization, had its own organization, as did the smaller eastern and western regions. And bishops from large, rich dioceses like Emmett

Carter's Toronto, swollen in the 1950s and 1960s by Catholic immigration from Italy, Portugal and Poland, had more power than those from Hubert's Saint-Jean–Longueuil, where the proportion of Catholics who practised their religion fell from 65 per cent in 1961 to 27 per cent in 1971. All the time-honoured Canadian questions are always emerging at the CCCB: Who does what? How autonomous should the regions be? Added to these were the questions that can confound any organization, large or small, national or local, private or public: What is the role of staff? Is the organization structured in the best possible way? How is the place managed?

John Sherlock had approached Ryan about taking the job as general secretary. The bishop of London was just ending his tenure as CCCB president and was confident that the Jesuit was what the Conference needed at the time. "Bill Ryan is an idealist but also a cold-blooded realist," Sherlock said. "It didn't take him five minutes to perceive the situation at the conference." One element in that situation, Sherlock noted, was simmering regional resentment of the national office: "It was the feeling of many bishops that they had no say over the affairs of the Conference." Sherlock also recalled that some bishops were becoming anxious about the political tilt to the left among the leadership of Catholic organizations, citing the Canadian Catholic Organization for Development and Peace and the Conference's own Social Affairs Commission: "Bishops perceived that the social affairs office was working with social advocacy groups that contained people hostile to the Catholic view of the sacredness of life. It is the task of the general secretary to make sure that everyone maintains complete coherence with the policy of the conference."

The bishops had established the CCODP as an independent Third World development group during the heady days of expansion in the 1960s, but its critique of capitalist development agitated Emmett Carter. Long a sturdy anti-communist, Carter saw the CCODP as too radical, doing too much social justice work and not enough evangelizing. He couldn't rein it in because it was controlled by a lay board and influenced by Quebecers, so he simply cut his annual contribution, causing a flap in Catholic circles.

"The sacredness of life" is, of course, shorthand for vigorous Catholic opposition to abortion. Tony Clarke, lead staffer at the Social Affairs Commission, was in the years following "Ethical Reflections" participating in active coalition-building. It was a time when many on the left were searching for effective alternatives to orthodox notions of class struggle and theorizing about the potential political traction of "social movements." This meant the peace movement, then swollen by citizens worried about the Reagan Administration's arms build-up and cruise missile testing in Canada (the Church funded the disarmament group Project Ploughshares). It meant the Central American solidarity movement opposed to the obscene brutalities being inflicted by U.S.-funded death squads in El Salvador (the Church was in the vanguard, funding the Interchurch Committee on Human Rights in Latin America and numerous other "development" organizations). It meant the environmental movement, the anti-poverty/social justice movement, and other movements with which the dozen-odd interchurch coalitions spawned in the 1960s and 1970s identified. It also meant the women's movement and, as such, groups that countered the official Catholic support of "life" with a vigorous defence of "choice." When John Sherlock tackled Social Affairs for its ties to pro-abortion feminists, Clarke countered by pointing out that while some bishops might be feeling the heat from their colleagues close to the anti-abortion movement, they should also put themselves in the shoes of movement-building feminists trying to defend themselves for working in coalition with the Catholic hierarchy.

All of which put Bill Ryan in a bit of a spot. He had in the past been a keen backer of the idea of a Coalition of Canadians for Development, a (rather fuzzy) amalgam that lumped business and government with labour, youth, minority and citizens' groups as those "most actively concerned with poverty problems."[18]

In that context in 1969, he had urged the Church to embrace people's power and the "Saul Alinsky approach of confrontation." Ryan had also spent his career in leadership positions providing political space for people, such as Bill Callahan at the Center of Concern and Doug McCarthy at the Ignatius Farm Community, who were inclined to radical experimentation of the sort that he never engaged in himself. He had made a determined effort to ensure that the Center of Concern was independent from the control of the official Church. And as Jesuit provincial, he had ample room to manoeuvre. Things at the CCCB were different. Although he was a shrewd institutional poker player, he was now part of an institution that had its limits. In the end, the idealism and realism described by John Sherlock brought home the hard fact that institutional politics are like other politics – the art of the possible. And what had seemed possible fifteen years previously was not necessarily possible in the mid-1980s.

As soon as Ryan and Hubert started working together at the CCCB, it was obvious that they were under pressure to cut the budget. Ryan, who was used to working in organizations that were in expansionary mode, balked and suggested a move that would both buy time and placate anxious bishops who felt that they didn't have a handle on the organization. A task force of prominent bishops could look into all aspects of the organization. When Hubert asked how such a task force might work, Ryan suggested approaching Emmett Carter, with whom Hubert differed on many important issues although they always maintained cordial personal relations. With an early sign of approval from the influential Toronto cardinal, Ryan was confident that the project would float. And it did.

"Hubert put it before the board and Carter seconded it," explained Ryan. "Well, you had it." For Ryan, running this task force was a high point of his period at the CCCB, a chance to undertake a project with "top bishops" like Sherlock, Hubert, James Hayes of Halifax and Robert Lebel of Valleyfield (bishops Ryan described as "open and really fearless"). Once the bishops gave their go-ahead for a task force, Ryan contacted the consulting arm of the same firm that had done the audit on the papal tour. Three management consultants from Touche Ross would undertake a study of the organization of the Conference, its structure and priorities, under the guidance of Ryan and the task force of bishops. To fund the study, Ryan secured a grant from a Dutch Catholic foundation he had tapped in the past that was particularly disposed to Jesuit-backed initiatives. Cost-conscious bishops who had been eager to acquire Ryan's services in the first place were doubtless impressed.

On one level, the task force was a straightforward organizational review of the kind that had by the 1980s become standard operating procedure for corporations, government departments and even non-governmental organizations. Management consulting had become big business and a growing number of people with MBAs sold their services to organizations anxious to rethink the way they did things. A blizzard of buzzwords – from downsizing and rightsizing to the ubiquitous "excellence" – began to blow. Canada's bishops had never brought in outside professionals to help analyze the way their conference worked and Bill Ryan, who was always keen on those he considered the Top People, was glad to engage three management consultants from Touche Ross. The leader of the Touche Ross team was Bob Brouillard, an articulate organizational analyst with a wide range of experience in the million-dollar world of public- and private-sector consulting. Although the

CCCB contract was a small engagement in dollar terms, Brouillard found it to be one of the most interesting jobs he had ever undertaken because the bishops and their employees were interesting people and their organization highly complex. He recalled the bishops themselves as being open, trusting and "almost naively unquestioning" about recommendations from those who had their confidence. He also discovered that there was no one in whom the bishops placed more confidence than Bill Ryan. Brouillard described the bishops as "phenomenally" respectful of their general secretary: "He had an absolutely superb political nose."

Ryan needed every ounce of his political savvy to handle the social justice dossier at the CCCB. Of course, Ryan had long been pushing anti-poverty issues and prided himself on his contacts with Latin America's leading liberation theologians. But at the bishops' conference the difficult and often contradictory business of the Church's leftward tilt was further complicated by a number of factors. One was the centre-versus-regions dynamic. "It does not do much good to continue to have excellent social justice statements made nationally unless there are regional and especially local facilities to put legs on these statements for ordinary Catholics," he said later. "It was just such pressure that set the task force to rethink the shape of the CCCB and its services."

In addition, as general secretary, Bill Ryan was in charge of the Social Affairs Commission staff, but the bishops who defined the direction of the Commission were in turn his bosses. This bureaucratic tangle made for unclear lines of authority. Although Ryan might have been tempted to dive into social justice issues, they were not part of his direct job description. Dennis Murphy, whose background was in religious education, recalled the very real difficulty he had not sticking his nose into the workings of that office when he took over as general secretary. What's more, added Murphy, the Social Affairs Commission was in the vanguard of Conference activity, "always riding out like scouts ahead of the Conference, searching out the enemy." It was the commission, after all, that had come out with the much-publicized "Ethical Reflections" document criticizing capitalist development.

This made Ryan's relationship with Tony Clarke – and the task force's approach to the Social Affairs Commission – particularly fraught with tension. By this time Clarke had been working at the CCCB for some fifteen years, usually in alliance with outspoken, left-leaning bishops who sat on the Social Affairs Commission: Remi De Roo, Bernard Hubert and Adolphe Proulx of Hull. An outspoken radical and Canadian nationalist, Clarke was suspicious of the task force, in part because he distrusted management consultants from a firm that he identified with the draconian policies of the Thatcher government in Britain, in part because of the strains then emerging at the CCCB. Clarke later attributed the tensions to a right-wing coup by an alliance of business interests and conservative clerics, a coup that he believed effectively led the bishops to retreat from their position of leadership on social justice. He would eventually accuse the bishops of a "moral abdication."

What prompted Clarke to conclude that Bill Ryan's Task Force on Future Directions was part of this coup? Was there indeed such a coup? The answer to the second question is "not really," although the Church was becoming less socially engaged for a complex set of reasons that included an increasingly conservative episcopate. The answer to the first is no less complex. It is bound up with changing times, organizational infighting and a clash of personalities. Both questions point up what would be one of the most difficult periods in Bill Ryan's career, a career that had hardly been devoted to moving the Church in a conservative direction.

⎯⎯⎯➤◦◄⎯⎯⎯

Remi De Roo, bishop of Victoria, spent seventeen years on the Social Affairs Commission of the CCCB. More than any other bishop from English Canada, De Roo was associated publicly with the increasing radicalism of the Canadian Church in the years after Vatican II. A Manitoban of Belgian descent, De Roo had been a stalwart supporter of the CCCB's social justice and interchurch coalition work. He was the bishop most often called on by the media to explain the Church's latest statement against the arms race or in favour of workers' rights. In a 1981 public letter promoting a new international economic order, he had urged the Canadian government to abandon policies that ruin the environment while benefiting the rich and exploiting the poor. Conrad Black, the caricature corporate mogul whom the left would have had to invent had he not sprung unbidden from Upper Canada College, once slammed De Roo as "egregious" in the course of an attack on Catholic social activism. Black, a convert to Catholicism, was glad that De Roo had been "sacked" as chair of the Social Affairs Commission.[19]

At the 1985 annual meeting that elected Bernard Hubert president of the CCCB, Remi De Roo was indeed defeated in his bid for another term as chair of the activist commission. Whether he was "sacked" or not is a matter of interpretation. Tony Clarke attributed the end of De Roo's tenure as chair, coming as it did a few months after the controversial statement mentioning Eaton's that so offended Emmett Carter, to a "carefully orchestrated strategy" by Carter, who managed to get De Roo replaced by a Calgary bishop "who had openly challenged the Commission in the late seventies on behalf of the petroleum magnates." According to Clarke, De Roo's confidence was "temporarily shattered."[20]

For his part, Bill Ryan attributed De Roo's departure to bureaucratic rather than political reasons. Ryan maintained that Clarke failed to mention that the new rules of procedure adopted by the Conference two years previously "foresee a Bishop remaining a member a commission for a maximum of two terms of two years each" and that De Roo had been with Social Affairs for eleven years, chairing it for five. Yet Ryan still used the verb "dumped" to describe what happened in 1985.[21] Whatever the origin of De Roo's failure to be elected chair of the commission in 1985, the aftermath was clear enough to Clarke. It unfolded on Bill Ryan's watch. This was how Clarke characterized it:

> In the period between 1986 and 1988 steps were taken behind the scenes to work out some sort of compromise between church and state over the economy. The central issue over which this compromise was eventually reached was the free trade deal. To some extent, the foundation for such a church-state compromise had already been laid during the papal visit, which had served to cement working relationships not only between the bishops' conference and the federal government, but also between business leaders and local dioceses. Now that De Roo was out of the way, there were many people in Ottawa and on Bay Street who were confident that the Commission would no longer cause trouble.[22]

Tony Clarke liked to mix it up with people on the other side of the political fence and had little use for what he called the "elite accommodation" approach to social change that he saw as the dominant trend at the CCCB when he first arrived in the early 1970s, soon after Ryan's departure for Washington. "The important thing [was] for the social action office to know the ministers and who's shaping things on Parliament Hill and that's how we bring about change," Clarke recalled. "That was a model that Bill certainly promoted." Soon after Clarke arrived he was surprised to learn that a Liberal minister like Allan MacEachen would ask the Social Affairs office to prepare speeches for him to deliver. Although maintaining working links with an influential left-leaning member of the governing party – and one who happened to be a Catholic – would have been just the ticket as far as the pragmatic Bill Ryan was concerned, it was not a strategy that appealed to Clarke: "I have a different kind of formation in terms of how you bring about change." For Clarke, the most important allies were not the Top People but the ones at the bottom – or at least those who represented them or acted on their behalf. Trade unionists, anti-poverty organizers, Native and feminist leaders and other opponents of the status quo – these were Clarke's comrades-in-arms. His approach to politics was different from Ryan's, which he described as "the priest in relationship to the king – the Jesuit model."

The differences between Clarke and Ryan emerged before Ryan and Hubert came up with the idea of their Task Force on Future Directions. A notable confrontation took place at a meeting of the Social Affairs Commission in 1986, in the aftermath of the second consecutive CCCB statement on the feast of St. Joseph the Worker. If the May Day statement the previous year had irked Emmett Carter because it was too strongly pro-union, the 1986 statement, "Supporting Labour Unions: A Christian Responsibility," must have also stuck in the cardinal's craw. But the main antagonist in this case was not Toronto's conservative cardinal but Clarke's former ally Bernard Hubert, who had often clashed with Carter in the past. The Conference president lashed out angrily at the commission staff for the statement on labour unions, arguing that this was an issue best handled in the regions and that there had been inadequate consultation with the bishops. It was a decisive moment for Clarke, who felt that he had been ambushed in the meeting. The statement had called on the churches to join with trade unions and other social movements in building a broader social movement to create a new society based on social justice. Clarke told Hubert that it had received the required approval of the general secretary. He later recalled: "In my defence I said I had the authority to proceed. [Ryan] just cowered when I said that. I can almost remember his physical moves. Instead of the president asking Ryan, he went on. It was a difficult moment for me. Hubert could have asked Ryan and Ryan could have said, 'I did give him the authority.'"

Bernard Hubert, who died in 1996, cannot give his version of what was surely a pivotal event in the relations among three of the most highly placed promoters of social justice in the Church. Bill Ryan corroborates Clarke's version, at least as far as the ambush aspect of it was concerned. "I remember very well making a deal with Hubert: 'Okay, let's let this thing go. You talk to Clarke,'" remembered Ryan. "Up until then I had carried all these fights and I just said, 'To hell with this. I'm not going to talk to him.' I wasn't going to try to defend Tony. I was happy to see him blasted."

Ryan had been back at the CCCB for eighteen months and was frustrated with what he saw as Clarke's lack of consultation with both himself and Hubert. The way he saw it, Clarke tended to arrive with a social justice statement at the last minute, pressuring him into giving him the go-ahead. As general secretary, he did not want to be rushed into things and felt that the statements should be going through a wider consultation process. "What he was doing more and more was keeping Hubert and myself out of this until the last moment," said Ryan. "And Hubert was getting frustrated."

Another reason for the growing tension between Clarke and his bosses was the Quebec lens through which Ryan and Hubert viewed Canada's episcopal conference. They were both ultra-conscious of the delicate Canada-Quebec dynamic at the CCCB. For Ryan and Hubert, restructuring the CCCB through the task force was at the top of their agenda. Tony Clarke, on the other hand, was very much a Canadian nationalist whose energies were soon to be focused on the fight against a free trade pact that Brian Mulroney had once rejected out of hand but was now promoting. By 1987, Clarke suspected that Hubert was not opposed to the looming free trade deal that he saw as an attack on Canadian sovereignty and a step on the road to a Thatcherite dismantling of the Canadian welfare state.

The contretemps at 90 Parent after 1986 was also rooted in a clash of personalities. Clarke, Hubert and Ryan all had strongly held beliefs. Each saw himself as a leader. None was without significant ego. Clarke felt a sense of betrayal that his former ally Hubert had now, as CCCB president, developed a close working relationship with Ryan. He did not have the same comradely relationship with the Jesuit that he had with bishops Adolphe Proulx and Remi De Roo, long-time social justice stalwarts on the Social Affairs Commission. For his part, although he very seldom wore a Roman collar, Ryan saw himself first and foremost as a man of the cloth while Clarke was a man of the left. Both were believers in social justice, but their tactical priorities did not mesh. By the mid-1980s, Clarke was embroiled in building a movement against the free trade agreement and the wave of privatization and deregulation being pushed by the business class, while Ryan's priorities were tied up with the workings of the CCCB. If Ryan thought that movement building was important, it was secondary to the task force and the job at hand.

The Task Force got the formal go-ahead at the CCCB's annual meeting in the fall of 1987. By this time Bernard Hubert's two-year tenure as president had run its course. But James Hayes, the new president, readily agreed with Bill Ryan's proposal that Hubert continue on as chair of the task force with the result that the Quebec bishop, according to Ryan, "never got out of Tony's hair." The task force included several of the most influential bishops in the country but was still a Bernard Hubert–Bill Ryan show, with Ryan as point man. Although it was a restructuring and not primarily a cost-cutting exercise, Ryan was well aware that local bishops were very conscious of the money they were forwarding to Ottawa. He also knew that if the organization was to continue to be effective, the bishops had to maintain a sense of what would soon be called "ownership" of a conference that was not the only organization to which they belonged. Each region now had its own episcopal assembly. There was a feeling of decentralization in the air.

Such were the organizational issues that were on the minds of Bill Ryan and the Canadian bishops who trooped off to the Vatican's long-awaited Synod on the Laity in 1987.

⟫·◦·⟪

Jokes about the slowness and conservatism of the Vatican bureaucracy abound. Asked how many people work at the Vatican, John XXIII quipped, "About half." In the early 1990s an apocryphal story made the rounds. A newborn baby had been found in the Congregation for the Doctrine of the Faith. Cardinal Ratzinger, the supremo of the Congregation, was apparently shocked and appalled. The squalling babe might, after all, belong to one of the priests. One of his assistants assured him that this was not possible: "Nothing is completed in nine months around here." Another monsignor backed his colleague up, adding, "A baby is the product of love, so it's surely not by us."

The Vatican is a feudal institution, the pope is the presiding monarch, and it is the job of his courtiers to carry out his will. For the Roman curia, the Church is the pope and vice versa. It is not surprising that governance is highly authoritarian. When the bishops who gathered at the Second Vatican Council got a taste of participation in the governance of a massively complex global institution that had long been dominated by Italians in Rome, they appreciated it. If there was one channel through which reform-minded bishops could institutionalize the Council's momentum, it was the synod, or representative meetings of bishops (the term that had once been applied to local, regional or even ecumenical meetings where Church issues could be discussed and even resolved). Synods are common in Eastern churches and it was Patriarch Maximos IV Saigh who suggested at the Vatican Council's second session in 1963 that synods continue after the Council. What the Church needed, said Maximos, was a college of bishops "to assist the pope, only at his request, in governing the Church and providing for its needs."[23] The patriarch would go on to extend the idea, suggesting that the synod of bishops be "supreme" and that "all the Roman departments must be subject to this."[24]

By 1987, when Bill Ryan attended the Synod on the Laity, the meetings had been much diluted. The extraordinary synod two years previously had been a flop. Janet Somerville, a Catholic journalist and friend of Ryan's who accompanied him and four Canadian bishops, concluded that the Synod on the Laity "certainly did cottonwool into nothing" all the practical suggestions on women in the Church. But Somerville, who served as an adviser to the Canadian bishops at the synod, added hopefully that "we certainly didn't pedal backward." Romeo Maione, another seasoned Canadian student of the Vatican scene who went to the synod as a lay observer, observed that bishops had yet to win the right to participate in decision making.[25]

This was Ryan's third Roman synod. A high point of his career had been the Justice in the World synod in 1971, when he had written speeches for a group of high-profile Canadian bishops fired with the spirit of Vatican II. Ryan attributed the success of the 1971 synod to momentum from Vatican II that had been boosted by Pope Paul's 1967 encyclical *Populorum Progressio* and the historic Latin American bishops meeting in Medellín the following year. "It was to be the closest the synod would ever get to being deliberative," said Ryan. Ryan's former teacher and colleague Phil Land, who had more Roman experience than Ryan, agreed that 1971 had been a success, in good measure because the Vatican curia had on that occasion not "corralled" the general secretary of the council of the synod. But times had changed. Land felt that the 1987 synod on the laity "failed miserably."[26]

The failure occurred despite the efforts of the Canadian contingent. Along with a handful of *periti* and lay observers, Ryan was accompanied by CCCB president James Hayes, John Sherlock, Maxim Hermaniuk, Jean-Guy Hamelin and Donat Chiasson. Ryan said before the synod that the biggest challenge for the meeting – and the Church in general – was to encourage co-operation between clergy and laity, that the Church had to consult honestly and openly at every level and on every question.[27] Ryan's hopes were echoed in the opening address by Hayes, who urged the Church to allow the laity more participation, accrediting lay men and women as well as priests at future synods. This was the Church envisioned by Vatican II. For Hayes, it was a matter of making sure that the "whole people of God" have an active role in dealing with matters affecting their church.[28] Jean-Guy Hamelin, the former Social Affairs director of the CCCB and by this time bishop of Rouyn-Noranda, followed by pointing to the striking contrast between the position of women in Canadian society and in the Church. Hamelin noted that women had been intimately associated with the Christian mission in the earliest Christian communities and that the Church had to "face some facts," including the women's movement, a sign of the times by the 1980s. He called on the Church to rescind rules that bar women from altar service and prevent lay Catholics from assuming positions of responsibility – save those requiring ordination.[29]

The synod itself relied on a traditional format, having each participant (there were some 220 bishops in attendance in 1987) give an eight-minute speech outlining his views. Such a way of proceeding, which one delegate described charitably as tedious, is not designed to stimulate debate or constructive exchange of ideas. It was also time-consuming. The official language was still Latin and, although many spoke in their own languages, simultaneous interpretation was spotty and in the wake of the meeting Ryan recorded an official plea for the use of vernacular languages in the final working documents. The long days of speechifying were followed by more fruitful meetings of small groups (*circuli minores*) in which participants got a chance to discuss the issues and thrash out resolutions. Written in several languages, these were submitted back to a large group of theologians, workshop reporters, secretaries and translators. What Romeo Maione described as "the debacle" and Ryan called "the overnight meltdown" ensued. This group met in the evening and had to produce a final document by eight the next morning. The result reflected the speed and unwieldiness of the process.

"The Canadians rightfully felt that the fruit of the bishops' work was truncated or even often ignored," recalled Ryan. "It was clear that by this synod the Canadian bishops were getting fed up with the heavy-handedness of the curia and the synod secretariat. Their love for secrecy and Latin showed up continually."

Frustration threatened to boil over. The Canadians had tried to consult the people in the pew, surveying thousands of practising Catholics. Two years after Ryan became their general secretary, the bishops

learned that although 86 per cent of Catholics believed that their Church
had changed for the better since Vatican II, 57 per cent felt that its
health was fair, poor or very poor.[30] The survey data seemed to confirm
what most clerics could see: there was disquiet among the laity who
were still showing up regularly. The Canadian bishops knew that the
laity – and especially lay women – wanted Rome to open up decision-
making at all levels of the Church. Yet the Vatican officials who ran the
synod were ignoring these concerns. Although few bishops had any
illusions about the synod's influence – its role was strictly advisory –
they found the ham-handed approach of the authorities frustrating. The
bishops were proud men, accustomed to getting their way. And if they
didn't always get their way, they certainly expected to be heard. Archbishop Chiasson, a newcomer to this sort of meeting, jumped at Ryan's
proposal that the Canadians move a vote of non-confidence in the procedures. But no sooner had he started to speak than the chair cut him off
and dressed him down for impropriety. Chiasson was badly shaken by
the experience, although Ryan recalled being proud of him and the other
bishops that day. "I came away knowing that no paths had been closed,"
recalled Ryan. "It would take a little longer. Even a lot longer."

This from-here-to-eternity feeling reflected the general mood
of a meeting where a strong sense of good will was much in evidence.
The optimism of faithful Catholics confronted with an institution steeped
in intransigence can be remarkable. Soon after the synod Janet Somerville
remarked that although no progress was made with respect to the public role women could play in the Church, there was certainly no
backpedalling because the meeting affirmed the equal human dignity of
men and women.

Another observer was Parmananda Divarkar. As one of Pedro
Arrupe's general assistants, the Indian Jesuit had been witness to endless
Roman intrigues. Admitting that the ancient forum that was the synod
had been rendered toothless by its consultative status and that there
was unlikely to be any starling change in the position of women in the
Church, Divarkar still insisted that it was a safe bet that this would eventually happen because so much had been said so forcefully on the
subject:

> On this point Jesus uttered a warning: You cannot put new wine
> in old bottles. It is very human to cherish a fond hope that per-
> haps old bottles will do if adequately reinforced.... But they will
> inevitably develop cracks and waste a lot of good wine.... For-
> tunately our supply of new wine is inexhaustible, for its source is

none other than the Lord and Giver of Life. So the good old church moves forward – staggering under the burden of our weaknesses, but ever faithful to God – as it inches its way to the third millennium.[31]

The synod offered up a lot of old bottles that had been patched and polished. Bill Ryan could not draw anything but a sunny conclusion from it all. Soon afterwards he explained it as a learning experience, describing the task of getting lay people fully accepted into the Church as "enormous," "huge" and "difficult." Yet in spite of this he explained that the further he got from the synod, the more hopeful he became about the constant growth that he saw in the Church.[32]

If the message that Ryan and Canada's bishops took to Rome was more participation in a more open Church, the reality of life in the Church was surely sobering. The social justice message, together with the injunctions against birth control and divorce, were not trickling down to the laity, so, not surprisingly, neither did the admonitions to participate in the life of the Church. In a conversation leading up to the synod, Julien Harvey pointed out that, twenty years after the Council, fewer than 80 out of 240 parishes in Montreal, his own diocese, had parish councils. Janet Somerville, another close friend of Ryan's, acknowledged that lay people had not yet occupied the space that had already been made available for shared decision making and shared pastoral life. She also pointed to the many parishes and dioceses without pastoral councils. Catholic lay people had not yet built up the organizational capacity that would enable them to participate.[33]

They came from a tradition steeped in authoritarianism and paternalism. Participation was not part of the culture that Catholic women and men had grown up in. Nor was it on the agenda being set by the men at the top, or by the men they were appointing to replace the bishops Bill Ryan had been working with for twenty-five years.

⋙●⋘

Back in Ottawa, Ryan continued to work closely with the Touche Ross consultants who were doing the CCCB's organizational review. The consultants interviewed each of the country's 100-plus bishops, canvassing their opinions about their relations with the Conference, asking questions, preparing slide presentations. There were also consultations with the various commissions, the committees of bishops who, together with staff, concerned themselves with missions, ecumenism, theology, social affairs, canon law and so on. Ryan attempted to use the

Touche Ross consultants, people who were well versed in organizational theory, to come to a better understanding of how the CCCB actually worked and how it might work better.

The organization was already structurally loose and decentralized, with individual bishops – the so-called "princes of the Church" – enjoying considerable autonomy. The job of general secretary was a tricky one, described by lead consultant Bob Brouillard as "like managing a club – the guys have to want to go where you want to take them." The autonomy of the bishops was also duplicated in the commissions. Staff reported to both the bishops on their particular commission and the general secretary. But, as Dennis Murphy explained, the general secretary was accountable to the bishops as well. So the general secretary had the job of coordinating a relatively independent staff. Brouillard recalled the uncertain authority invested in the job: "Was he just providing bed and breakfast for everybody?" In other words, the old question "Who's in charge here?" was as important at the CCCB as in any organization. Coupled with the inclination to regionalization, it made for a complex dynamic.

As far as Social Affairs was concerned, its commission recognized that things had changed in the five years since "Ethical Reflections." Tony Clarke had lost one of his main allies with the sudden death of Adophe Proulx in 1987. The bishop of Hull, outspoken in his defence of human rights in Central America, had chided the Vatican for the inaction of its regional representatives during the civil wars there. Following Bernard Hubert's moving eulogy at the funeral mass, the papal nuncio rose to lecture the mourners, telling the two thousand people present that the Church ministered to the rich as well as the poor and reminding the laity to respect the authority of the hierarchy.

Tony Clarke acknowledged that the "solidarity" generated by "Ethical Reflections" had "almost evaporated" and that a new strategy was needed to reconnect with the majority of bishops. In 1988, just as the controversy over free trade was building to the political crescendo of the federal election that fall, the CCCB's annual plenary approved a "Work and Solidarity" project designed by the Social Affairs Commission for implementation on a community and diocesan level.[34] The hope was that the CCCB could reconnect with its local base by addressing the disconnect between economic growth and mass prosperity then becoming apparent across the country as the boom of the 1980s failed to trickle down and the gap between good jobs and bad jobs widened.

When the task force issued its preliminary report in early 1989, Clarke felt that the Social Affairs Commission was being "targeted," pointing to several bits of phraseology that he found particularly galling. The task force accused the commission of building an "independent empire," applying Catholic social teaching in "unsatisfactory ways" and issuing statements that showed signs of "hasty and uncritical preparation." An angry Clarke pointed out that these accusations were unsubstantiated. From Ryan and Hubert's point of view, the criticisms were all about the Commission's lack of consultation with the bishops, who saw Clarke as having become involved too deeply in too many coalitions and social movements, wearing the hat of the Catholic bishops and, implicitly or explicitly, acting and speaking on their behalf. A few months later, in May 1989, Clarke issued a formal rebuttal, charging that the task force's goal was not to reorganize but to neutralize the commission and that "in recent years there have been plenty of signals from certain quarters of the CCCB and the corporate elite calling on the Commission to abandon its prophetic approach to…social justice concerns."[35] This was a reference to the Emmett Carter–Conrad Black nexus that Clarke was convinced was operating behind the scenes to scuttle Catholic social justice work.

The task force was concerned with the organization of the CCCB and not primarily with its social message. Its most important recommendation was to eliminate the CCCB's "Pastoral Team," a consultative committee of six bishops and six commission directors (CCCB employees) that had been the only central forum for bishop-staff discussion. This was where the "harmonizing" of the work of the CCCB commissions had, in theory, been taking place. The Social Affairs Commission had for several years not even been part of this Pastoral Team. The task force consultants came up with the idea of a more conventional corporate structure, a powerful programs and priorities committee comprising the bishops heading up the commissions and the two general secretaries. Commission directors would not be part of this new committee, an arrangement designed to clarify the confused lines of authority under which the directors had had two bosses, the bishops who chaired their commissions and the general secretaries.

Shuffling the bureaucratic furniture would take care of some of the conflicts concerning the relative importance of social justice work at the CCCB; certainly, the fact that the commission that worked on social justice had not even been participating in the organization's main coordinating team had been a key factor giving rise to such tensions.

Other factors at play included the clash of personalities between Clarke, on the one hand, and Ryan and Hubert, on the other. Clarke's tendency to ride out like a scout "ahead of the Conference, searching out the enemy" cannot be ignored, nor can the fact that Ryan's ability to play the game of institutional politics tended to trump Clarke's charismatic energy, some of which was perhaps misplaced, at least in tactical terms. Clarke, preoccupied with coalition-building and assuming that the institutional landscape of the late 1980s was similar to that of the late 1970s, overestimated the willingness or ability of the Catholic hierarchy to take radical – or even liberal – stands on the hottest issues of the day.

Remi De Roo recalled the heyday of the Canadian bishops' social activism, describing a "fledgling bishops' conference that caught fire with Vatican II." The Victoria bishop extended the metaphor by comparing the CCCB to "a football team that's on fire" and described his friend Tony Clarke as something akin to a star quarterback. "Not that he didn't work in a team," explained De Roo, "but he was just so strong that he would carry the team." By contrast, Ryan was more like a quiet coach carefully mapping the play: "Ryan by temperament would be more inclined to diplomacy, trying to understand everybody. And Tony Clarke as a result would see Ryan as too soft on the transnationals, as closer in a sense to Emmett Carter who hobnobs with the big powerful people, the Conrad Blacks…. He was more confrontational, more argumentative, not the listener that Bill Ryan was." De Roo and his more conservative colleague John Sherlock each used a figure of speech from another sport, horse racing, to describe the dynamic at the CCCB. "Bill had to rein Tony in," said Sherlock. De Roo concurred:

> I could see Bill Ryan as general secretary having to pull in the reins on Tony Clarke. Put Bill Ryan in his position as general secretary as distinct from the Bill Ryan of social justice of 1964–70. You have a Bill Ryan who has to try to keep all the Canadian bishops happy and is no doubt listening carefully to the more cautious wing, the Emmett Carters. [Carter] was quite offended that the bishops had been harder on the transnational corporations than they deserved. [Ryan and Clarke] had a similar vision of social justice. When it comes to tactics, they're considerably different. Ryan's strategy would be to listen far more and be a little more careful. It's not that he would be against Marxist analysis and would just use it very cautiously, whereas the Alinsky

school, Tony Clarke, would spend less time on the intellectual/academic side of that: "Let's get this thing done."

The reining-in process culminated in the final report of the Ryan–Hubert task force. Aside from the new programs and priorities committee, the Task Force recommendations on reorganization – overwhelmingly accepted by the bishops at their 1990 plenary meeting – included the elimination of the research position from the Social Affairs Commission and the need to "rethink" its work with ecumenical social justice coalitions, collaborate more with other commissions and conduct more consultation both with bishops and with "popular and professional groups."[36] Needless to say, Clarke saw these moves as part of a retreat from active social justice work. His office lost its research staff person and he was particularly irked with the description of his work with social movements and interchurch coalitions as "excessively time-consuming," a phrase repeated three times in his 1995 book *Behind the Mitre: The Moral Leadership Crisis in the Canadian Catholic Church.*[37] Clarke did not notice the irony: Ryan, who had helped to lay the foundations for the interchurch coalitions (particularly the radical Ecumenical Coalition for Economic Justice), who had long seen impeccable research as something crucial to an effective social critique, now found himself in the position of urging the bishops to rethink their support of these groundbreaking initiatives.

How did this come to pass? Ryan himself emphasizes organizational factors, especially the lack of consultation between the Social Affairs Commission and the bishops and the need to decentralize the Conference according to the principle of subsidiarity. All of these certainly came into play during the protracted wrangle: Clarke likely got carried away with the success of "Ethical Reflections," neglecting his political base and devoting insufficient energy to cultivating sympathetic bishops, consulting them, bringing them along and thereby strengthening support for social justice.

But these were not the only factors. The final recommendations of the Ryan–Hubert Task Force noted hopefully that the 1988–89 "Work and Solidarity" project was an example of an undertaking that promised to address the reservations and concerns the task force had about the Social Affairs Commission's approach to social justice.[38] Work and Solidarity was supposed to involve Catholics at the grassroots, in dioceses across the country. However, the project that had been backed by all the bishops at their annual assembly was a failure. Decentralization is a good idea, as is consultation, but the old saw about the spirit being willing but the flesh being weak came into play. The CCCB's fiftieth anniversary history of its social justice work observed delicately that "it was not easy to maintain an animation exercise of this magnitude, given varying staff capabilities and commitments to social justice in diocesan offices across the distinct regions of the country."[39] Work and Solidarity fizzled out halfway through its second phase.

The problem was those "varying" commitments. The Catholic Church is an odd combination of a highly centralized authority (Rome, the pope, the Vatican) and decentralized outposts under the control of individual bishops. The centre has the power of appointment. But, once appointed, local bishops cannot be forced into supporting the initiatives of particular groups, whether the local Right-to-Lifers or social justice activists. The pope may rail against birth control or scold bosses for trampling the rights of workers, but the local episcopal authorities decide for themselves what to emphasize. Some bishops may tackle global poverty by doing everything they can to work for a moratorium on Third World debt while others may just choose to support the Save a Family Plan. By the late 1980s, enthusiasm for social justice work was on the wane among Canada's bishops.

The intense debates over free trade contributed to the strained relations between Bernard Hubert and Tony Clarke, while underlining the tricky position in which Bill Ryan found himself as a leader of a binational episcopal conference. English-Canadian nationalists like Clarke were passionately opposed to the free trade deal being pushed by the corporate sector and the Mulroney Tories. But Ryan, who might have been expected to be wary of trade deals that strengthened the rights of capital, was preoccupied with the task force. Though Quebec nationalists like Bernard Hubert might oppose the free trade deal on economic grounds, they did not do so on the basis of the threat to sovereignty that worried Canadian nationalists. This made it difficult for Clarke to sell opposition to free trade to a group of bishops that included establishment clerics like Emmett Carter and standoffish Quebecers as well as people who shared Clarke's view of social justice. Ryan saw his job at the CCCB as managing these tensions, keeping all the balls in the air. His concern for social justice and Canadian sovereignty came second.

In 1987 free trade opponents convened a "Maple Leaf Summit" in Ottawa, which in turn led to the Pro-Canada Network, described by Tony Clarke as potentially "the largest broad-based coalition of its kind in the country."[40] The PCN eventually emerged as a key player in the

1988 election and Clarke, ignoring the advice of Ryan's assistant Bernard Daly, accepted the post of co-chair of the organization just as the task force was getting underway. The problems that the free trade opponents would have with Quebec were reflected in the name they chose for their organization. Calling the group "Pro-Canada" was not likely to ingratiate the otherwise dynamic coalition to most Quebecers, particularly those with whom the Canadian nationalists wanted to connect. The Quebec left is also an unalloyed nationalist and essentially sovereignist force. Playing the English-Canadian nationalist card at a Maple Leaf Summit and pointing to the threat free trade posed to Canadian sovereignty was unlikely to play well in Quebec. The PCN had realized this by 1991, when it changed its name to the "Action Canada Network."

The CCCB was wary of getting involved in "politics" in the run-up to the election. While Tony Clarke jumped into the free trade fray, in 1987 the bishops' conference issued a study document entitled "Free Trade: At What Cost? Ethical Choices and Political Challenges." The CCCB's own history of its social justice work described the document as a "non-position" with a "previously unheard of" disclaimer explaining it as a set of working documents that did not represent the official teaching of the church.[41]

As it turned out, most Canadians needed all the information they could get because of the government strategy of selling the free trade deal rather than explaining it. The Tories and the private-sector boosters played to people's fears of being left out of an increasingly globalized world while Canadian nationalists invoked the image of the border with the United States being erased – along with Canada's sovereignty and its social programs. In the end, those opposed to free trade made electoral gains in English Canada in the crucial 1988 election but lost out in Quebec, where the vote for the Mulroney Tories rose by 2 per cent over 1984. In the rest of Canada it declined by 10 per cent. As in the Trudeau years, the party that won Quebec won the country. It was a country that would be marked by a Tory victory that brought free trade and Meech Lake.

Because of the Ryan–Hubert task force, the CCCB was set to become a more streamlined organization. But streamlined or not, it is uncertain whether the CCCB as transmission belt for the Church's social teaching would have made a difference in debates over free trade – or the other big issues of the day. The challenge faced by Bill Ryan, Tony Clarke and other social justice advocates was clear: how to get a moral or ethical message across to the mass of Catholics at a time when fewer of these people were showing up. In the ten years between 1976 and 1985, the percentage of Canadian Catholics attending weekly Mass fell by 19 per cent. What's more, among those who did attend church regularly, only an infinitesimal number felt that Catholicism might have some impact among decision makers. Only 2 per cent of those answering a CCCB survey of the laity said that politicians or business people would be affected by their faith.[42] And Rome was still extremely cautious about "lay involvement" – the participation of Catholics in the life of their own church.

Why hadn't the social justice message trickled down from the episcopate? In an article in *Compass*, the Jesuit journal Ryan had founded as provincial, Ian Drummond, an academic critical of the bishops' social justice efforts, referred to a decade of "hectoring from the hierarchy," arguing that it had had but little effect because of human nature: "Most people are still greedy, self-seeking...reluctant to pay taxes or submit to external authority, and not deeply interested in the Third World."[43]

John Williams, a Catholic ethicist who pondered the issue at the same time, provided an alternative explanation. In an article entitled "Why Isn't Anyone Listening?" Williams noticed that the social justice statements from Canada's bishops were overwhelmingly dependent on Vatican documents and the Bible. They did not consider why biblical principles of social justice should have much traction in a pluralistic, secular society such as Canada. Williams also pointed out that "leadership of an authoritarian or hierarchical nature does not necessarily compel assent. In the post–*Humanae Vitae* age, even the most devoted church members do not accept official statements or decrees simply on the authority of the hierarchy." If Catholics were ignoring the Church on birth control, why should they pay attention to teachings about social justice?

Furthermore, said Williams, "Some Catholics perceive a great inconsistency between the bishops' outspoken promotion of social justice in Canadian society and overseas and their relative lack of action for justice within the church." Examples included "the denial of equality for women...and discrimination against homosexuals." Finally – and this spoke to Church reluctance to become involved in small-*p* politics – Williams focused on the unwillingness of powerful Canadians, Catholic and non-Catholic, to heed the teachings of the bishops. Of course, while Canada's corporate and government potentates could ignore the ethical arguments of the bishops, they do react to political pressure; however,

Williams noted that the bishops have been "reluctant to attempt the mobilization of Canadian Catholics to exert concerted pressure."[44]

Bill Ryan had been working inside various Church structures for more than twenty years and felt that the way to get the social justice message across was to get the laity involved. During his busiest period of work on the task force in 1988, he agreed that Canada's bishops had had "only very limited success" in persuading Catholics that social justice was inseparable from the Gospel, arguing that bishops' statements were still only calling for docile consent, not critical engagement. Ryan claimed that finding solutions to social problems was up to the laity. With an eye on the situation at 90 Parent, he noted that bishops' messages were still crafted by CCCB staff. And with an eye on the task force recommendations for decentralization, he asked, "Are there not better ways to recognize the special charisms and competences of the laity?"[45]

Ryan hoped that, as the CCCB changed its approach to social justice, the initiative would get picked up at the local diocesan level. It didn't happen. In 1993 Janet Somerville wrote a feature for *Catholic New Times* called "Who's Minding the Faith and Justice Store." Bernard Hubert told her that justice had to pass through local Christian communities, that the national effort would once again be strong "only when all regions and dioceses have found their own voice." Ryan, with his Vatican II–inspired belief in the Church as the People of God, observed that the bishops are not the whole Church. But, he added, "In Canada we have no national structures of lay people, no national lay council, very few participatory forums where lay people can stimulate or put on their feet the teaching of the bishops."[46]

By this time Bill Ryan had left his post at the CCCB. The end of his six-year term had coincided with his turning sixty-five. Tony Clarke was about to leave the organization and the Catholic activists who had had the wind at their backs in the years since Vatican II were now leaning into a stiff breeze. But although sixty-five is the point the secular world has come to view as the signpost of retirement, this is not the case in the world of religious orders. And retirement was certainly not something that seems to have occurred to Ryan, who simply continued his career as an energetic Jesuit who persisted in both travelling the world and confronting its apparently intractable problems.

1   Doug McCarthy SJ, "The Church in Canada: A Golden Autumn and a Dark Night," in Robert Chodos, ed., *Compass Points: Navigating the 20th Century* (Toronto: Between the Lines, 1999), 339.

2   *Maclean's*, April 16, 1984, 61.

3   John J. English SJ, *Spiritual Freedom: From an Experience of the Ignatian Exercises to the Art of Spiritual Guidance*, 2nd ed. (Chicago: Loyola Press, 1995), 20.

4   Tony Clarke, *Behind the Mitre: The Moral Leadership Crisis in the Canadian Catholic Church* (Toronto: HarperCollins, 1995), 81.

5   Episcopal Commission for Social Affairs, "Defending Workers' Rights: A New Frontier," in Edward F. Sheridan SJ, ed., *Do Justice!: The Social Teaching of the Canadian Catholic Bishops* (Sherbrooke, QC: Éditions Paulines, 1987), 449–51.

6   Michael W. Higgins and Douglas R. Letson, *My Father's Business: A Biography of His Eminence G. Emmett Cardinal Carter* (Toronto: Macmillan, 1990), 211, 220–21.

7   Gregory Baum, "Call for Social Justice: A Comparison," *Christianity and Crisis*, vol. 44, no. 22 (1985).

8   Quoted in Thomas J. Reese, *Inside the Vatican: The Politics and Organization of the Catholic Church* (Cambridge, MA: Harvard University Press, 1996), 52.

9   Ibid., 255.

10   Penny Lernoux, *Cry of the People: The Struggle for Human Rights in Latin America – The Catholic Church in Conflict with U.S. Policy* (New York: Penguin, 1991), 109.

11   Bernard Hubert, "Canadian Participation in the 1985 Extraordinary Synod," CCCB mimeo, February 10, 1986 (Document 1178), 3–6.

12   Jamie Swift and Ecumenical Coalition for Economic Justice, "The Debt Crisis: A Case of Global Usury," in Jamie Swift and Brian Tomlinson, eds., *Conflicts of Interest: Canada and the Third World* (Toronto: Between the Lines, 1991), 21.

13   Quoted in Paul Longpré, *Malgré tout, l'espoir: Rencontre avec Bernard Hubert, évêque* (Montreal: Fides, 1994), 21.

14   Bernard Hubert, "Seeds of Life, Seeds of Death: Quebec's Church at the Crossroads," *Compass*, May 1990, 35.

15   Ibid.

16   Bernard Daly, *Remembering for Tomorrow: A History of the Canadian Conference of Catholic Bishops 1943–1993* (Ottawa: CCCB, 1995), 159–60.

17   Reginald Bibby, *Fragmented Gods: The Poverty and Potential of Religion in Canada* (Toronto: Irwin, 1987), 20.

18   Joint Strategy Committee, "Poverty and Conscience," in Sheridan., ed., *Do Justice!*, 166, 171.

19   Conrad Black, "A Naïve, Sophomoric Mishmash," *Compass*, summer 1987, 13.

20   Clarke, *Behind the Mitre*, 103–4.

21   William F. Ryan SJ, "Some Tentative Observations on Tony Clarke's 'Behind the Miter' [sic], February 8, 1995," Ryan files, mimeo, 3–4.

22   Clarke, *Behind the Mitre*, 105–6.

23   Quoted in Xavier Rynne, *Vatican Council II* (New York: Farrar, Straus and Giroux, 1968), 220–21.

24   Reese, *Inside the Vatican*, 42.

25   "Synod on the Laity Redux," *Compass*, July 1988, 28.

26 Philip S. Land, *Catholic Social Teaching: As I Have Lived, Loathed and Loved It* (Chicago: Loyola University Press, 1994), 35.

27 William F. Ryan SJ, "Labouring at Reading the Signs of the Times," speech to *Catholic New Times*, November 17, 1986, mimeo.

28 James M. Hayes, "Open the Doors," speech to Synod on the Laity, October 2, 1987.

29 Jean-Guy Hamelin, "The Participation of Women in the Life of the Church," speech to Synod on the Laity, October 9, 1987.

30 CCCB survey cited in Bibby, *Fragmented Gods*, 18, 12.

31 P.R. Divarkar, "A Letter from Rome: On the Synod of Bishops," *America*, November 14, 1987, 350.

32 "Synod on the Laity Redux," 30.

33 Julien Harvey SJ, "A New Church in the Making? An Interview with Bishop Bernard Hubert," *Compass*, October 1987, 19; "Synod on the Laity Redux," 30.

34 Clarke, *Behind the Mitre*, 134–35.

35 Ibid., 132–33.

36 Canadian Conference of Catholic Bishops, "Task Force Proposals on CCCB Future Directions," September 1989; addendum no. 12, Plenary Meeting, October, 1989, 61.

37 Clarke, *Behind the Mitre*, 134, 138, 142.

38 Canadian Conference of Catholic Bishops, "Task Force Proposals," 62.

39 Joe Gunn and Monica Lambton, *Calling Out the Prophetic Tradition: A Jubilee of Social Teaching from the Canadian Conference of Catholic Bishops* (Ottawa: CCCB, 1999), 36.

40 Clarke, *Behind the Mitre*, 120.

41 Gunn and Lambton, *Calling Out the Prophetic Tradition*, 34.

42 Bibby, *Fragmented Gods*, 19, 152.

43 Ian Drummond, "Needed: Patience with the System," *Compass*, summer 1987, 23.

44 John Williams, "Why Isn't Anyone Listening?" *Compass*, summer 1987, 27–29.

45 William F. Ryan SJ, "Ethical Reflections on the Economic Crisis: Comments on the Canadian Experience of Catholic Social Teaching," *Notes & Documents*, nos. 21-22 (January–August 1988).

46 Janet Somerville, "Who's Minding the Faith and Justice Store," *Catholic New Times*, June 13, 1993.

Chapter 7

Keeping the Faith

A ray of light unifies the figures in a fresco at Il Gesù, the Jesuit church in Rome. The light beams down from the heavens to Christ and then to Ignatius of Loyola, from whom it is reflected into four streams that travel to the four corners of the world – Asia, Europe, Africa and Latin America. As much as they have been known as educators and diplomats, preachers and confessors, scientists and even economists, the Jesuits have been a travelling band, roaming the world, spreading the word of their God.

Through the 1990s, Bill Ryan made no fewer than thirty-two trips outside Canada. But unlike his peripatetic forerunners in the Society of Jesus, this itinerant priest did not hit the road hoping to convert the heathen masses. In 1994 he travelled to Guyana to work as an election monitor with the International Centre for Human Rights and Democratic Development. In 1998 he visited Washington before making a round-the-world trip in the spring, stopping in southeast Asia, south Asia and the Middle East. Then it was a short visit to Havana followed by summertime trips to Minneapolis and Boston before heading to Zürich and Milan in the fall. The next year he participated as a judge in a Toronto human rights tribunal looking into a massacre in Colombia. For someone whose parents rarely left the Ottawa Valley, the Jesuit from Renfrew had, literally, gone a long way.

Since he left the bishops' conference in 1990, Ryan has not had the responsibilities of a day-in-day-out job. As a result, he has been free to write reviews for Catholic papers, respond to requests for speeches and interviews ("Priest sees hope for 21st century," read the Pembroke *Observer* headline) and undertake projects that come in over the transom. He has always enjoyed the role of travelling writer and commentator and professor of things-in-general, but after 1990 he had the opportunity to indulge this taste more than he had before. And as he settled into the role, he managed to refine his speaking style. He got away from his old habit of reading long quotes and began to leaven his presentations with anecdotes and jokes. He realized that self-deprecation could be useful in warming up the audience and his credentials as an economist provided ideal grist for that mill. So he would tell of the time he fell into conversation with a Hindu physician on a flight from Sri Lanka to Madras. When the doctor found out about the Canadian, he leapt to his feet and announced to the startled passengers, "Break out the champagne! We have a man here who is both a priest and an economist. It's a Hindu fast day, but I think this deserves a toast."

Ryan related this story in a 1996 keynote talk to a crowd of businesspeople attending a conference on "Values and Ethics for the 21st Century" sponsored by the Alberta Congress Board. In the same address, Ryan told the audience that economic growth was failing a quarter of the world's people, that international debt was sucking the poor countries dry, and that fetishizing unregulated global competition only played into the hands of the biggest transnational corporations, making "nonsense of the vaunted free-market ideal."[1]

Because he did not have a formal institutional affiliation, during this period he would often go by the official title of "Director of the Jesuit Project in Ethics and Politics," a one-man enterprise he had initiated soon after leaving the CCCB. The idea was to use his Ottawa connections to promote dialogue on social ethics with members of Parliament and senior civil servants. It was a notable failure, giving credence to the cynical view that pushing ethics in politics was as oxymoronic as the concept of an industrial park. Although Ryan described the small evening get-togethers he arranged with top civil servants in their homes as "highly successful," in fact nothing came of them. Why? Ryan, who had always been based in institutions and was a quintessential organization man, had tried his ethics and politics initiative on his own, without institutional support. And his effort coincided with the final months of the moribund Mulroney government when politicians were occupied elsewhere. Like many others, Ryan noticed that people were becoming increasingly critical, even scornful, about politicians who, he said, "lump even the Churches among…special interest groups" rather than view-ing them as sources of "enlightenment, strength and encouragement for them to live out their vocation as faithful servants of the common good."[2]

Although Ryan may have displayed uncharacteristic naïveté about the possibility of turning things around, he did bring his usual energy to the task, arranging personal meetings with fifty-five civil serv-ants and sixty-three MPs – as always, he was keeping track.

Ryan had set the stage for this life of travel, meeting, informa-tion-gathering, writing and speaking as soon as his job at the CCCB ended when he undertook a fellowship at the Canadian Institute for International Peace and Security. His task was to spend three months in eastern and central Europe to evaluate the role of religion in the recent collapse of communism. Ryan interviewed bishops, intellectuals and Canadian diplomats in Poland; politicians and priests in Ukraine; Catho-lics in the former East Germany; former Charter 77 activists, journalists and politicians in Czechoslovakia; and academics and former commu-nists in Hungary. Everywhere he used the still-extant Jesuit network to get the lay of the land. It was a remarkable time to travel in the region, less than a year after the end of authoritarian regimes that had tried with varying degrees of enthusiasm and varying degrees of success to sup-press organized religion and all its works.

Admitting that he had no particular expertise in eastern Euro-pean affairs and that his communications were limited because his in-formants were speaking in their second or third languages (unlike some Jesuits, Ryan had never become much a linguist), he nonetheless came up with a comprehensive socio-political analysis of the situation. Ryan acknowledged the basic antagonism at the level of ideas between Chris-tianity and Marxist ideology, but he also noticed that the two sides had settled for a pragmatic modus vivendi over the years. The Polish pope, who had kept a strong hand on his homeland since his accession in 1978, was well aware of the subtleties of the conflict between the cross and the hammer-and-sickle. "I personally evidenced an ambiguous mo-ment in this basic confrontation in a visit with Pope John Paul II in January 1990," recalled Ryan the following year. "It was just a few days after Gorbachev had visited him at the Vatican. In a short conversation the Pope repeated several times, 'Gorbachev may be a Communist, but he is certainly not a Marxist. He believes in human rights and values.'"[3]

Tensions between Marxism – or, for that matter, liberalism or John Paul II's own values – and human rights notwithstanding, Ryan noted that the bishops at Vatican II had avoided the usual denunciations of communism, leaving the door open for a Catholic *ostpolitik*. He concluded that, though the situation differed from country to country, the Church had played a role in the demise of communism in the region by providing a "space for nonconformity." But he also cautioned against any Catholic triumphalism or exaggeration of the Church's role, noting that this energy for nonconformity was usually restricted to a few leaders and a small group of intense believers. Ryan delineated other factors, including the failure of the command economy, the international human rights movement and the Helsinki process, and resistance by the main elements of civil society that were not part of the Church. He did not ignore the crucial role of Gorbachev and his programs of glasnost and perestroika. And as a creature of Vatican II, he was careful not to begin the story of the Church's role with John Paul II but to credit John XXIII with pioneering support for basic political and economic rights in his 1963 encyclical *Pacem in Terris*. Ryan added a careful caveat to his analysis: "The Pope was listened to – but selectively. For example, his strong encyclical *The Social Concern of the Church* (1988) that emphasized social responsibility was read in Poland more as support for private property and personal initiative. More and more, local Bishops' Conferences and Catholic associations are exercising a certain autonomy in interpreting and applying Church teachings locally."[4]

The next investigation topic that took Ryan to far-flung corners of the world was even more complex: the links between spirituality and development. By the early 1990s, the *idea*, the mindset of development had become frayed at the edges. For one thing, world inequality was worsening just as the word *globalization* began to enter popular conversation and markets reigned supreme. In 1992, when Canada bumped Japan from the top of its human development index, the United Nations revealed that the richest 20 per cent of the world people got at least 150 times more income than the poorest fifth – up from thirty times in 1960.[5] For another thing, the Cold War that had done so much to impel the development enterprise was over. And more people – theorists as well as veteran development practitioners – were asking a big question: Has faith in progress and development cut people in the south off from the essence of life? "Progress impelled these people to become their own God and make their own history," wrote José Maria Sbert, a Mexican who once worked with the radical Catholic critic Ivan Illich. "It ridiculed their old beliefs, fears and superstitions as well as their reverence for nature, the past and their ancestors.... Disembedded from his community and caring only for himself, free from his elders' beliefs and fears, having learned to look down on his parents and knowing he will find no respect in what they could teach him, [the common man] and his fellows can only become *workers* for industry, *consumers* for the market, *citizens* for the nation and *humans* for mankind."[6]

Ryan had been interested in questions of development ever since his doctoral studies at Harvard, an institution that helped provide the theory behind the conventional model that equated development with modernization and growth. Thirty years later he was still reading the signs of the times: he knew that there were environmental limits to growth, but these limits were being ignored by what hardbitten marketeers were calling the "real world." It was a world of capitalism, unabashed and triumphant.

So Ryan was intrigued when, in 1993, he got a call from Pierre Beemans of the International Development Research Centre (IDRC), an Ottawa-based crown corporation that funds researchers in the Third World, or "the South" as it had become known. Established during the first Trudeau administration, the IDRC had managed to survive the funding cuts and was still "enabling people of the South to find their own solutions to their own problems." The IDRC is a uniquely Canadian institution, highly regarded internationally by those in the development enterprise. Beemans, a Catholic who had done undergraduate studies at Loyola College in Montreal, was a veteran of that enterprise, describing himself as a "career development manager." He had volunteered for CUSO before heading up that agency's Latin America desk, and by the mid-1990s he was vice-president of the multi-million-dollar IDRC, closing in on retirement and disturbed by something at the heart of the development enterprise. Twentieth-century missionaries like Beemans had headed south, preaching the good news of development – modernization, poverty eradication, human rights, basic human needs, sustainable development. Though the terminology and the politics shifted, the impulse remained the same. But Beemans, like Illich, Sbert and scores of other thinkers, was wondering, as Peggy Lee asked in the song, "Is That All There Is?"

"I could never understand why, in development, we talked about everything except religion, spirituality and morality," explained Beemans. "Those were not just non-words, they were dirty words."

The development enterprise has its roots in materialism and the Enlightenment. Traditional belief systems were not generally considered by mainstream thinking about development as it had evolved since Beemans first went to Latin America. The keepers of these belief systems were marginal to the development process and frequently (Iran springs to mind) hostile to it. Beemans wanted to make some links. "I needed someone who could walk both sides of the street," he recalled, "who would be listened to in the development community because of his credentials and at the same time was a believer, who took religion seriously and would be listened to by people who also took religion seriously."

A Latin American Jesuit friend told him that he knew a priest who had a doctorate in development economics from Harvard. Intrigued, Beemans set up a meeting with Bill Ryan: "I was expecting some sharp young snappy Jesuit and instead I meet this guy who's semi-retired and looks like Hollywood central casting for the wise old Irish priest." Others in the IDRC were wary, with one Latin American refugee from a right-wing dictatorship suspecting any priest of being connected with the shadowy Opus Dei. Chris Smart, who would work closely with Ryan at the IDRC, was keen on having a Jesuit on board. While teaching in Papua New Guinea, Smart had befriended two Jesuits who sat back and chuckled after sending the visiting papal nuncio into the interior to spend a few days with some nuns who worked in rigorous upcountry conditions. The Jesuits knew that such conditions would be completely foreign to the comfortable Vatican diplomat.

Ryan's work with the IDRC involved a 1994 trip around the world to investigate the links between spirituality and development, a voyage that found him visiting both the Jesuit curia in Rome and the Indian Social Institute in New Delhi, where the dormitory was ridden with bedbugs and Jesuits were working with dalits (or untouchables) on issues of land rights, food and the environment. He knocked on doors at the Third World Network in Malaysia and renewed acquaintance with liberation theologians Gustavo Gutierrez in the slums of Lima and Juan Luis Segundo in Uruguay. In Africa he met Pete Henriot, his old friend from the Center of Concern, along with Cecil McGarry, a Jesuit theologian who had been with him at GC32 and GC33. In Manila there were two more Jesuits who had been at GC33; one, noted Ryan, had been a personal adviser to President Corazon Aquino. In Jordan he conferred with Dr. Leila Sharaf, wife of the former prime minister and cousin of the king. There was an Egyptian adviser to the World Bank, a Jesuit who had been research director at the Venezuelan finance ministry and the director of the Institute of Management at the University of Senegal. Although Ryan met with some people working at the grassroots level in what the Jesuits call apostolic communities (social centres, schools, colleges and parishes), most of his contacts were Top People – economists, directors, Ph.D.s, professors. He was in his element and, from the IDRC's point of view, he was the ideal person for the job. His contacts in the global Jesuit network gave him access to intellectuals from all faiths and he talked to nearly two hundred people in the course of his intense five-month journey.

He reported back to the IDRC that the dominant notions of development were crumbling. Segundo and Gutierrez, each of whom Ryan described as a "co-founder of liberation theology,"[7] expressed relief at the demise of state socialism because it meant that they could criticize capitalist development without being dismissed as communists. Ryan noted that the "enthusiastic revival of neo-liberal market ideology has few defenders among those interviewed." His contacts viewed Western-trained experts and technocratic approaches to social problems with suspicion. He was told time and again that the IMF and the World Bank acted as enforcers for neo-liberalism and that cultural values were being sacrificed on the altar on the market. The people he met, wrote Ryan, were frustrated and impatient that it was taking so long for Westerners to realize that

> their basic development model has failed and is continuing to fail hundreds of millions of poor people in the developing world. Experience has shown that Western free-market models, which ignore spiritual and cultural values as "externalities" while establishing dependency and vulnerability in their place, do not work in developing countries. The clear opinion was that fundamental reworking of the current development paradigm is long overdue. Gustavo Guttierez summed up his frustration as he spoke about the extreme poverty of many of his parishioners who live in one of the poorest barrios in Lima: "How much longer do people have to suffer?"[8]

Ryan looked for the bright side and found it in NGOs and social movements – "one of the most hopeful signs of the times." For him, leadership had to come from the people, and although NGOs included charlatans and were sometimes inexperienced or incompetent, he felt that they were the social forces most able to nurture the genius of grassroots organization. It was NGOs, not governments, that would take the initiative in building a sustainable global community. Women's movements, human rights movements, environmental movements and the emerging links between "groups of groups" gave him hope for "a living breathing global body!" Ryan went on to explain that although he had been retained by the IDRC because of his training in economics and theology, he felt he had to explain the origins of his sanguine world view. Those were Ignatian, a spirituality of perseverance: persevering, with God's help, in learning to contemplate God everywhere, in all things and in all creation.

"I like the intuition of Teilhard de Chardin," Ryan wrote, "that the evolution we experience is not chaos, it is 'directed chance.'" Admitting that he had not fully grasped the idea, he said he was comfortable with the Jesuit paleontologist's "hopeful vision of a growing global *noosphere.*" He explained it as a sphere of thinking including consciousness, interaction, sympathy and mutual concern. The Jesuit economist felt that the future of the planet was based not on the expansion of GDP but "the growth of genuine love." Ryan's *noosphere* represented a unity of hearts and brains: "Perhaps the rich experience I have had in interviewing people of different backgrounds in many parts of the world gives some small witness to the existence of this mysterious phenomenon." He concluded his report in an unconventional fashion, at least for an international development consultant. Ryan quoted his old friend Barbara Ward, who had died at age sixty-seven in 1981: "The scientist and the sage, the man of learning and the poet, the mathematician and the saint repeat to the human city the same plea and the same warning: 'We must love each other or we will die.'"[9]

———

Bill Ryan's reports on his global sojourns were nothing new for his order. Jesuits have always been keen correspondents, filling archives and books with voluminous accounts of their travels. The Jesuit *Relations*, the annual reports sent from the Society's missionaries in Canada to its Paris office from 1632 to 1672, provided colourful and detailed documentation of their enterprises, an ethnographic and documentary record for today and a genre of travel literature that was eagerly devoured in the eighteenth century.

Provincials and consultors still file endless reports to headquarters at Borgo Santo Spirito. By the 1990s, keeping up with the times, they had exchanged the quill pen for the computer. Curiously, however, they have never seized on another modern invention, retirement. In fact, the order has no retirement policy. As the average age creeps up, in Europe and North America at least, one of the most difficult tasks of a provincial is to get his old colleagues who have become too sick to work to move to the infirmary. The Jesuits try to act like families of old, postponing the inevitable for as long as possible by integrating the elders into daily life. Apostolic communities, particularly parishes, try to hold onto older Jesuits to help retain a sense of brotherhood and to assist in pastoral work. The Jesuits feel that their older members tend to be approachable and make good confessors and spiritual directors.

Bill Ryan, however, had never been much for pastoral work. Although approachable and certainly talkative, he had not taken to the life of a priestly father-confessor. His world has always been bound up with ideas and organizations. So while the superior of his Ottawa community, a Jesuit of Ryan's generation named Norman Dodge, concentrated on visiting seniors and shut-ins, Ryan continued to focus on writing and meetings, e-mail and the phone. Ryan and Dodge share the Jesuit house on Sunnyside Avenue in upscale Ottawa South with Art White, the long-time support staff worker for the Upper Canada province, and Martin Briba, a Jesuit from Burkina Faso doing doctoral studies in political philosophy. Another member of the community lives – and works – apart; he spends his days carrying anti-abortion signs around Parliament Hill.

Consisting of two semi-detached houses used as one, the Sunnyside residence is a large complex, and with so few permanent residents it has ample room for travellers passing through Ottawa. It is a typical Jesuit house. The bright, roomy kitchen, the social focus of most family households, has an institutional feel. The common rooms, neat and comfortably furnished, somehow lack anyone's personal touch. Two small framed pictures – a photo of Kolvenbach and a sketch of seventeenth-century Scottish Jesuit martyr St. John Ogilvie, his neck in a noose – adorn an otherwise austere front hall. Only the rooms occupied by the individual residents project personality. The tiled gas fireplace (unused) and handsome leaded window in Ryan's large ground-floor office reflect the age of the house. The room is extremely tidy, its sheaves of papers and files carefully organized. Above the computer is the same pen-and-ink rendering of Sancho Panza and Don Quixote that used to decorate the publications of the Center of Concern. Another sketch of Renfrew's St. Francis Xavier churches, old and new, adorns the wall above a writing desk that features a colour photo of Bill Ryan meeting John Paul II. Above one of two comfortable leather reading chairs is a 1997 poster denouncing corporate rule, published by the Jesuit Centre for Social Faith and Justice.

Impersonal or not, the Sunnyside residence is Ryan's home, and the Jesuits are his true family. The Society resembles a family because, like all families, it has a culture bound up with common stories and experiences. Jesuit fathers and brothers, like everyday sisters and brothers, share a common formation. It may not involve play or adolescence or, most important, common parents, but it is still an intense experience, more unifying than simply going to school together. Jesuits have all lived together "in community," worked together, taken the same courses in theology and philosophy taught by other Jesuits, made the same Spiritual Exercises. They share meals and daily prayers and 500 years of family stories, tales of superiors who were good and wise and those who were malicious or just plain crazy. Many of the stories of great Jesuits have taken on the mythological stature that is such an important glue in the cementing of cultures.

Whenever and wherever he travelled, Ryan had a Jesuit house where he could feel at home among men who had all gone through exactly the same formation and shared his faith. Anyone who has ever arrived cold in a strange land without contacts or the ability to speak the language will realize that this is no small advantage, and it was important in making Ryan into a global citizen. What better way to find out what is happening in the world? What better way to feel at home in the world? When Bill Ryan hit the road for the IDRC, sixty of the 188 people he met with were Jesuits, of whom eight had been with him at GC32 or GC33. Many more were people whom he had met as provincial, at various synods or in his other travels. Many were also academics – economists, theologians, sociologists.

Bill Ryan's identity as a Jesuit is also a central part of his place in his other family: his siblings and their spouses, children and grandchildren. Helen Hanniman, Bill's sprightly youngest sister who takes responsibility for many matters in the Ryan family, keeps track of her brother's whereabouts, letting the others – all of whom still live in the Ottawa Valley – know where he has gone and when he is returning. She keeps a maternal eye out for his appearance, seeing to any of his sewing needs. Along with her husband, Merv, Helen is very proud of "Father Frank" and his accomplishments. She is always amazed at the pace he has been able to maintain, attributing it to the ease of the priestly life. "This is why he is so young," she laughs. "He never had any worries. The rest of us had to worry about making a living. Everything's taken care of for him. He comes back from a trip and he's ready to go tomorrow. We have responsibilities to others."

It was on an extended trip that took him from Rome to the Soviet Union, Japan, Vietnam and Sri Lanka in 1970 that Ryan heard that his mother, who was living in a Renfrew nursing home, was not well. He immediately flew back from India in time to see her before she died. Lena, the deeply religious family woman who had devoted her life to her children, thought the world of her high-achieving son. And once he became a Jesuit his stock rose even further. For his part, Ryan suspected that his mother's powerful intuition – which he felt bordered on psychic power – prompted his quick return to her deathbed. Five years later, when the family gathered for a big Easter meal, Bill Ryan, Sr., informed his children that his time was coming and that time was not far off. He said he had done his bit. A few weeks later, Bill Ryan, Jr., was talking long distance at the Center of Concern when another call came, this one from Renfrew. Ryan suspected that his father had died but asked Eileen Olsen to take the call. He returned to Renfrew to preach the homily at his father's funeral and later recalled that he spent little time grieving for either parent, opting instead to try to understand them better.

Ryan's siblings have a deep, though sometimes grudging, respect for their Jesuit brother whose world is foreign to them. His younger brother Bob, the clan's impish self-styled black sheep, recalled that their other brother, Father Jim Ryan, the Oblate who died of a heart attack at age fifty while cross-country skiing in Ottawa, used to be "up home" more often than Father Frank. Bob's wife, Ann, tells of the time Father Frank was visiting their cottage and disappeared into the wilderness for several hours. They were worried because Ryan was completely unfamiliar with the country, but he eventually returned, explaining that he had simply gone for a walk in the woods. "He does what he does," shrugs Helen, explaining her brother's singlemindedness. "He just has so much energy. He has a talent that I admire: he can be doing something very concentrated and then he can cut off and go and do something else."

Though close to his family, Bill Ryan is not one to spin yarns of the old days or wax sentimental. As Helen Hanniman readied the old Ryan house at the corner of Quarry and Lynn for sale in 2000, picking her way among family memorabilia that included her mother's old treadle sewing machine, a novelty book titled *The Wit of the Irish*, and a coffee mug adorned with a picture of the pope, she paused to reflect. "Dad didn't live here at all," she recalled, adding that two of her sisters never really left home. "Those two girls who lived here were married to their jobs." Her brother "Father Frank," on the other hand, showed little apparent interest in reminiscing about the house where he had grown up.

He did remark that, though the rest of the clan will be buried in Renfrew, "I'll go with the Jesuits."

—⇒»·◦·«⇐—

Ted Hyland is a Canadian who spent sixteen years in the Society of Jesus. He lived with Jesuits in Paris, travelled to eastern Europe before 1989 and visited Central America when the killing was at its height. He met Jesuits who had become angry and embittered, seeking refuge in alcohol or leading extravagant lifestyles. He knew of whole communities that turned themselves inside out to try to compensate for these lifestyles. He met many who were wrestling with a vow of poverty that allowed them to enjoy access to a fleet of cars and have their laundry, shopping and housework done and not have to worry too much about how the bills were getting paid. He shared stories of good superiors and eccentric superiors, community members who were great cooks and those who were so crazy that they would bark at strangers. Although he left the Jesuits in 1996, Hyland says he could never imagine being a priest and not being part of the Jesuit family.

"I don't think I've ever met any group of people as remarkable as the Jesuits," explained Hyland, describing his encounters with them from Marseille to San Salvador. "I felt at home wherever I went. There wasn't a lot of dancing around. You got straight to it. Even though this was the first time you had met this person, it was almost as if you had known each other for years." He got to know men who told him about their work in refugee camps all over world. There were, of course, men he did not get along with at all, but "you still had the feeling you'd go to the wall and die for them."

But if the Jesuits are an extraordinary family, they are also a shrinking one, especially in the wealthy countries of North America and western Europe. The disturbing trends Ryan had pointed to in *Our Way of Proceeding* in the early 1980s intensified in the last years of the century. By 2000, the number of Jesuits in the Upper Canada province had declined to 264 from 307 in 1983, and of these, just under half were over sixty-five years of age while only thirteen (5 per cent) were under thirty-five. The age structure of the province was almost the reverse of what it had been in 1943, just before Ryan joined the Society, when 60 per cent were under thirty-five and only 9 per cent were over sixty-five. Of the seven Jesuits who started in the novitiate with Ted Hyland in 1980, only one remained in the order twenty years later. The number of recruits had become so low by the early 1990s that the province gave up the Guelph novitiate that Ryan had attended in the 1940s, sending the few who entered to the novitiate in Wisconsin. A projection of current trends (and Bill Ryan would be the first to point out that a projection of current trends is not the only possibility) would lead to an Upper Canada province of about a hundred members in 2030, with only thirty of them under sixty-five. All of this, of course, reflects a broader problem faced by the Church in general: the priesthood is aging, its numbers not being replenished. As Berkeley sociologist of religion John Coleman SJ wrote in the Jesuit magazine *America* in 1981, "Any profession for which the following facts are true – declining absolute numbers in the face of growth of the large population, significant resignations, a declining pool of new recruits and an aging population – can be referred to as having a deep-seated identity crisis, whatever the internal morale of the group."[10]

The decline in Jesuit numbers, especially in the younger age groups, was one factor – although far from the only one – in a dramatic cutback in the programs that had been initiated or expanded while Bill Ryan was provincial. David Nazar, Ryan's housemate in Ottawa back in the 1980s, was appointed provincial in August 1996, and about six months into his term he announced the end of province funding for the Jesuit Centre for Social Faith and Justice, *Compass*, the Jesuit Companions (since renamed the Jesuit Volunteers) and more than a dozen other apostolates. In a separate move, the Ignatius Farm Community was closed in 2001. Rumour linked the closure of the Jesuit Centre to a controversial poster the Centre had issued a few months before, and there was much speculation about the reasons for the closure of the Farm Community. But the primary reason invoked by the province for the closures was money.

Budget-cutters are generally seen by some as courageous leaders who are not afraid to make tough decisions, and by others as soulless bean counters whose concern for the bottom line has led them to ignore human realities. Nazar was no exception. Forty-three when he became provincial, fresh from Wikwemikong on Manitoulin Island where he had been pastor of a Native parish, informal in his style, Nazar became a controversial figure. Was he an "innovator" as Ryan had been in the late 1970s and early 1980s, tailoring the province to new circumstances? Or was he someone who had lost sight of what the Jesuits were supposed to be about and why they had undertaken the new initiatives in the first place? There was also a question of priorities: the French-Canadian Jesuits, facing similar problems, abandoned their educational institutions but kept their Centre justice et foi in Montreal and their magazine, *Relations*. Controversy surrounded even minor decisions. In

2000, Nazar moved the provincial's office from the west-end Toronto location it had occupied since the Jesuits abandoned their Rosedale mansion in the 1970s to a more central venue in a converted Persian rug showroom on Bay Street. Although the new office was at the north end of the street, far from the financial district that gives it its reputation, the symbolism of a Bay Street address did not sit well with some Jesuits.

Few would argue that the Upper Canada province of the Jesuits could have continued to spend money at the rate it did during Bill Ryan's years at the helm. While one Jesuit did suggest that there was no genuine financial crisis, there seems to be little doubt that the human and financial resources of the province diminished significantly in the last twenty years of the century. The reasons for the financial decline are less clear, although there are plenty of candidates. Bill Ryan suggested that it came about largely because of the salaries that had to be paid to lay employees of the new apostolates. The apostolates were never able to become financially self-sufficient, so they continued to draw on the province apostolic fund that he had originally established to provide them with seed money. A related factor was declining Jesuit manpower and the aging of the Jesuit population, which meant that fewer Jesuits were working at high-paid university jobs and more were in need of expensive care at the province's Pickering infirmary. For Bill Addley, the main culprit was a sexual-abuse case involving the late Father George Epoch, who had been a pastor in the Native parish of Cape Croker on Ontario's Bruce Peninsula. When the case came to light in the early 1990s, Addley, whose term as provincial had just ended, was involved in the negotiations with the Native people and sought to work out a just settlement. This settlement included a multi-million-dollar payout that represented a serious drain on the province treasury. Others pointed to the souring of the province's investments, which had provided handsome returns in the 1970s and early 1980s but were no longer performing as well.

These explanations can be mixed and matched in various proportions, but in any case, by the time Eric Maclean took over as provincial in 1990, the Jesuits' financial picture was considerably bleaker than it had been in the Ryan and Addley eras. Money was tighter in the early 1990s than it had been before and there were reductions in subsidies to apostolates, but no drastic measures were taken until Nazar's appointment as provincial in 1996. "His inexperience helped," commented Bill Ryan. "He felt he had to do something." What he did was twofold: he appealed for help to American Jesuit provinces that were in better fi-

nancial shape, and he cut way back on the funding of apostolates, virtually dismantling the structure that Ryan had created some fifteen years
earlier.

➤•◀

When the American-trained army slaughtered six Jesuits together
with their housekeeper and her daughter at the Jesuit university in San
Salvador in 1989, Michael Czerny moved to El Salvador to help fill the
vacuum left by the martyred Jesuits, and Ted Hyland succeeded him as
director of the Jesuit Centre for Social Faith and Justice. Hyland stayed
for five years and for most of that time was the only Jesuit on staff,
surrounded by lay activists. One of these was Joe Gunn, a Saskatchewan
native who returned from his work in Central America in 1989 and began working for the Jesuit Centre on Central American issues. Gunn
described a "collective type of operation" with an emphasis on process,
consensus and non-hierarchical decision-making. (This in an organization founded and sponsored by a religious order known for obedience
and usually mythologized by military metaphors – the Company of Jesus, soldiers of God, papal commandos, the army of the Reformation,
hammer of the heretics.) Though the staff included active feminists sympathetic to the pro-choice movement, both the secular leftists and the
Jesuits were savvy enough to wink at the contentious abortion issue.
There was enough work lobbying the government on human rights and
immigration, doing refugee casework, organizing sessions called "naming the moment," fundraising and attending all the meetings generated
by any expanding organization – particularly one striving for collective
decision-making. While the social affairs office of Ottawa's CCCB was
shrinking in the early 1990s, Toronto's Jesuit Centre was getting bigger.

Sandra Kowolchuk, who helped to administer the Centre's million-dollar budget, described it as a staff-run organization and recalled
someone making the casual remark that "it's our centre." As time passed,
the Jesuits had less ownership of the place and when Ted Hyland took a
leave of absence in 1995 and left the Jesuits the following year, this
became even more apparent. The search for a new director was carried
out in the classified section of the newspaper, not by scanning the pages
of the annual catalogue that lists every Jesuit in the Upper Canada province. The new director was a lay Catholic, Kevin Arsenault, and the
Jesuit presence evaporated further. "I found it strange," recalled
Kowolchuk, "that this centre was so important to them but they couldn't
come up with a Jesuit to lead it." The hard reality was that the Canadian

Jesuits simply could not supply men fired with the vision of social justice who were experienced enough and young enough to provide the leadership for a place like the Jesuit Centre.

The link between faith and justice that Bill Ryan had helped forge in 1975 was central to the identity of the Jesuits. Why, then, did secular social justice activists become the mainstay of the principal social justice apostolate of the English-Canadian Jesuits? The declining number of Jesuits is part of the answer, but it is more complicated than that. Venerable institutions made up of older people are not easily transformed, as is evidenced by the experience of the post–Vatican II Church. Despite the efforts of Ryan and others, the social justice imperative had not yet taken root among Canadian Jesuits, trained as they were to be theology professors and spiritual directors, not organizers or lobbyists. "By the time I got to the Jesuit Centre," says Joe Gunn, "there was only a minimal Jesuit presence and this was a fundamental flaw that I often brought up to them. I knew a bit about Catholic social teaching and could not understand why we had entire teams of people working there who weren't familiar with that. I could not understand why we were not engaged with other Jesuits." As Ted Hyland explained, "It was fulfilling a mandate of the province and the Society in terms of its work for justice but it was removed from much of the day-to-day experience of Jesuits."

It wasn't long after Hyland's departure that the Canadian Jesuits decided to pull the plug on the Jesuit Centre. After consulting with other Jesuits and people at the apostolates, Nazar put Bill Ryan, by then chairing the Centre's board, in charge of winding the place down and turning its assets over to a new, secular Centre for Social Justice that would soon emerge. As Ryan put it at the time, "You haven't got the money to do what there is to do."[11]

The fact that director Kevin Arsenault had made front-page news in Toronto when he publicly criticized Aloysius Ambrozic, the city's conservative archbishop, for hobnobbing with the rich while more people fell into poverty was not a direct factor in the Centre's demise. Nor was the catchy "Exposing the face of corporate rule" poster – "Here are the men (one woman) who reaped record profits while slashing jobs" – that identified individual corporate bosses along with their large salaries and the number of workers their companies had laid off. Although widely distributed, the poster was banned from churches in the Toronto archdiocese. Ambrozic's public-relations officer charged that it might give "divine sanction" to a "homicidal maniac" bent on going after corporate leaders. Ryan responded by defending the Jesuit Centre's "very professional" staff, saying his concern was that the information on the poster was correct and that it was "deplorable" and "a clear social injustice" that CEOs were making ninety times what workers earned. "All Catholic social teaching is that unaccountable power is not acceptable," said Ryan in response to the controversy that erupted when auxiliary bishop John Knight issued a letter banning the poster. He added that he regretted that Knight's letter did not address the social justice issue, saying that he wished that the bishop "would show as much concern for the poor and the unemployed as he did for the rich."[12]

Ryan managed to hand off the Centre's assets – including its all-important mailing list – to two groups: Horizons of Friendship, a small NGO that supports projects in Central America, and another group made up of secular leftists who continued research and publication on the growing gap between rich and poor in Canada. By spinning the Centre off rather than simply shutting it, Ryan was being consistent with his long-standing pattern of pragmatism, creating as much space as he could, given institutional constraints, for those more inclined than he to front-line action. In the end, the Jesuit Centre's rise and fall can be attributed to two things: the funding crisis that was the order's official explanation, and its inability to come up with even one of its own people to provide the faith-based leadership that would have integrated the two basic tenets of GC32, faith and justice. A complicating factor was the Centre's inability to take advantage of its growth years, when it was headed by Jesuits, to incorporate the spirit of that Congregation in a sustainable way.

Compass maintained broader Jesuit links than the Jesuit Centre, with four Jesuits on the magazine's editorial board through the 1990s and others (including Bill Ryan, who wrote about development, Quebec, Catholic social teaching and other topics) involved as contributing editors, writers and members of the Publishing Policy Committee. As financial times became tighter in the early nineties, *Compass* responded with cost-cutting measures, scaling back fees for writers and editors, downgrading the quality of paper, and eventually reducing the number of pages in each issue. But the essential character of the magazine was preserved and it continued to develop new features, notably a series on the decades of the twentieth century, initially conceived by Michael Czerny and launched in 1990, and a column by its astute and eloquent former managing editor, Martin Royackers SJ, who was posted to Jamaica in 1994. Its quality continued to win recognition, including a silver National Magazine Award in 1995. But it also continued to be one of the Jesuits' more expensive projects, even as funding declined through the 1990s, and so it became a casualty of Nazar's drastic cuts. Unlike the Jesuit Centre, the editors of *Compass* were not able to find alternate backers for their activity, and the magazine suspended publication after its May/June 1997 issue, transferring its assets to a consortium of the magazine's editors and other principals who set themselves up as the Compass Foundation.

Unlike *Compass* and the Jesuit Centre, the Jesuit Communication Project continued to operate, although it was now simply a tag for the work of a single persistent and media-savvy Jesuit, John Pungente. Also still in operation was the Anishinabe Spiritual Centre in Espanola, Ontario, even as the goal of a Native church that had underlain the Jesuits' choice of this project as their priority apostolate in 1979 and had been stated in Ryan's *Our Way of Proceeding* document two years later remained a distant dream.

Beautiful and peaceful as ever on the shore of Anderson Lake, the Spiritual Centre was used primarily for marriage-preparation programs, Alcoholics Anonymous retreats and similar programs. The Jesuit presence consisted of Clair Fischer, a retired Jesuit in his late seventies; Michael Stogre, a younger Jesuit (and medical doctor) who also had four parishes on Manitoulin Island to attend to; and others who came for short periods to teach in the ministries program. The Spiritual Centre was also rented out to other groups, with preference given to Native organizations such as band councils. Other Christian denominations were regular customers: "The Anglicans love to use this place," commented Dorothy Regan, one of two Sisters of St. Joseph who were the core of the Spiritual Centre's staff. In 1993 the Spiritual Centre hosted an international workshop of Jesuits working with Native peoples, with Father General Kolvenbach as one of the honoured guests. "Native people will seek their own justice; no one can do it for them," Kolvenbach said. "Our ministry is to promote Native organizations and accompany their movements, build up local power in communities, and help them get their own rights."[13]

In the Jesuit parishes that dot Manitoulin Island, a handful of deacons trained at the Spiritual Centre were leaders in their communities. At the largest of the parishes, Wikwemikong, a new Jesuit team arrived in the fall of 1999: Bert Foliot, who had been pastor of the Jesuits' bustling downtown Toronto parish, Our Lady of Lourdes, and Doug McCarthy, who had lived in a L'Arche house in Toronto since leaving the Farm Community in Guelph in 1994. Foliot had revelled in his role as parish priest in a culturally diverse community in Toronto[14] but found that this experience had not prepared him for either the richness or the deeply ingrained problems of Wikwemikong. "I don't know how to be a pastor here," he said in the summer of 2000. McCarthy, convinced of the deep resonances between Christianity and Native spirituality, believed as Mike Murray had twenty years earlier that a key step in moving towards a Native Church would be for Rome to recognize an Anishinabe rite, with a married priesthood. Rome under John Paul II was not providing any encouraging signs. From that golden moment in Guelph in 1979, when the Jesuits had awarded Bill Ryan's $100,000 prize to Murray's plans for the Anishinabe Spiritual Centre, they had done much to establish the sincerity of their desire to transform their centuries-old relationship with Native people. But as with much else undertaken under Ryan's leadership, it was proving to be a longer and harder road than he had anticipated.

Although the closure of the Jesuit Centre attracted more attention, perhaps no closure was more painful than that of the Farm Community at the end of June 2001. Since it had never represented a major financial commitment on the province's part, the financial argument did not carry as much weight as it did with the other apostolates (which is why the Farm Community escaped the initial round of closures in 1997), and so its principals searched for explanations for the province's ending of its commitment to the community. Interviewed a few weeks before the closure, director Bill Clarke, sixty-eight at the time, acknowledged that there was no younger Jesuit available to succeed him. Those who were capable of and interested in doing the work, such as Martin Royackers, who had grown up on a southwestern Ontario farm and lived at the Farm Community in the 1980s and early 1990s, were fully occupied elsewhere (in Royackers' case, in Jamaica, where he served as a pastor, taught at the seminary, drafted episcopal statements and helped run a rural-development project, among other activities). Others pointed to the inherently unstable and chaotic nature of the community as a reason why the province would want to close it. "Living there means living in the middle of the broken bits, of your own life and others' lives," wrote former Farm Community volunteer Louisa Blair in 2000. "It means walking straight into the wound and lying down in it."[15] Founder Doug McCarthy, for whom the closure of the community represented a "paradise lost," suggested that it just may have been "too messy an apostolate."

Like *Compass*, the Farm Community made unsuccessful attempts to arrange alternate sources of support. The most obvious solution would have been to turn it into a L'Arche community, but that would have meant complying with a whole new set of rules, and in Clarke's estimation it would have taken five years to make the transition – time the Farm Community didn't have. And so, in the spring of 2001, Clarke arranged new placements (L'Arche houses, group homes) for the people living in the community, and this messy, radical and deeply Christian apostolate came to an end. The farm itself stayed open as part of a community-shared agriculture project. The five Jesuits remaining at the Guelph site (retreat directors, a pastor and an ecologist) all moved into the Red House, across the road from the large greystone main building on the site, the former novitiate where Bill Ryan had entered the order as the Second World War came to its end. It was here that hundreds of young men who wanted to join the Society of Jesus got their first exposure to the the rigours of Jesuit life, Jesuit training, Jesuit spirituality. In 2001 that rather forbidding building no longer had any Jesuit presence at all.

Ten days before the closure of the Farm Community took effect, Martin Royackers was gunned down as he locked his church office in Jamaica. Forty-one years old at the time of his death, Royackers had joined the Upper Canada province in August 1978, the same month that Bill Ryan became provincial, and was nurtured in two of the apostolates that grew under Ryan's leadership, *Compass* and the Farm Community. Deeply disenchanted with North American consumer society, he found his niche in rural Jamaica, where he worked with Jim Webb, who had been among the first English-Canadian Jesuits to live the spirit of GC32 when he took up residence in a poor Toronto neighbourhood in the mid-1970s. Until his death Royackers also remained close to Doug McCarthy, who had been led by the same spirit to start the Red House in 1976; the two exchanged letters in which they shared their spiritual lives.[16] Webb and Royackers had been working on a land redistribution project, and had been the target of death threats in connection with that project. It was assumed that the gunman who took the life of this committed, singleminded, brilliant and difficult Jesuit was carrying out those threats.

Inevitably, Jesuits placed Royackers' name in the line of those who had died in the service of faith and justice since GC32. Michael Czerny, who had gone from the Jesuit Centre for Social Faith and Justice to El Salvador to Rome as the order's secretary for social justice, made this connection when he spoke on behalf of Father General Kolvenbach at a memorial service in Royackers's home town of Parkhill, Ontario, and again at his funeral in Jamaica two days later. He specifically linked Royackers with the first post-GC32 Jesuit martyr, Rutilio Grande, who had also been killed while working on land redistribution. There is a positive side to martyrdom in Christian theology, and it was emphasized especially in a pastoral letter from provincial David Nazar and socius Jean-Marc Laporte, read by Laporte at another memorial service in Guelph. Placing Royackers' death in the context of the deaths of several other relatively young Canadian Jesuits in the previous year or so, he said, "God took Martin and the other men I mentioned earlier to teach us something about being free and fully alive.... And God chose to take them when their light was strongest and they were at their best, not to deflate us, but to encourage us." For others not quite so committed to seeing the murder through the theological lens of Christian martyrdom, such consolation was harder to come by. Royackers' mother captured a widespread sentiment when she said, "I would rather have a living Marty than a dead martyr." And Royackers' death left a deep hole not only in his stricken family but also in the thinly stretched Upper Canada province, which could ill afford to lose one of its most vital and talented younger members.

—»·◊·«—

And what of the other organizations to which Bill Ryan devoted so much energy during the peak years of his working life, the Center of Concern and the Canadian Conference of Catholic Bishops? The Center of Concern, a group that has no formal Jesuit connection but whose staff comprises people whose work is informed by their faith, has followed a different path than the Jesuit Centre for Social Faith and Justice in Toronto. The Center remains independent, supported mostly by foundation money and direct-mail appeals. It did go through a period when it did not pay much attention to matters spiritual, and according to Jim Hug, its director and sole Jesuit staffer, it hired people, often Catholics, who "had no truck with dealing with the spiritual side of it all. That really didn't work well, so we've given more attention to it now." One Jew who grew up in a secular household has reconnected with spiritual Judaism by working at a place where important planning meetings start with prayers and reflection. The idea is to create a unifying bond. One day will start with Christian prayer and the next morning a Buddhist will lead a prayer and a chant. People speak of what motivates them in their work, explaining their sense of call. "It's when you get to that level that you know it's all one," says Hug. This reintegration of faith and justice reflected Ryan's initial hopes for the Center. In 2001 the Center was immersed in NGO networking around racism and the links between trade policy and gender. It was also working on ways to make corporations more responsive to the common good. In the issue of its newsletter, *Center Focus*, marking the organization's thirtieth anniversary, Hug quoted from "a particularly insightful reading of the current global situation" that he had come across "during a recent review of social justice literature." It read in part:

> Cruel facts have exploded the myth that individual goods and individual values add up to a common good and a social value for all. People are not looking for mechanical or even wholly "rational" solutions to development problems; they want to participate in the decisions that control their destiny. Increasingly they want to do this within a framework of recognized human rights, a framework of national and international social justice that comes to grips with the problems of power, privilege, of unemployment, social services and income distribution.[17]

Then Hug revealed the source of the quotation. It came from the second issue of *Center Focus*, published nearly thirty years earlier, and was written by the organization's director at the time, Bill Ryan.

In Canada, the CCCB has dramatically scaled back its social justice work. By the turn of the millennium, in the wake of the Ryan–Hubert task force, the bishops reduced the social affairs staff from five people to two. The Conference was even having trouble finding bishops to volunteer to sit on the Social Affairs Commission, once a hotbed of activity. While social justice had not vanished from the episcopal radar screen, it had most certainly faded. By the end of the 1990s there were still many Catholics and a few Catholic institutions like Development and Peace – products of the *engagé* years just after Vatican II – challenging the way unfettered capitalism is creating wealth while generating savage inequalities both in Canada and globally. As the millennium approached, strong Church support provided the momentum for the jubilee campaign against Third World debt. But the CCCB's efforts on the social justice front flagged in the 1990s just as those inequalities grew. As early as 1993, Janet Somerville noted that long-time CCCB Social Affairs director Bernard Dufresne (since dismissed) did not "sound like the captain of an enthusiastic team."[18]

Bill Ryan always insisted that in sizing up a meeting room it was important to identify where the energy was, who had momentum, who didn't. Canada's bishops have intervened eagerly in the political process in opposition to rights or benefits for homosexuals (a group well-represented within its own priesthood) at the same time that the official history of their social justice efforts pointed out in 1999 that "the Social Affairs Commission has now been reduced to the smallest number of members in its history."[19] Ryan felt that "part of the problem is that the bishops are not the whole Church" but that Canada had no national structures of lay people or forums where lay Catholics could "put feet on the teaching of the bishops."[20] Another Ryan, long-time social justice advocate Sister Frances (no relation), agreed that the laity were crucial because younger clergy weren't taking the lead in justice work. But she cautioned that the way to get to the laity was through "parochial pipelines."[21] By century's end, the pipelines were getting clogged.

The decline in CCCB social justice activity was part of a larger set of changes taking place within the Church, both within Canada and internationally. The momentum that was generated by Vatican II – the moves to collegiality, ecumenism, religious liberty, social justice – has not been reversed; it has simply stalled. Institutions as old and complex as the Roman Catholic Church – arguably the oldest and likely one of the most complex on the planet – certainly do not change easily, particularly when headed by a self-perpetuating and unaccountable leadership whose prevailing response to change has historically been to hunker down and adopt a siege mentality.

The Church is a very large tent sheltering both reactionaries and open-minded, creative people eager to adapt to changing circumstances. But the balance has shifted, especially in the episcopate, as bishops who shared Ryan's sensibilities became thinner on the ground. To be sure, even though it is still organized like a Renaissance monarchy, the Catholic Church is in a way a decentralized organization. Ryan's years of working inside the complex institution had shown him that bishops and bishops' conferences operated with considerable autonomy from the Vatican. This was illustrated in the bitter dispute involving Raymond Hunthausen of Seattle, a liberal archbishop who during the 1980s had incurred the ire of the Vatican for, among other things, not defending unambiguously enough the exclusion of women from the priesthood and being wishy-washy about "the intrinsic evil of homosexual activity." The case had enough twists, turns and schemes to qualify as a Venetian court drama, but in the end it was apparent that the Vatican's power over the affairs of a local bishop is extremely limited. Jesuit sociologist Tom Reese concluded that the first lesson to be drawn from the Hunthausen case was that "the Vatican could do to Archbishop Hunthausen only what he allowed it to do.... The power of the Vatican is based on its moral authority and the willingness of Catholics to agree and obey."[22]

Consent is a crucial factor in the legitimacy and staying power of any system of authority. It is just as critical to the Church. A willingness to agree and obey is both the strength and the weakness of reformers and social justice advocates like Bill Ryan who identify themselves with the energies of Vatican II. A strength because it's so intrinsic to his faith, allowing him to persevere optimistically, confident that, in the end, the People of God will witness the remaking of their beloved institution and the loosening of the bonds of magisterial authority. A weakness because there is little evidence that this is happening. Instead, more people are living outside the Church. The pope may have moral authority among the priesthood and the hierarchy, he may be respected by the laity, but his doctrines – on contraception, divorce, social justice – have little or no effect on the way lay Catholics in a country like Canada live their lives. Ryan's friend and skiing buddy Everett MacNeil, a career Church official and, like Ryan, a former general secretary of the CCCB, put it bluntly: "The laity walked."

Because of the way the Church is organized, one of the most important Vatican powers is the power of appointment, and especially the power to appoint bishops. Dennis Murphy, another close friend of Ryan's and another former general secretary of the CCCB, believes that in recent years there is "no doubt at all that in the naming of bishops Rome tried to assure that those names would have a strong Roman loyalty.... Rome was naming people who would have a greater propensity to be inspired by Rome in the directions they would take." Shifts to a more conservative episcopacy are discernible in North America as the Vatican II generation fades into retirement to be replaced by more recent Vatican appointees. In the 1980s the U.S. bishops launched a remarkably open process, getting the laity involved in the preparation of pastoral statements on economic justice and peace. But, as the changing of the guard progressed, things became much quieter on the social justice front. Milwaukee's Rembert Weakland, one of the brightest members of the American hierarchy and a man who made no Vatican friends when he observed that the pope could work a crowd better than any actor, was preparing his priests for the inevitable conservative succession in his diocese. "It seems that we are now coming to a period of more uniformity, less creativity and less space for personal preferences," he wrote in a confidential 2000 letter to the priests.[23]

The use of Vatican appointments to cool down the social justice thrust in the Church has been most pronounced in Latin America and among Vatican diplomats who have served in Latin American postings. If a socially engaged Church is surviving and thriving in Latin America, it seems to be doing so in spite rather than because of the Vatican. Cardinal Angelo Sodano, Vatican secretary of state, had served as papal nuncio in Chile in the 1970s, during which time he publicly criticized priests and laity who demonstrated against torture by the regime. The Brazilian Lucas Moeira Neves was appointed a cardinal by John Paul II in 1988 and eventually became prefect of the Congregation of Bishops in Rome. Neves, as much as anyone, was responsible for engineering the Vatican effort to bring the Brazilian Church, long a stronghold of social justice, under control by ensuring the appointment of right-wing clerics to the Brazilian episcopacy. In 1983 John Paul II appointed Alfonso López Trujillo, the highest-profile opponent of liberation theology, to the College of Cardinals at the age of forty-eight. Trujillo would later become president of the Pontifical Council for the Family.[24]

Meanwhile, Bill Ryan, contacted in 1992 by a Vancouver *Sun* journalist doing a story on John Paul II's approach to politics, said that the pope was not as inconsistent as he might appear: the pope believed that some liberation theologians had moved too close to Marxism, opposed any form of totalitarianism, and felt that some liberation theologians were so strident in their denunciation of oppression that their teachings could lead to violence. (The journalist could not cull a quote from his interview with Ryan, likely because his way of speaking proved too rambling and circular.) Ryan's cautious analysis was part of an article dealing with John Paul II's support for unions and human rights and questioning of the sanctity of private property.[25]

While loath to point out the Church's contradictions to inquiring outsiders, when addressing the cognoscenti inside the tent Ryan still nurtured the hope that he had gained at the 1971 synod. It was this synod, he pointed out in 1991, that had acknowledged that "the credibility of the Church's message would be diminished unless it were accompanied by prophetic witness to justice...in its own administration." In an article in *Compass*, Ryan tipped his hat to Richard McBrien, who had just noted that the 1971 synod report was the only Vatican document in the past century to point out this inconsistency and who had made the further point that the Church had a responsibility to practise what it preaches. That said, Ryan ended on a loyal, hopeful note: John Paul II could rejoice and thank God that Catholic social teaching had improved over the course of that century and this was surely a good sign as the number of Catholics grew in the Third World.[26]

Patience, like faith, is a virtue. "What is needed…is not short-term effort," wrote the noted American spiritual writer and social justice advocate Sister Joan Chittister OSB in 1992, "but a spirituality for the long haul, an internal energy for justice that comes unbidden and simply will not die, even in the face of defeat."[27] Reformers and social justice advocates seem to need ample reserves of both faith and patience to keep the vision of Vatican II alive. Bill Ryan has had those reserves, with a cautious Jesuitical pragmatism thrown into the mix. When Dennis Murphy described Ryan as having "very deep faith," he was asked whether the same couldn't be said of all priests. "Not necessarily," he replied. "A lot of us would probably struggle more than Bill. He's just rock solid in his faith."

---

[1]   Alberta Congress Board, *Values and Ethics for the 21st Century*, Proceedings of conference October 31–November 3, 1996, 2, 8.

[2]   William F. Ryan SJ, "Proposed Jesuit Project on Ethics and Politics," Ryan files, mimeo, n.d.

[3]   William F. Ryan SJ, "Dynamics and Significance of Two Belief Systems in Confrontation in the Demise of Communism in Eastern Europe," Ryan files, mimeo, May, 1991.

[4]   Ibid.

[5]   United Nations Development Program, *Human Development Report 1992* (New York: United Nations, 1992), 1.

[6]   José Maria Sbert, "Progress," in Wolfgang Sachs, ed., *The Development Dictionary: A Guide to Knowledge as Power* (London: Zed, 1992), 197. Emphasis in original.

[7]   William F. Ryan SJ, *Culture, Spirituality, and Economic Development: Opening a Dialogue* (Ottawa: International Development Research Centre, 1995), 64.

[8]   Ibid., 13–14.

[9]   Ibid., 42–43, 50.

[10] John Coleman, "The Future of the Ministry," *America*, March 28, 1981, quoted in Garry Wills, *Papal Sin: Structures of Deceit* (New York: Doubleday, 2000), 131.

[11] *Catholic New Times*, March 9, 1997.

[12] *Catholic New Times*, February 23, 1997.

[13] Peter-Hans Kolvenbach SJ, *New Vigor for the Church: Conversations on the Global Challenges of Our Time* (Toronto: Compass: A Jesuit Journal, 1993), 11.

14   See "A Parish Priest's Faithful Presence," an interview with Robert Foliot SJ by Curtis Fahey and Judy MacDonald, *Compass*, May/June 1997, 6–10, 29.

15   Louisa Blair, "Love and the Booby Hatch," *Canadian Forum*, April 2000, 12.

16   McCarthy and Michael Czerny read excerpts from the letters at the memorial service for Royackers in Parkhill, Ontario, on June 26, 2001, and some quotations appeared in a detailed and sensitive profile by Leslie Scrivener, "Father Martin, the man," Toronto *Star*, July 8, 2001, F1.

17   Jim Hug, SJ, "30 Years of Struggling for Social Justice," *Center Focus*, June 2001, 1.

18   *Catholic New Times*, June 13, 1993.

19   Joe Gunn and Monica Lambton, *Calling Out The Prophetic Tradition: A Jubilee of Social Teaching from the Canadian Conference of Catholic Bishops* (Ottawa: Canadian Conference of Catholic Bishops, 1999), 43.

20   *Catholic New Times*, June 13, 1993.

21   *Catholic New Times*, May 2, 1993.

22   Thomas J. Reese, *Archbishop: Inside the Power Structure of the American Catholic Church* (New York: Harper & Row, 1989), 337–43.

23   New York *Times*, September 10, 2000.

24   John L. Allen, Jr., "These paths lead to Rome," *National Catholic Reporter*, June 2, 1990.

25   Douglas Todd, "Politics of the Pontiff," Vancouver *Sun*, September 19, 1992.

26   William F. Ryan SJ, "Social Teaching for Modern Times: A Century of Catholic Social Documents," *Compass*, November/December 1991, 39.

27   Joan Chittister OSB, "Spirituality for the Long Haul," *Compass*, May/June 1992, 12.

Epilogue

In May 2000 Bill Ryan celebrated his seventy-fifth birthday with a special mass at St. Francis Xavier in Renfrew. A purple Buick in the church's spacious parking lot had a bumper sticker with the Virgin Mary in profile. "Pray the rosary!" it urged. Some 250 of the faithful arrived for the service on a cool, grey Sunday morning. That same morning, Anglican priests across Canada mounted their pulpits to read a special message from the primate, who attempted to assure the faithful that the money they dropped into the collection plate would not line the pockets of the lawyers arguing over the 1,600 abuse claims by Native people against their Church.

By the turn of the millennium, many ecclesiastical verities had been shaken. Things had changed since the young Bill Ryan trotted off to Mass each morning and gazed up at the priest in his lofty pulpit. One priest served the Renfrew parish, down from five in Ryan's youth. The modern St. Francis Xavier Church, designed in the 1960s, has no pulpit. A plain communion table is a few carpeted steps up from the rest of the wide, fan-shaped sanctuary. An equally simple lectern stands off to the side. There were altar girls as well as altar boys that morning. Ryan entered the sanctuary carrying a thick binder ("I hope that's not his homily," his brother Bob grinned). His friend Janet Somerville, executive director of the Canadian Council of Churches, read from the Acts of the Apostles. Thanking Ryan for his years of Jesuit service and leadership, J.P. Horrigan SJ presented Father Bill, as he's known in Renfrew, with an icon of Mary "as a token of the importance that Mary has played in your life." But when he stepped up to the lectern to give his homily, the white-haired Ryan made only brief passing mention of the Blessed Virgin.

Wearing an immaculate white surplice embroidered with a tall, slender cross, Ryan used the Easter season to speak of life and its renewal. Never having been a preacher or a pastor, he does not speak spontaneously. Reading from a prepared text, he discussed love, not simply the love of physical touch but the love that is friendship and caring, the love expressed when people feed the hungry, shelter the homeless, visit prisoners. He talked of hope, his hope that our problems can be addressed by dialogue across gender, racial and religious lines. Through dialogue, he insisted, we can become one with the person with whom we are communicating. In that there is hope. It was a simple, optimistic message, simply delivered. It did not sound terribly inspiring, for though he has been a leader, Ryan has never been charismatic. Nor has he been one to declaim from on high.

"There are key people who make a difference and Bill is one of them," said Ted Scott a few weeks before the Renfrew Mass. The former Anglican primate, one of Canada's pre-eminent Christian leaders of Ryan's generation, described his Jesuit colleague's contribution as quiet and steady: "He challenged other people to move in the way he moved but he had a profound respect for people. That quality of respect for people is something we just need much more of."

"This guy gave me hope," said Pauline Lally, a Sister of Providence of St. Vincent de Paul who is about a dozen years younger than Ryan and chair of her order's Justice and Peace Committee. While Sister Pauline does not know Bill Ryan well, she drew spiritual sustenance from what he said when they did meet: "He removed the paralysis of guilt that had been dumped on me. He was the first person I ever listened to who challenged me about justice without making me feeling guilty."

In his Renfrew homily Ryan went on to thank his family, his friends, the congregation at St. Francis Xavier and his Jesuit family for the spiritual sustenance they had offered him over the years. A modest but proud man, he did not fail to mention his doctorate from Harvard. Ryan described the most dramatic event of his life as having unfolded in the dorm of St. Patrick's College when he received the sudden call to join the Jesuits. The three daunting challenges that shaped his Jesuit ministry, he explains, all happened within the space of four years. Being sent to Washington by his "dear friend and holy Jesuit" Pedro Arrupe to start a new social justice centre. Being adviser to the Canadian bishops at the Justice in the World synod of 1971. Being elected in 1974 as a Canadian delegate to the Jesuits' 32nd General Congregation.

Ryan's daunting challenges have met with mixed results. The Center of Concern survives as an independent, faith-based group active on several global social justice fronts. The lofty goals expressed at the 1971 synod – a Church that practises internally the social justice message it preaches to the world – have remained just that, as hopes have been stymied by a conservative pope and intransigent curial bureaucracy. As for the Jesuits, they deftly weathered the storm of having a papal delegate superintend their affairs but found that marrying faith and justice, a wrenching task at GC32, would prove even more difficult in the order as a whole, and in the world at large. The experience of Toronto's Jesuit Centre testified to that difficulty. Of course, no one, and particularly no canny Jesuit, could have realistically expected either the Church or the world to change very quickly. But many of those who were animated by the heady spirit of the 1960s and 1970s and subsequently disappointed by the grim realities of the 1980s and 1990s have withdrawn into cynicism or pessimism. Many in the priesthood simply left.

Ryan would always keep the faith. He echoed one of his major intellectual influences, Pierre Teilhard de Chardin, as he insisted to the congregation gathered in his home town that "despite so many blatant evidences to the contrary, I believe that the Spirit of God is ever at work in helping us to realize and finally to live out the great scientific and spiritual fact of our existence, namely that we are all one human, divine family."

Two years previously, Ryan had faced another daunting challenge. As he prepared to travel to Renfrew for Christmas, he had learned that he had prostate cancer. His first reaction was to follow his physician's advice and undergo radiation treatment. But he was in no hurry. He had arranged a trip to the Holy Land and that was his immediate priority. Making an appointment to start the radiation, he began a course of hormone therapy that would last until his return and headed off to Jerusalem. Returning to Ottawa, Ryan happened to be talking to a woman he knew who had had breast cancer. She and her husband urged him to reconsider the conventional medical approach and opt for a different path. That night, after weighing his options, Ryan decided to take their advice.

He cancelled his date with nuclear medicine and instead embarked on an intensive series of tests lasting several weeks. The theory was that cancer, rather than being a proliferative disease, is an immune-system disorder unique to each patient. The goal was to conduct a detailed analysis of his immune system so that the alternative practitioners could come up with a treatment regime to help boost his immunity as a way of attacking the tumour. Many people opt for alternatives to conventional cancer treatment, but most do so only after exhausting what the mainstream system has to offer. Ryan changed his mind about radiation therapy before he tried it, even though his physician expressed his doubts. After months of taking thirteen capsules containing vitamins, minerals and acids (from folic acid to epigallocatechin), Ryan learned from his skeptical physician that his tests were showing a dramatic shrinkage in the size of the tumour. Within two years of his diagnosis, the patient felt confident that he had done the right thing. Of course, there was no guarantee that prostate cancer, notoriously slow to develop, would not return. But no form of treatment offered any guarantees and, in any case, Ryan was not worried.

"It's hard to believe I'm seventy-six," he said a year after his celebratory Mass in Renfrew. "I am going to bed a little earlier than I used to. Less serious reading at night, but I did manage about thirteen good cross-skiing jaunts this winter so far." Ryan, being Ryan, was still counting. As he entered his seventy-seventh year he was cooking up a new scheme called the Catholic Social Teaching Implementation Project: although there was a wealth of such teaching, it had little traction among lay Catholics or in the world at large. In the spring of 2001 Ryan drove across Canada and back, visiting bishops and pitching to them the idea of setting up groups "to enhance their knowledge of and ability to apply Catholic social teaching in their own circumstances." Ryan would initiate the project, though younger Jesuits might be involved later. He was also involved in reviving the Jesuit Centre for Social Faith and Justice, in a modest way. The reborn Centre was launched in 1999, although for the moment it remained primarily an umbrella for social justice work that Ryan and other Jesuits were already doing. In the early going, its most innovative wing was its Ecology Project in Guelph, where Jim Profit SJ was giving eight-day ecological retreats based on the Spiritual Exercises, among other endeavours. The Centre did give Ryan a new calling card: he now described himself as "Ottawa Office Co-ordinator, Jesuit Centre for Social Faith and Justice." In addition, he would continue his work on development and spirituality, this time with the Canadian International Development Agency.

"He doesn't like to lose," said Dennis Murphy, a frequent skiing and golf partner. "He certainly is very self-assured. And I must say he's not always encumbered by logic. If he were sitting here and we were discussing something and he was putting forward a thesis that you drove a truck through, it would not bother him in the least. He would just stop and move in another direction."

In 1999 Ryan and Everett MacNeil were driving home to Ottawa from a golfing visit to Murphy's cottage on Lake Nipissing. They had visited their old friend Alex Carter, the outspoken bishop at the 1971 synod who was now in a nursing home (and has since died). The three career Catholic backroom boys had done some reminiscing over drinks and dinner, but it had been reminiscing tilted to the future and how they might be trying to improve things if they were still operating today. As Ryan and MacNeil headed south past Kiosk and the entrance to Algonquin Park, Ryan suddenly had an idea.

"My dad used to work in the Park near Brent and Mackie," he piped up. "Let's take a look in the woods back there and see if we can find where the sawmill was."

"But Bill, that was eighty years ago," said MacNeil, who had done a lot of hunting in the backwoods of Nova Scotia. "It'll be gone by now. Just completely overgrown."

"That's okay. Don't worry, I'll find some old-timer who can give us directions."

There was a bit of a pause.

"Bill, you *are* the old-timer."

If Bill Ryan had not gotten the call to join the Jesuits that springtime afternoon in the college dorm, if instead of spending his life travelling he had stayed on in Renfrew like the rest of his family, he would likely have been a successful lawyer or hardware merchant. He would also, surely, have been a spark plug in the local Optimists Club.

Also available from Novalis

A Faith that Challenges

The Life of Jim McSheffrey

By Maura Hanrahan
Foreword by Helen Porter

A Faith that Challenges, the second book in the series *Out of the Ordinary: Novalis Biographies,* tells the story of Jim McSheffrey, a Jesuit brother who shared all he had with those around him. For Jim, a commitment to the Gospel values of justice and peace meant living among the poor – sharing their burdens, learning from their struggles, celebrating their spirit and opening his home and heart to them. He marched on St. John's City Hall with his neighbours when the provincial government instituted a fee for children who took the bus to school. He started a community garden to feed the neighbourhood families, who couldn't afford the high prices of fresh vegetables at the grocery store. He greatly valued his friends and proudly presented them with garage-sale bargains or items he found in people's curbside trash, sure that the broken-down lawnmower or propane stove he had picked up would come in handy. He refused to attend fancy dinners at expensive hotels. He brought many people together, and more than once got under the skin of people in authority.

Jim McSheffrey died in Newfoundland in 1999 at age 54. A huge outpouring of grief paid tribute to this quiet, determined, good man who lived his faith every day, never losing hope that justice would triumph.

Gem: The Life of Sister Mac

Sister Geraldine MacNamara

By Eleanor Stebner
Foreword by Rosemary Radford Ruether

GEM is a "social-spiritual" biography that explores how Sr. Geraldine MacNamara – a privileged, middle-class, well-educated religious sister – lived into her vocation and became converted to social justice. This is the first book in the series *Out of the Ordinary: Novalis Biographies.*

A member of the Sisters of the Holy Names of Jesus and Mary, MacNamara in 1976 founded Rossbrook House, a drop-in centre in one of Winnipeg's most troubled neighbourhoods. From Rossbrook, MacNamara and her "kids" addressed issues crucial to their community – including social services, substance abuse, truancy, the justice system, and urban development. MacNamara herself became a well-known local and national advocate for the rights of the disenfranchised, especially the young urban poor.

MacNamara was influenced by her personal experiences, idealism, and sense of commitment; by the vision of Vatican II and its uplifting of the people of God; and especially by the young people she met, the friendships she made, and the struggles she witnessed.

The Doctor Will Not See You Now

The Autobiography of a Blind Physician

By Jane Poulson

Jane Poulson was dealt a difficult hand of cards as a child: diabetes. Blinded by this disease at 27 and about to graduate from medical school, Jane pushed herself to become Canada's first practising blind physician. Then, when cancer and heart disease took their toll on her, she continued to live the only way she knew how – with every ounce of strength and courage and hope she possessed. She embraced life as a uniquely gifted doctor with a special understanding of disease that only her degree of affliction and hard-earned faith could teach. In recognition of her exceptional medical skills and insight, she was awarded the Order of Canada at the age of 35. Although her life was cut short, she lived it to the fullest and leaves her readers with a joyous account of her triumph over incredible odds.

From Corporate Greed to Common Good

Canadian Churches and Community Economic Development

Edited by Murray MacAdam

Despite record profits and low interest rates and inflation, the mainstream economy fails to meet the needs of many Canadians. Yet there is a glimmer of hope on the horizon: a growing grassroots movement called "Community Economic Development" (CED). These efforts encourage citizens to take action for social and economic development. Author Murray MacAdam offers practical suggestions for individuals and groups who wish to participate in community economic initiatives.

This hopeful vision of alternative economic movements "…should be top choice for discussion groups in parishes across Canada. The book should be ordered in bulk." —*Catholic New Times*

NOVALIS

To order these books, contact Novalis
1-800-387-7164 or <u>cservice@novalis.ca</u>